Chapter 1

The Country and the People

*B*URMA LIES BETWEEN India on the west and China on the east. In the extreme north it borders on Tibet, and to the south it reaches half-way down the peninsula which ends in Malaya and Singapore. From its most northerly point to its southernmost tip is roughly the distance from Liverpool to Gibraltar, and it is the largest country in what used to be called Further India or Indo-China, and what is now more generally known since the Second World War as South-East Asia.

Except along its coasts it is surrounded by hills, in the shape of a horseshoe: the Arakan Yoma in the south-west, the Chin and Naga Hills along the Indian frontier, the Kachin Hills – the eastern end of the Himalayas – in the far north, and the Shan plateau in the east. Down the centre of the country, from north to south, flows the Irrawaddy (with its principal tributary the Chindwin), whose waters enter the Bay of Bengal through the many creeks of its delta. Burma proper, the country of the Burmese, is the fertile valleys of these

Chin coolies

9

rivers. Around it in the hills live the Chins, Nagas, Kachins and Shans and kindred tribes, and in the coastal strips of Arakan and Tenasserim live peoples who are akin to the Burmese, but who have a strong admixture of non-Burmese blood – Indian in Arakan, Siamese and Malay in Tenasserim. There were no road or rail links between Burma and any of her neighbours except for a road from the Shan States into northern Siam and the 'Burma Road' into China, which crossed Yunnan from the Burmese frontier and was built by the Chinese in 1938 to make it possible for military supplies to be brought into China from Rangoon.

Geographically Burma falls into five distinct areas: the two coastal strips with an annual rainfall of 160 to 220 inches; the southern wet zone – including the Irrawaddy delta – with an average rainfall of about 90 inches; the northern wet zone with 70 to 80 inches; and the central dry zone with only some 30 inches. In the dry zone are most of the old Burmese capitals, for this was the original homeland of the Burmese.

The Burmese have a history which goes back at least a thousand years. Their first great king Anawrahta was a contemporary of William the Conqueror, and most of the great Buddhist temples which still stand at Pagan on the Irrawaddy were built in the twelfth century. Throughout the greater part of Burma's history the dry zone was occupied by the Burmese while the delta was ruled by the Mons (or Talaings), an offshoot of the Khmer empire of Cambodia. At one time the Burmese, at another the Mons, would establish a hegemony over most of the country. At the end of the thirteenth century Burmese power in the north was temporarily eclipsed by an invasion of the Shans from Yunnan. These people, who are the same race as the Siamese, penetrated northern Burma, spread westwards into Assam and eastwards into what are now the Shan States, and finally reached Siam or Thailand. The Burmese of the plains of northern Burma still call themselves Shan-Burmese and are generally rather fairer-skinned than the pure Burmese of the dry zone.

It was Alaungpaya, founder of the last Burmese dynasty, who finally destroyed the power of the Mons in a short reign lasting from 1752 to 1760. His son Bodawpaya annexed Arakan, which had until then been a separate kingdom, and of all the Burmese kings came nearest to ruling the country which we now call Burma. But no Burmese king ever had more than a loose suzerainty over the Shan States or over the hill peoples of the north and west. Bodawpaya's annexation of Arakan and his intervention in the internal affairs of the Shan kingdom of Assam brought him to the borders of British India. He and his successor made the mistake of thinking that the

East India Company was no more powerful than the other neighbouring rulers. The Burmese violated the British frontier and a number of provocative acts led to the first Anglo-Burmese War of 1824–26. Rangoon was captured without a blow by the British forces, and after far more of the troops had died of sickness than in battle, the war ended with the cession by the Burmese of the two coastal provinces of Arakan and Tenasserim, and their agreement that a British Resident should be sent to their capital Ava.

But, as the years went by, the Burmese Government became more difficult to deal with, the Resident was withdrawn, and British merchants and sailors made constant complaints of ill-treatment at Rangoon. This led to the second Burmese War of 1852, which resulted in the annexation of Lower Burma – the old Mon country – including Rangoon and the Irrawaddy delta. Lower Burma had never recovered from the destruction wrought by Alaungpaya, and vast areas were uninhabited wilderness. But, as peace was established, Burmese who had fled to Upper Burma – the name by which the northern and central areas were known to the British – returned; natives of Upper Burma were attracted to the new British province and vast numbers of Indian immigrants were brought in as labour. The result was that these desolate wastes became one of the world's great rice-growing areas.

The rule of the Burmese kings was now confined to the dry zone – the old Burmese homeland – and the country to the north of it. During the twenty-five years' reign of King Mindon relations between him and the British were good, but they deteriorated under his son and successor, the weak and incompetent Thibaw. The British Residency, which had been re-established after the second Burmese War, was again withdrawn as a result of anti-British incidents. The Burmese Government began to flirt with the French, now in Indo-China, and a pretext for British intervention was given when the Burmese imposed a fine of a quarter of a million pounds upon a British timber firm, the Bombay Burmah Trading Corporation. The British Government of India sent Thibaw an ultimatum, in which he was required to refer the case to arbitration and in future to submit his foreign relations to British control. The ultimatum was rejected, whereupon independent Burma was invaded (November 1885), and in a fortnight the capital Mandalay was occupied and Thibaw was a prisoner. Upper Burma was formally annexed by Britain on the 1st January 1886. Thibaw was exiled to southern India, and his kingdom might well have been administered as a protected state, had there remained a member of the royal family with any character or following. But there was none – Thibaw had put most of them to death on his accession – and it was decided to bring the country under direct administration like the rest of British Burma. Many Burmese officials took service with the new government, and an advisory body of former ministers was established with the chief minister at the head. But, though the Burmese Government had been overthrown so speedily, it took the British five years and an army of 30,000 men to bring peace to Upper Burma.

The whole of Burma now became a province of the Indian Empire, the highest posts in the administration being held by European officers of the Burma Commission, a service made up partly of members of the Indian Civil Service, partly of Indian Army officers and partly, in the early days, of persons who had had commercial experience in Burma. From about 1920 onwards natives of Burma, whether Burmese or Anglo-Burmese, began to enter the Burma Commission. In later days the administration of the hill peoples was largely in the hands of the Burma Frontier Service, a new service created after the First World War and having a status lower than that of the Burma Commission.

The population of Burma, as recorded in the 1931 census, numbered rather more than 14½ million, of whom over 9 million were Burmese and kindred races. The next largest indigenous groups were the Karens with fewer than 1½ million and the Shans with 1 million, both peoples of similar origin. The Karens are found in the eastern hills south of the Shan States, but most of them have gradually spread into the Irrawaddy delta, where they live side by side with the Burmese, keeping, however, in their own communities and showing no great love for the Burmese. The Shans live mainly on the Shan plateau, but, as I have said, they are intermingled with the Burmese in the north. The Chins and Kachins are more primitive people who live entirely in the hills; the Kachins were still moving down into Burma at the time of the annexation in 1886. Of the non-indigenous peoples the largest in numbers were the Indians with over a million.

The Burmese are a Mongolian race, speaking a language which belongs to the Tibeto-Burman group. They have straight black hair and brown skins, the cultivator who leads an open-air life being generally darker than the town-dweller. The Burmese male grows practically no hair on his face, though some of the older men cultivate small moustaches at the corners of the mouth. The Burman is small of stature, but well-built and generally above the average in good looks. He is easy-going and cheerful, quick to see a joke and, though often regarded as lazy by those who have been used to Indian labour, he works hard enough when he has to; the seasons entail intensive

Kachin with carrying basket

labour in the fields during and immediately after the rainy season and at harvest-time, but permit long periods when there is little or nothing to be done in the fields. His formal costume consists of a turban called a *gaungbaung*, a long-sleeved collarless shirt, a short cotton jacket (the *eingyi*) and a *longyi*, which is a wide tubular skirt like the Malay *sarong*, and is knotted in the front of the waist. The official class – and on gala occasions all classes – frequently wear a silk *gaungbaung*, *eingyi* and *longyi*, but the ordinary peasant in the fields wears a cotton *longyi* and generally a short-sleeved cotton shirt. When he needs to be particularly active, he lifts his *longyi* to the height of his knees, passes the lower part through his legs and tucks it into his waist at the back. Tattooing of the thighs to just below the knees used to be the universal practice, but it is fast dying out; in the rural districts, however, the older men are still tattooed. Men used to wear their hair long, tied into a knot on the top of the head; the country people still do so, but the modern practice of cutting the hair in the European fashion is general in Lower Burma and is spreading fast in the north. The women's dress is similar to that of the men. The *htamein*, the feminine equivalent of the *longyi*, is more gaily coloured and often has a flowered pattern, and it is fastened at the side, not in the front. The Burmese woman wears a tight bodice, for it is considered indecent to show any sign of protuberance in front; over the bodice is a jacket which is even shorter than the male counterpart. She normally wears nothing on her head, except as protection from the weather, though she often puts flowers in her hair; on high days and holidays she may build up her hair high on her head by means of false tresses.

The Burmese have no family names and consequently there is nothing in his name to identify a man with his father. In the old days a child's name depended to a certain extent on the day of the week on which he was born; a group of letters of the alphabet was allocated to each day and a child born, for instance, on a Monday would be given a name beginning with a k̲, k̲h̲, g̲, or n̲g̲. Though this practice no doubt persists in parts of the country, it is certainly ignored nowadays by very many Burmese. In Burma proper a boy will be given one or two names – in Arakan three is the usual number – and will be addressed by all his names, prefixed by an honorific, which is in origin a term of relationship. For most practical purposes there are three of these: U meaning uncle, Ko meaning elder brother and Maung meaning younger brother. The honorific used depends not only on the status of the person addressed, but also on his standing vis-à-vis the person addressing him. A young man will bear the names, let us say, of Ba Chit. Men who are considerably his seniors will call him Maung Ba Chit, while his contemporaries will call him Ko Ba Chit. When he grows older, his juniors will address him as U Ba Chit, and in fact all older men, and men in positions of importance, will be addressed as U by all but their own familiar friends. The principal honorifics for women are Daw (or aunt) and Ma (or sister).

Great care is needed in the choice of the personal pronouns 'I' and 'you', since the words used indicate the relative positions of the persons concerned. In speaking to Buddhist monks – and in the old days to royalty – not only must special pronouns be used, but for many actions (speaking, living, eating, walking, etc.) an entirely separate vocabulary is *de rigueur*.

By religion the Burmese are Buddhists, their Buddhism being of the southern (Hinayana) type similar to that practised in Ceylon, Siam and Indo-China. Many scholars regard this as the purest form of Buddhism, and it differs from the northern (Mahayana) Buddhism of Tibet, China and Japan most noticeably in that it does not recognise a multiplicity of gods. In Hinayana Buddhism there is, strictly speaking, no god at all, since the Buddha is regarded as a great teacher on whose life his followers should model their own, and not as a god. His image in a pagoda is there not to be worshipped, but to be used as an aid to meditation. Nevertheless, the peasants draw little distinction between their teacher and a god. In theory the Buddhist should look upon this life as a vale of tears, for his religion teaches him that the world is full of misery, and that it is a misfortune to be born and to have to live in it at all. The only way in which a man can avoid being reborn after death – for the Buddhist believes in reincarnation – is for him to amass so much merit by a good life that he will not be reborn, but will attain to Nirvana, where self-consciousness ceases. I say a man advisedly, for a woman must first accumulate sufficient merit to be reborn as a man before she can hope to reach Nirvana. The Catholic Bishop Bigandet, who wrote the standard work on the Buddha of the Burmese, calls their religion one of annihilation, and so in theory it is. But, despite its teaching of the misery of life – in which it does not differ so very much from some other religions – there is little sign that the Burman does in fact find life miserable.

His religion lays down five commandments: not to drink alcohol, not to take life, not to steal, not to fornicate and not to speak falsely. The Burman says that the prohibition on the drinking of alcohol is the first and greatest of these commandments, inasmuch as the man who breaks it is liable by becoming drunk to break any one of the others. But this again is theory rather than practice. For the villager drinks distilled spirit and the fermented juice of the toddy-palm or nipah-palm and rice-beer, and the townsman drinks western beer and spirits when he can afford them. The Burmese official would frequently drink for the greater part of his life and, when old age approached and he began to think of the life to come, would become a teetotaller.

As his religion forbids him to take life, one might suppose the Burman to be a vegetarian. But the Buddha is said to have adopted the attitude that, though he could not himself take life or eat anything which had been killed specifically for him, he could properly eat the flesh of something which had not been killed for him. The Burman will eat fish, flesh and fowl, though many will not eat beef; possibly this is due to the Hindu origin of Buddhism. Fish and chicken are among the favourite ingredients of a Burmese curry, and goat mutton is much eaten. Animals are slaughtered mainly by Indians and Chinese, but fishermen are predominantly Burmese and they are regarded – being takers of life – as being of a lower caste than other people, though in practice there are no caste distinctions among the Burmese.

His religion plays a very real part in the life of the Burman. Every village has one or more pagodas, and some are centres of worship for the countryside around. The number of pagodas far exceeds the number of places of worship which would be found in a western country; not only in the villages, but on hill tops far removed from the centres of population, are to be seen the gold or white spires of pagodas, and the reason for this is that the man who builds a pagoda acquires more merit thereby than by the performance of any other act. The pagoda usually contains an image of the Buddha set in a small niche, but it is otherwise of solid brick construction. The great national pagodas are said to enshrine a hair or some other relic of the Buddha, or one of the sacred books, and it is indeed remarkable that any one country can have acquired so many such relics! The vast majority of pagodas, however, contain only models of these sacred objects in metal, precious stones or clay. Social life in the villages revolves to a great extent round the pagoda and its festivals, and any villager who was not a Buddhist would find himself very much cut off from the rest of his village.

But, despite his attachment to his religion, the Burman retains a very strong belief in spirits (nats). Some of the nats are historical persons, believed to have been rewarded for their good lives by becoming spirits. But most of them are simply nature spirits: nats of the house, the air, the water and the trees. And it is very important that they should be propitiated, for they may at any time turn hostile.

The Burman is intensely superstitious and a believer in magic. Some days, for example, are regarded as propitious for performing certain actions, some are not; and many a Burman would not dream of setting out on a journey without consulting the local astrologer as to the best day to do so.

The Buddhist's profession of faith runs: 'I take refuge in the Buddha, I take refuge in the Law (or teaching), I take refuge in the Order', and the Order of monks holds a very important place in the life of the people. Every village has at least one monastery, where the yellow-robed monks (or *pongyis*) live their communal life. Unlike the members of western monastic orders, Burmese monks do not necessarily remain such throughout their lives. It is perhaps the general practice for them to do so, but it is not uncommon for a man to return to lay life after some years as a monk, and no-one thinks the worse of him for doing so. In theory the monk has no property except the bare necessities of clothing, a begging-bowl, an axe, a needle, a water-strainer (to ensure that he does not inadvertently take life by swallowing an insect) and a fan, and he must depend for his existence on the charity of the faithful. Early every morning the monks leave their monastery in single file, each holding his begging-bowl before him, and proceed slowly through the village, looking neither to right nor to left. As they pass, the villagers come out with food and place it in their bowls, and on their return to the monastery the monks make their meal out of these offerings. Such at least was the old practice, but now it is not uncommon for this food to be given to the young novices while the monks have a better meal already cooked and awaiting their return. They are not permitted to eat between midday and dawn the next day.

The Burmese monk is not a priest in our sense of the term, for he does not officiate at any religious ceremonies. If a private person holds one of those social ceremonies which are generally intimately connected with religion, the monks from the local monastery will be invited as a matter of course and will be treated as honoured guests, but they will sit apart by themselves and take no active part in the proceedings. Their most important role so far as the people at large are concerned is that of schoolmasters. Long before the British annexation of Burma, Burmese boys learned their reading, writing and simple arithmetic at the village monastery, with the result that a far higher degree of literacy was found in Burma than in most eastern countries. After the British occupied Burma, an attempt was made to graft the monastery school system on to the general government educational system, but this was unsuccessful. Even so, the first education which many village boys receive is still in their local monastery. Girls have to learn at home, for it is not proper for females to enter monasteries.

The decline of discipline over the monastic order which followed on the British annexation, and which was mainly due to the traditional British attitude of neutrality in religious matters, resulted in the assumption of the yellow robe by many men who were quite unsuitable, and some monasteries even became places of refuge for criminals. Though a monk is supposed not to interest himself in the affairs of this world, many came to take an active part in politics. But the great majority remained simple, pious members of the order, fully deserving the respect which is accorded by the Burmese to all wearers of the yellow robe, whether good or bad.

A few words must suffice for the other races of Burma. The Shans, like the Burmese, are Buddhists; they dress in much the same fashion, except that the men wear loose cotton trousers in place of the *longyi*, and the Shans proper are virtually confined to the plateau of the Shan States, though there are a few small states in northern Burma. Each state had its own chief, usually called the Sawbwa; in the smaller ones he was a simple rustic gentleman, while the chief of one of the larger states might have had an English education. The Karens, Chins and Kachins are essentially hill peoples, animists by religion, though, as I have said, large numbers of Karens now live in the plains of Lower Burma, where they have adopted the dress of the Burmese and to some extent their religion. Christianity has found many converts among them, though it has made little headway among Buddhists.

The principal immigrant races are the Indians and the Chinese. In British times the bulk of the trade of Burma was in the hands of Indian merchants. Indians provided much of the labour for the rice-fields of the delta and Indian money-lenders financed the Burmese peasant. In up-country towns the Indian would be found managing the bazaar and the cattle slaughter-house and running many of the shops. The Chinese were mainly town-dwellers, living in Rangoon and the delta centres, engaged in trade. But they too would be found in rural areas as liquor-shop and pawnshop licensees and managers of pig slaughter-houses. The Anglo-Burmese (Eurasians) were employed principally in the railways, the telegraphs, the police and other public services. In their ways of life they were generally more akin to the European than to the Burmese, but they assimilated themselves with neither.

Burma was – and is – predominantly an agricultural country, and two-thirds of her people owed their livelihood to the soil. Before the Second World War she exported about three million tons of rice a year and was the world's largest exporter. Timber was her second most important produce, Burma teak being known throughout the world, and forests covered more than half the total area of the country. The oilfields in the dry zone produced enough oil for Burma's own needs and for export to India. Other minerals, found in the hills, were silver, lead, zinc and wolfram.

From the outset British Burma was administered as a part of India. The provinces of Arakan and Tenasserim, after their annexation in 1826, were first placed under the direct supervision of the Governor-General, but were later transferred to the Government of Bengal. In 1862 the province of British Burma was formed under a Chief Commissioner, and to this Upper Burma was added in 1886. In 1897 the Chief Commissioner became a Lieutenant-Governor, and a Legislative Council was established, consisting of nine members, all of whom were nominated and four of whom were officials. In 1909 the Council was increased to thirty members with an unofficial majority, but they were still nominated, and the Council had little power and was hardly more than an advisory body to the Lieutenant-Governor.

The Montagu-Chelmsford reforms of 1919, which introduced into India an advance towards self-government known as 'dyarchy', were not applied to Burma, as her people were considered to be insufficiently educated and politically experienced to be able to work a constitution of this nature. This slight – as it appeared to the Burmese – had the effect of rousing the national sentiment, and the unexpected strength of feeling on this issue led to the application of 'dyarchy' to Burma too in 1923. This meant that the functions of government were divided between the central Government of India and the provincial Government of Burma, while the provincial functions were further divided into 'reserved' and 'transferred' subjects. 'Reserved' subjects were controlled by the Governor through two Members nominated by him, one of whom was always a Burman – and they included defence, finance, law and order and irrigation. 'Transferred' subjects – education, health, agriculture, forests, local government, and public works other than irrigation – were the responsibility of two Ministers selected from the members of the Legislative Council. The Council was considerably enlarged, and now contained seventy-nine elected members out of a total of one hundred and three. In 'transferred' subjects it had the final power of legislation, subject to the approval of the Governor, and the Ministers held office only so long as they could command the confidence of the Council.

From the time that the pacification of Upper Burma was completed until 1930 Burma was, comparatively speaking, an oasis of peace in the Indian Empire, disturbed only by occasional communal riots. In

1930, however, a rebellion broke out in Lower Burma, which was essentially an anti-foreign movement, directed principally against the Indian money-lenders into whose hands most of the delta rice-lands had passed. The leader of the uprising was one Saya San, a professional magician, and, though the insurgents were armed only with knives, ancient guns and charms which bestowed invulnerability, it took more than a year to quell them.

It was natural, but unfortunate, that Burma should have been administered as a part of the Indian Empire. Her people were totally different from the Indians, and there was resentment at the large numbers of Indians who had been imported into Burma under British rule, many of whom were employed in the lower ranks of the Government service. When, therefore, the time came for the next stage in India's constitutional advance, it was recommended that Burma should be separated from India and should become a distinct territory under the Crown. Though this could in the long run prove nothing but advantageous to the Burmese, opposition was roused to the proposal. Many Burmese became suspicious, mainly, it would seem, because they found the British, both officials and business men, in favour of separation, and thought there must be some catch. They thought that, once Burma was no longer part of India, a brake might be placed upon her constitutional progress; and they feared that the capitalist activities of British firms, which had to some extent been controlled by the Indian Government, would be allowed a free rein in a separated Burma. An Anti-Separation League was formed, which won a complete victory in the 1932 elections. Its members had suggested that Burma should join the proposed Indian federation, but with the right to opt out should she so desire. This, however, was rejected, and Burma was given the alternatives either of complete separation or of unconditional adherence to the Indian federation. There was naturally considerable hesitation on the part of the Burmese to accepting the second alternative, and in the end the issue was decided in favour of separation. Burma was promised that this would be accompanied by a more advanced constitution.

Separation and the new constitution came into effect on the 1st April 1937. The Burma Government became directly responsible to Parliament in London, and it consisted of a Governor, a Council of Ministers – which was limited to ten, but in practice varied between six and nine – and a Legislature with two Houses, the Senate and the House of Representatives. The Governor was solely responsible for defence, both external and internal, for monetary policy, currency and coinage, for foreign affairs and for the 'scheduled areas' of the Shan States, Karenni and the Tribal Hills; he was provided with up to three Counsellors to advise him in the exercise of these responsibilities. In all other matters he was bound to act on the advice of his Ministers, who were responsible to the Legislature. The Governor was given 'special responsibility' powers, which he could exercise in emergency – for example, to prevent grave menace to internal peace, to maintain financial stability, to protect the interests of minorities and of officers in the public services; and in such matters he could refuse to accept the advice of his Ministers. Yet, even when allowance was made for the Governor's 'reserved' and 'special responsibility' powers, the Burmese Cabinet now had effectual control over practically all internal affairs in Burma proper.

The first elections under the new constitution took place, and after prolonged negotiations a coalition was formed under Dr Ba Maw, a flamboyant character said to be of Armenian descent, who had first come into prominence by his defence of Saya San and other leaders of the 1930 rebellion. He had been Minister for Education under 'dyarchy', and had later been an anti-separationist who expressed his determination to wreck the new constitution. His coalition included the Indian and Karen groups, but had a very small majority, and depended to a great extent on the support of the European group, which maintained an independent position.

A concomitant of the introduction of parliamentary government into Burma was the appointment, for the first time, of a politician as Governor. Hitherto the Governor had been a senior member of the Indian Civil Service, but in 1936, in time to introduce the new constitution, Sir Archibald Cochrane arrived in Burma as Governor. He had had a distinguished naval career and a less remarkable one as a Member of Parliament, and rumour had it that he was the eleventh MP to whom the Governorship of Burma had been offered.

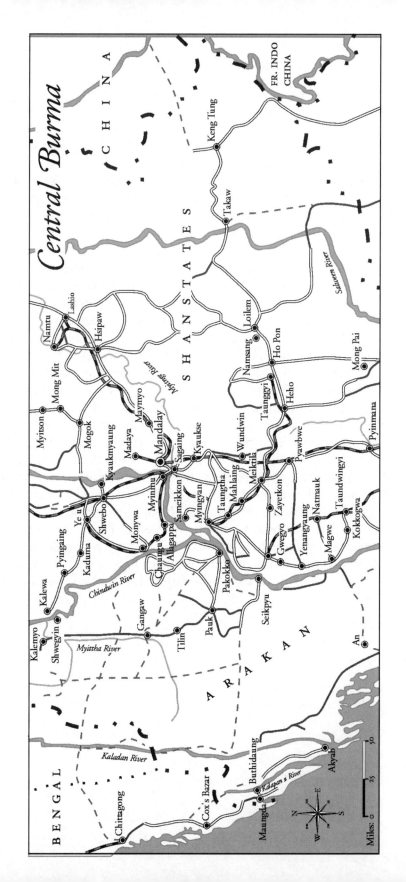

CHAPTER THREE

Under Training 1938-39: 1

ON TUESDAY THE 15th November, I was up on deck soon after dawn for my first sight of Burma. It was sunny, but cool, at that time of day, and we were moving up the Rangoon River between green paddy (rice) fields which stretched as far as the eye could see. After what I had read of the 'steaming Irrawaddy delta', I was pleasantly surprised by the crisp, cool atmosphere; but this was the 'cold weather', which lasted from November to the end of February. As we approached Rangoon, the great golden mass of the Shwe Dagon, the most famous pagoda in Burma, appeared high up on the horizon with the sun gleaming upon it, a most impressive sight. Soon we could see the city ahead. We passed the Burma Oil Company's refinery at Syriam, crossed the mouth of the Pegu River, and shortly after 8 a.m. tied up alongside one of the Rangoon wharves.

On board the ship to meet us came Swithinbank, the Commissioner of the Pegu Division, with another senior member of the Indian Civil Service. Merrells had met Swithinbank in England and was to stay with him, while my host, I was told, was to be Craw, one of the two Financial Commissioners; a Financial Commissioner was one of the highest-ranking government officials. This attention shown by those in high places to the insignificant was typical of Burma. The senior grade of the Civil Service was small, everyone knew everyone else, even if only by name and repute, and the sense that all were members of one service was strong. Later I found this conspicuously lacking in the Colonial Service, where it was rare for the more senior officials to put themselves out for a junior. In some colonies this was probably due to the size of the European element in the Service, and partly no doubt to the fact that the Administration was but one branch of the Colonial Service, while in India and Burma it was *the* Civil Service *par excellence*.

Before we left the ship we were told that we were both to be posted to Sagaing District for training. By this time of course we knew pretty well where Sagaing was; it was in the heart of Upper Burma and only a short distance from Mandalay. It so happened that I had had a dream while still in England, in which I saw myself posted to Sagaing together with another officer. I had told my Burmese colleagues, who laughed: a European officer, they said, might be posted to Mandalay or to Magwe or Minbu, but not to a comparatively unimportant district like Sagaing. I think that my stock went up with them when they heard that I had in fact been sent there. The reason was probably that the country was only just recovering from the Shwe Hpi riots. Shwe Hpi was a schoolmaster, a Burma Muslim, who some years before had published a pamphlet in which he had made some uncomplimentary remarks about the Buddhist religion. It had gone unnoticed at the time, but a reprint was seized upon by those Burmans who had a political axe to grind and was used to foment religious discord between Buddhists and Muslims. The press gave publicity to passages from the pamphlet, the Buddhist monks made inflammatory speeches, and anti-Muslim riots occurred in many parts of the country. Mandalay had been one of the centres of the trouble, and it was doubtless thought best to post young officers fresh to the country – who were in any case likely to be of little use to anyone for some months – to a rather quieter district.

We were seen through Customs and advised to report ourselves to the Home Department in the Secretariat before noon, as otherwise we should receive no pay for the day! We were then carried off to breakfast in our hosts' houses.

Rangoon was the first eastern city that we had either of us seen, and it was natural that it should have a certain fascination for us. The streets, warming up as the sun rose higher in the sky, were full of colour. They were well planted with trees with brilliant blooms, and were crowded with brightly-dressed Burmese, white-clothed Indians and, from time to time, processions of yellow-robed monks carrying their begging-bowls and receiving gifts of food from the faithful. Rangoon, as we had already learnt, was more an Indian than a Burmese city; in fact it was pretty cosmopolitan, having a fair-sized Chinese population among its half million inhabitants as well as 15,000 or so Europeans and Anglo-Indians. Rickshaws, pulled by Indians, weaved among the traffic, giving car-drivers, one might suppose, many an anxious moment.

Later in the morning we reported at the Secretariat, a hideous building, and were taken to see the Home Secretary, who gave me some good advice about doing my best to pass my examinations while I was still undergoing training, 'Since,' he said, 'if you've not finished them, or most of them, before you're given charge of your first subdivision, you'll find them a millstone round your neck.' We were asked to come again in the afternoon to meet the Home Minister, Sir Paw Tun, but, when we duly reappeared, we found that he was at a meeting and we never saw him.

There were letters waiting for both of us in the Secretariat from John Hall, the Deputy Commissioner in charge of the Sagaing District, who was to be responsible for our training. He welcomed us to Burma and to Sagaing, which he assured us was one of the pleasantest districts in Upper Burma; yet another example of the kindness shown to a newly-arrived officer. In due course our arrival was notified in the official *Burma Gazette*, together with our posting to Sagaing District as Assistant Commissioners (under training), with the powers of Third Class Magistrates, and we each received an extract of the notification 'for information and guidance'.

On first arrival in Rangoon we should normally, after signing the Governor's book, have been invited to tea at Government House before we proceeded to our district ('to the jungle', in the Rangoon parlance, which somewhat amused me at the time). The Governor was, however, away on tour, and our only visit to his residence was therefore for the purpose of signing his book. It was to be eight years before I met a Governor of Burma.

The rest of our short time in Rangoon was occupied mainly with shopping. Mrs Craw and Swithinbank helped us with this, our principal needs being certain things which we had not brought with us, such as pressure lamps, camp beds and tables. Before I left England I had provided myself with a topee. The outfitters to whom I went, though they had for many years supplied persons going to India, were unable to advise on the correct type of topee; but, as they had only two kinds, one called a 'military topee' and the other a 'civilian topee', I settled for the latter. It was a pretty smart affair, with a red lining, and cost what in those days was the not inconsiderable sum of one guinea. I wore it for the first time when I disembarked at Rangoon. As we were doing our shopping, Swithinbank said in his kindly way: 'Of course you won't be wearing that topee in the jungle, will you?', and carried me off to buy another which cost only a few shillings. My expensive topee – I had bought a special tin to hold it – rarely appeared thereafter, except on ceremonial occasions such as the King's Birthday Parade.

In my host Craw – later Sir Henry Craw – I recognised the member of the Civil Service Commission interviewing board who had asked the question about Burma which had led to my choosing Burma rather than India. I reminded him of the incident, which he did not remember; his daughter, however, told him that it sounded just like him. He had a small dinner-party on the day after my arrival, at which the Governor's Counsellor, who was the most senior civil servant in the country, was present. I was placed next to the wife of one of the guests, a woman who obviously led very much the colonial social life in a purely European milieu. She told me what Europeans I should meet in Sagaing, of whom there would apparently be very few. When I asked if she knew any of the Burmese officers there, as I should be interested to meet them too, she looked at me in some surprise, and said: 'But do you want to meet any Burmans?' I said that, having come to Burma, I certainly hoped that I should meet Burmans, and conversation somewhat flagged thereafter.

Arrangements had been made for us to leave Rangoon on our third day, the Thursday. The train for Mandalay left at night, and we were taken to the station by Swithinbank and settled into our compartment. Merrells was bound straight for Sagaing. I had been invited by Ohn Maung – who had been posted to Meiktila, a little south of Mandalay – to break my journey and stay with him for a few days. He was at that time unmarried.

The following morning the train reached Thazi, the junction for Meiktila and a place noted for its tough women porters, where Ohn Maung met me and drove me the fourteen miles into Meiktila. The town lay between two lakes and he had a large rambling house overlooking one of them. The couple of days that I spent in Meiktila gave me my first acquaintance with a real Burmese town, and I left it with the impression of heat, glare and dust by day and, as the sun went down, of pagoda bells tinkling in the breeze, of bullock carts creaking as they lumbered home, and of beautiful sunsets over the lakes.

On Sunday morning, after an early breakfast, Ohn Maung drove me to Thazi to catch the train. At noon I was in Mandalay, where I changed trains, and was soon rattling across the Ava Bridge over the great Irrawaddy into Sagaing railway station, where Hall and Merrells were waiting to meet me.

John Hall was a bachelor, and Sagaing was the first district of which he had held charge. He was at this time about thirty years of age, a very capable officer, with a keen sense of humour and a great love of the Burman. This last he had doubtless inherited from his father, H. Fielding Hall, who had served in the country about the time of the annexation of Upper Burma and had written a number of books about the Burmese, in which he perhaps idealised their gentleness and charm. John Hall spoke Burmese with great fluency and with an atrocious accent, and I have a vivid recollection of his taking me into his office a day or two after my arrival to see how he dealt with petitioners. Beside him stood his clerk and every sentence that Hall uttered was repeated in correct Burmese by the clerk. Hall appeared to be not in the least put out by this, but I made a mental resolution that, when I knew the language better and had to interview petitioners, I would not have a clerk in the room. Hall's ideas of administration were of the paternalistic kind: he loved going on tour round his district, taking his horse with him, and riding from village to village discussing crops and other village matters with the headmen. This was after all the ideal way of governing a district; far too many officers in these latter days were tied to their office desks by the ever-growing mass of paper, and were unable to get out among their people as much as they could have wished.

Sagaing town, the headquarters of the district, was a fairly quiet little place. The civil station, which consisted of the bungalows of the senior government officials, the hospital, church and club, lay stretched along the bank of the Irrawaddy, which was here some 590 miles from its mouth and at least a mile wide. Only during the rains, between May and September, was the river full from bank to bank. For much of the rest of the year extensive sandbanks lay on either side of the channel and sometimes almost in midstream. When there were strong winds from the river, quantities of sand were blown through the windows of the houses nearest to the bank. In the districts of this part of Upper Burma these sandbanks were the cause of many disputes. When the waters receded, they were frequently planted with groundnuts or tobacco and, as they tended to shift their position from year to year, different farmers would lay claim to cultivation rights on them.

We lived as Hall's guests for a few days, but he had arranged for us to rent a large house a few doors away which belonged to the American Baptist Mission. This Mission ran a school and had a small church, and the house had been occupied by the headmaster of the school, who had been a European. He had now left and his place had been taken by a Burman who had his own house in the town. We were charged the large sum of seventy-five rupees a month for the unfurnished house; this was equivalent to about £5 12s. 0d. Teak furniture could be obtained quite cheaply; some we bought from a doctor who was just retiring, and some we ordered from Rangoon. The house was typical of the older type of official residence. The lower storey was of brick, the upper of timber. On the ground floor were a large sitting-room, a dining-room and a small office; upstairs were a spacious landing, which I used as my office, and about three bedrooms. The kitchen was separate from the house and connected with it by a covered way, to protect the staff and the food from rain. The compound (or premises) was large, for it contained not only our house, but the school, the church and quarters for some of the

Burmese staff employed at the school. There were also quarters for our servants.

Before we moved into our house, we had of course to have the usual complement of staff. Merrells had, while still in Rangoon, acquired a house boy who came from Sagaing, and no sooner did I arrive there than this man produced his young nephew, aged about eighteen, as my personal servant. He was a very young fellow in his ways and rather diffident, and at first I did not find it easy to converse with him. We then had to each find a cook, for Hall had warned us that we should be sent off on tour separately, and should require a cook to take with us; one cook between us therefore would not do. Two middle-aged Burmans were produced for our inspection, each with the usual sheaf of testimonials, and were duly engaged; neither was much of a cook. There was a very clear-cut division of work among the staff. The cook would buy the food in the bazaar and cook it, and that was as far as his duties went. The house boy would look after one's clothes and other possessions, keep the furniture clean and generally act as major-domo. But neither would attend to the walls or floors or wash up the plates. Water supply and modern sanitation were unknown in most up-country houses in Burma. In the compound there would be a deep well and water for all purposes – washing and drinking – came from that; the drinking water was of course boiled or filtered. It was customary to employ one servant to perform the functions of water-carrier and gardener, and he also washed up the dishes. We had no responsibility for the garden, so our water-carrier must have had quite an easy time. The sweeper, a low caste Indian, was employed to dispose of the contents of the commode (generally known as the 'thunder box') and to sweep walls and floors. His work did not occupy him long, and it was usual for the same sweeper to work in several houses, and to visit each several times in the day. Washing of clothes was done by the *dhobi*, also an Indian, who would come about twice a week to collect the laundry and take it down to the river, where it was subjected to the usual process of having the dirt beaten out of it. Later, when we acquired horses, we employed a *syce* (groom) each and, had we at this time possessed cars, we should doubtless have needed a driver each. Wages in Burma were said to be high compared with those paid in India, but a staff of house boy, cook, water-carrier, *syce* and driver, together with the services of sweeper and *dhobi*, would not have cost more than about £14 a month. They had to feed and clothe themselves.

The day began at 6.30 with the arrival of morning tea, with perhaps a boiled egg or some biscuits. We arose soon after 7 and would then

Water carrier at the entrance to his village

work till breakfast time; the work might be either office work at home or outdoor work. At about 10 we had an enormous breakfast, which served as both breakfast and lunch, and I have often wondered since how we managed to consume so much. We would start with a cereal, and continue with a fish course, an egg course and toast and marmalade, ending with fruit or fruit juice. At about 10.30 we left for the office, and did not return till 4.30 or later for tea. After tea we walked or played tennis at the club, and at about dusk we had our baths. There was no such thing as a long white bath in the house. There was cold water in the bathroom, kept in a large earthenware jar of the Ali Baba type, known as a Pegu jar. Beside it was a galvanised iron tub, which at bath time had a couple of tins of boiling water emptied into it. By ladling cold water out of the Pegu jar with a tin container called a water dipper, one brought the water in the tub to the right temperature, and one was then ready for the bath. Dinner was on much the same scale as breakfast; I am almost certain that we regularly had both fish and meat. And soon afterwards we were ready for bed. During our time in Sagaing I remember that we were both most abstemious. Sometimes we would buy half a dozen bottles of beer, which would last us for a considerable time, and I think that our usual drink at the club after tennis was a soft one.

All the doors and windows of the house would be shut when we left for the office in the morning, for this made it easier to keep the house moderately cool. We had ceiling fans in the sitting-room only, and at times it was so hot in our office rooms that we had to keep fanning ourselves with hand fans. The fauna of the house consisted in the main of lizards on the walls, and occasionally the large tuctoo (or gekko), an animal of the lizard family. From time to time we would find a scorpion lurking in the bathroom, so it was just as well not to walk about in bare feet. When the rains broke, the plague of insects at night would sometimes drive us early to bed to the protection of our mosquito-nets. The flying ants in particular used to harass us, dropping their wings all over the floor and in our hair and down our necks. I remember that on one particular evening when we had been more than usually exasperated by insects we picked up a left-wing periodical sent out from England, and learnt from it that one of the services performed by the overseas territories was to enable members of middle-class English families to live upper-class lives!

The District Office, to which we walked every weekday when we were not on tour, was set back from the river and was not far from our house. It was a long two-storeyed building, and outside it were always gathered groups of petitioners or of witnesses in a case. It had its own peculiar smell, a compound of betel-juice, urine and cheroot smoke. The betel-nut is chewed by most Burmese. A piece of the nut is cut and placed on a leaf of the betel-vine, on which a little white lime has been spread; the leaf is then wrapped round the nut and makes a quid, which is stowed away in the side of the mouth and squeezed from time to time. The juice turns the saliva red, and there is need for frequent expectoration; hence large enamel spittoons were part of the equipment of every office. The lime quickly corrodes and destroys the teeth. As for cheroots, most Burmans, male and female, smoke them in some form; it used to be a stock joke that the Burmese baby grasps his mother's breast with one hand, while he holds a cheroot in the other! The most popular cheroot is a green one, containing very little tobacco, which is mild and whose smoke tastes like cabbage water. The cover is made of a leaf, the ends of which are tucked in, and the contents are chopped tobacco leaves and pieces of the stem of the tobacco plant. It follows that, once the cheroot is lighted, it must be held well away from the clothes or hot cinders falling from it will burn holes in them. The rolled cheroot, made entirely of tobacco leaf, is also smoked; it is short and black and is steeped in spirit during its manufacture. The long, dark brown cheroots which we know as Burma cheroots were made almost entirely for European consumption. The women generally smoke the 'whacking white cheroot' of Kipling's 'Mandalay', whose contents are the same as those of the green cheroot, but which is much larger and whose outer covering is the thick integument which encloses the maize cob, often reinforced by a sheet from the local newspaper.

The residential and shopping area of Sagaing lay inland from the civil station. The shops, generally known collectively as 'the bazaar', lay along two streets at right angles to one another. There were not very many of them, and one could buy nothing much more than the bare necessities. A district headquarters generally had a larger shopping centre, and the reason why Sagaing's was so small was no doubt the proximity of Mandalay, the second city of Burma, which lay only fifteen miles away, and which the construction of the Ava Bridge had brought within little more than half an hour's journey by road or rail. The houses of the local population were generally of timber, though there was the occasional brick house covered with plaster, which was known as a 'pukka house'. The town roads were metalled, but along each side there was usually a dirt track for the use of bullock-carts, which always raised a considerable amount of dust. Strong lights and colours and the ever-present smell of dust in the air: those were the characteristics of a walk in the town. There was comparatively little traffic: a few cars, some ancient buses, horse-drawn gharries which looked like up-ended match-boxes on wheels, and a large number of bicycles. There were of course many pagodas, and the Sagaing Hills, which ran down from the north to the river, were covered with monasteries. Near the civil station there was a group of pagodas, some in a partly ruinous state. I remember in particular one very large round one, which Hall christened the 'Albert Hall'; it certainly bore some resemblance.

The senior government official in Sagaing was the Commissioner, MacDougall – later Sir Raibeart MacDougall – whose charge extended as far as the Tibetan border, and who spent a good deal of his time touring; his wife was in England at the time and I did not meet her. There were Bradley, the Judge, who dealt with the more important criminal and civil cases, and the Superintendent of Police, both of whom had their wives with them. The officials of the second rank, with the exception of Merrells and myself, were Burmese. Relations between the races were friendly. Hall would not infrequently give dinner parties to which both Europeans and Burmese were invited; the fact that he was himself unmarried no doubt made things easier, for the parties would be entirely male. I soon learnt that the presence of women, of whatever race, was a hindrance to easy social intercourse between Europeans and Burmese. The Burmese official's wife spoke nothing but Burmese, while the European's wife spoke only the type of Burmese required for giving orders to servants. At a dinner party, therefore, the two could do little but sit and smile at one another. Let me add that there were European women who spoke excellent Burmese, but they were very few.

The small government club in the civil station, which was used by officials of all races, provided tennis and billiards, but little else, and it was rare to find anyone using it after dark. Merrells and I played a fair amount of tennis, as we felt we needed exercise after a day in a stuffy office; Hall's usual form of relaxation was riding. Behind the club lay the 'government church', which was of course Church of England. Padre Caldicott from Mandalay used to spend almost all his time travelling round the districts in our area, sleeping a night here and two nights there, holding services and retailing the local news. He came to Sagaing once a month, and was as good as a newspaper with the gossip which he collected from each club. In the town there was a Catholic church, which was also visited periodically by old Father Lafon, who had lived many years in Burma and had built a church in Mandalay which looked as though it were covered with icing.

This seems a convenient place for me to digress and to describe briefly the district administration in Burma, which in practice covered the whole country except the Rangoon Town area. The civil service – by which I mean the administrative service only – was divided into three grades. At the top was the Burma Commission, consisting almost entirely of officers of the Indian Civil Service, and known officially after the separation from India as the Burma Civil Service (Class I). Next came the provincial civil service, entirely locally recruited, and called the Burma Civil Service (Class II). Below that came the Subordinate Civil Service.

The country was divided administratively into eight divisions, each under a Commissioner, who was a senior member of the Burma Commission. When I arrived in Burma, all the Commissioners were Europeans, two of them being former officers of the Indian Army. It was not until the Civil Government was re-established after the war with Japan that the first Burmese and Anglo-Burmese Commissioners were appointed. The Commissioner had a general power to co-ordinate policy in the districts of his division – on an average there were five – and was more particularly concerned with the supervision of the local authorities, such as Municipalities and District Councils. He had, however, no responsibility for law and order.

In some of the Indian provinces the post of Commissioner had been abolished and in Burma after the Second World War, when local authorities were temporarily suspended and the Deputy Commissioner took over their functions, the Commissioner had really very little to do.

The central figure in the administrative organisation was the Deputy Commissioner, who was the head of the district. He had three main roles: as Deputy Commissioner, he was responsible for the administration and the preservation of peace in his district; as District Magistrate, he was the head of the magistracy; and as Collector, he had to ensure that government revenues were duly paid and safeguarded. He was usually an officer of the Class I Service, and might be European, Anglo-Burmese or Burmese, though at this time there was still a majority of Europeans; in a few cases he might be a senior member of the Class II Service. Directly under him in his headquarters office he had four Burmese officers, usually of the Class II Service: the Headquarters Assistant was his deputy and principal assistant, particularly in matters of general administration; the Akunwun was in charge of the revenue side of the work; the Treasury Officer was the custodian of the cash and also a part-time magistrate; and the Superintendent of Land Records was responsible for the mapping of agricultural land, for producing town and village plans, and for maintaining the registers of land ownership.

The district was divided into two or more subdivisions under Subdivisional Officers. The Subdivisional Officer was either a junior member of the Class I Service (European or Burmese) or, more usually, a member of the Class II Service or, occasionally, a senior officer of the Subordinate Civil Service. His responsibilities within his subdivision corresponded with those of the Deputy Commissioner in the district, but he exercised them under the Deputy Commissioner's general control. Having a much smaller area to administer, he naturally knew it much better than the Deputy Commissioner could hope to know his district, and there were many senior members of the Services who looked back on their time as Subdivisional Officers as the happiest days that they spent in Burma.

Below the subdivision came the township, of which there were on an average three to a subdivision. The township was not, as its name might imply, an urban area; it was like a district or a subdivision, but was a smaller unit than either. It was administered by a Township Officer, who belonged to the Subordinate Civil Service. Some of the older Township Officers had started as clerks and a few knew no English, but the younger men were mostly graduates of Rangoon University. The Township Officer's work was much the same as the Subdivisional Officer's, but on a lower plane, and in some of the heavier Townships he had an Assistant Township Officer to help him.

Lastly came the village tract, the lowest unit in the administration. This consisted of a number of villages with their surrounding agricultural land, and was under the charge of the village headman. Since the headmen were far and away the largest class of administrative official, and were to a great extent the basis of the whole administration, their position deserves to be discussed in some detail.

The headman was a government official in the sense that he was appointed by the government and could be removed from his post at the government's pleasure. He was, however, appointed as the representative of his community and as the result of an election held in the village tract, except in the very few cases where the headmanship was hereditary. He could not be transferred by the government to another area, and he held office till he died, resigned or was removed.

Under the Burmese kings the village headmen were grouped together under a superior headman called the *myothugyi*, who exercised a sort of feudal lordship over certain classes of people in his area who were liable to perform services for the king, and who seems to have had a general criminal jurisdiction over the whole area. We are not familiar with the full details of the system, but under the British administration the *myothugyis* were allowed to die out. The Indian system of village administration was imported and the *myothugyis'* areas were broken up into village units. This was the subject of criticism in later days by British officials who served in Burma, on the ground that the village became a mere artificial administrative unit, which was foreign to the Burmese, and that the local self-government which depended on the *myothugyi* was replaced by a foreign legal system, since recourse to the courts took the place of reference to the *myothugyi*.

The village headman received no salary from the government, his perquisites being a commission on the revenues which he collected for the government and exemption from certain civic duties. The principal revenues which passed through his hands were the land revenue and the capitation tax, and he had to pay his collections to the nearest Township Office before receiving his commission. If he was unable to collect any dues, and was forced to apply to the Township Office for assistance, he received no commission on these particular sums, even though they might eventually be paid.

It was unsatisfactory that the largest class of government administrative officials and those who really lived among the people

Village headman, his sons and womenfolk

should have been remunerated in this way: a good headman in charge of a comparatively poor village tract would naturally receive less commission than, say, an indifferent headman in a richer area. From time to time proposals were made for the payment of fixed salaries to headmen, but these came to nothing. The principal arguments advanced against them were, firstly, that the headman, though admittedly appointed by the government, was not in fact a government official, and, secondly, that if he no longer received a commission on his revenue collections, he would cease to show such enthusiasm for this work. This last objection was met by a compromise proposal: that headmen should continue to draw a commission on revenue collected and should in addition be paid a sum sufficient to bring their total remuneration (inclusive of their theoretical commission) up to a fixed figure.

Early in the century, in order to combine adequate emoluments with efficient administration, a comprehensive scheme of amalgamation of villages had been undertaken. And even in later days, in order to ensure that a headman's commission was sufficiently large to make the job reasonably attractive, the occasion was taken of every vacancy in a headmanship to assess the amount of the revenues accruing from the area and, if they were small, to consider amalgamating it with a neighbouring village tract. This led over the years to a gradual decrease in the number of village tracts, and my own experience was that amalgamation was not welcomed by the people. The more villages a headman had in his area, the further some of his villagers would have to travel when they wished to see him on official business.

The occasions on which a man might have business to transact with his headman were numerous. Not only did the headman collect the taxes and compile the list of taxpayers for the purpose of the capitation tax, but he was also responsible for maintaining the official registers of births and deaths, for recording the names of all strangers spending a night in his area, and for reporting to higher authority outbreaks of smallpox, cholera, plague and cattle disease. The Village Act of 1889 laid on the villagers the duty of doing and reporting a number of things, many of which involved the headman. It empowered him too to try, either by himself or sitting with his village committee, certain minor criminal and civil cases, and to impose fines. He was also in some degree a village policeman, to whom reports of offences would be made, though with government approval he could appoint subordinates in the other villages of his tract to exercise certain of his police powers.

The government certainly got a considerable amount of work out of its headmen at comparatively little cost. Besides having to undertake the various duties outlined above, the headman was at the beck

A government inspection party – the luggage goes ahead

and call of every government official who visited his village tract. These would include not only the more important officers of the Administration and the Police on their periodical tours, but also subordinates such as police constables on surveillance duties, vaccinators, public health and veterinary inspectors, revenue surveyors and so forth. Not unnaturally friction sometimes arose between the headman and the host of minor officials; the latter would sometimes throw their weight about and treat the headman as a subordinate whose job was to do what any government official, no matter how lowly, told him to do; the headman would react by being as little co-operative as possible, and this would lead to complaints against him by the minor officials concerned. Moreover, the headman, as the chief representative of his people, was continually being summoned to the nearest government headquarters to give evidence in court cases or other inquiries. Officers of the Administration did their best to deal with such inquiries while on tour in the headman's area in order to inconvenience him as little as possible, but the volume of office work was such that, with the best will in the world, they had frequently to call the headman to the office. He was of course paid his travelling expenses and an allowance to cover the cost of food taken *en route*, but even so the headmen of large or disturbed village tracts must have spent a considerable part of their time in travelling to and from the office. Nevertheless, there was never in my experience any lack of candidates for a vacant headmanship.

The headman administered his tract with the assistance of a village committee of four, who held office for three years. They received no monetary remuneration at all, but were exempted from the performance of certain village duties.

A European officer of the Civil Service, on first arrival in Burma, underwent a course of training in the district to which he was posted, under the general supervision of the Deputy Commissioner. Burmese members of the Class I Service took the same training course, but young men joining, say, the Subordinate Civil Service would probably be appointed Assistant Township Officers at once and would have certain duties to perform while learning the job. They had not so much to learn as the Europeans, partly because the duties which they would be called upon to perform were more limited in scope, and partly of course because they already knew the country and were tolerably familiar with the general pattern of administration. The period of training for a member of the Class I Service lasted for a little under a year. He usually arrived in the country in November, took his first departmental examinations in

May, and two or three months later was placed in charge of a subdivision.

The course of training was designed to ensure that an officer would learn every branch of the work with which he would later have to deal, and the first and most important study upon which he embarked was that of the land. Not only was this the main interest of the people of the district, but it yielded the bulk of the locally raised revenue. The total revenue of Burma in 1939–40 was a little over 17 crores of rupees (a crore being 10 million); 5.7 crores came from customs and excise duties, and land revenue with 5.1 crores was second.

In theory all land, with a few exceptions, belonged to the state, and under customary law the Burmese king had had a right to a tenth of the produce. Rights in land could be acquired by gift, inheritance, purchase, original reclamation from jungle or by unchallenged occupation for a period of ten years. No rent was charged by the government for agricultural land, and the customary due of a portion of the produce was perpetuated under British rule in the form of a land revenue. The rates at which this was to be paid were fixed as the result of a 'settlement' of the district. About once in twenty years a settlement party went to the district, spent about two years surveying all the agricultural land, making detailed maps showing every holding, classifying types of land according to the fertility of the soil and assessing crop outturns from each class of land – with the assistance of local advisers called *thamadis* – and eventually submitted a report to the government with recommendations as to the rates to be charged per acre on the various types of land; these were of course to be paid in cash, not in kind. It was never my good fortune to be a member of a settlement party, for the war soon broke out and, to the best of my recollection, only one district was 'settled' during my time in Burma; but those who took part in these operations found the work most interesting and enjoyable. The members of the party, moving slowly from village to village in the best season of the year and able to take their time, came into much closer contact with the people and acquired a far fuller knowledge of them and their ways of life than any ordinary administrative officer could ever hope to do, with his many other preoccupations, particularly his office desk. The settlement report, usually a large volume, contained a mass of interesting information about the district.

The revenue to be paid was based on what was called the 'nett produce value', and this was arrived at by calculating the normal gross outturn and deducting the assumed cost of production. Once

A zayat where a government officer would stay on tour

the recommendations had been approved by the government, the actual revenue payable on each particular holding was calculated by the district Land Records staff with reference to acreage and soil class, and every year the tax tickets were prepared and submitted to the Revenue Department of the Deputy Commissioner's office, where they were stamped with his name stamp before being sent out to headmen for collection of the revenue.

An accurate system of field mapping and recording of changes in land ownership had of course been devised and this was, as I have said, the responsibility of the Land Records Department, a most important and useful department. It was staffed entirely by Burmans, though in a very few cases the Superintendent might be Anglo-Burmese. The lowest member of the department – apart from menials such as chairmen – was the revenue surveyor. On this lowly-paid, but frequently very knowledgeable, person depended the efficacy of the whole system. Surveyors were stationed throughout the district, each having a number of village tracts within his charge. They were responsible for keeping the field maps up to date, recording all physical changes in boundaries, noting every year what crops were planted on a holding, what plots were left fallow, and so forth. They also maintained registers showing changes of ownership, tenancies and mortgages.

Being, as I have said, but lowly-paid, they were of course open to the temptation of trying to augment their salaries by making false entries in their records. If, for example, they marked a certain plot as lying fallow when in fact it was planted with rice, the owner's land revenue would be assessed only at the fallow rate, which was very low. Their work was therefore subjected to as much verification as possible. Immediately above the revenue surveyor was the inspector, who was continually moving round and checking the work of his surveyors. Above the inspector was the superintendent himself, who was expected to spend the greater part of the 'cold weather' – the season during which the rice crop was reaped – out in the fields inspecting. As a further check on the work of the Land Records Department, officers of the administration from the Deputy Commissioner downwards were expected to do a certain number of inspections every year. Any errors or omissions found during the inspection were entered on a standard form and at the foot the inspecting officer recorded his opinion of the surveyor's work.

As soon as we had settled down in Sagaing, Merrells and I were attached to the Land Records Department for training. Hall invited us to dinner to meet the Superintendent of Land Records, U Ba Thaw, a portly, cheerful and altogether very likeable and competent officer, to whom I owe a great deal for introducing me to the country. We spent a week or so in his office learning about the various registers and the method of calculating land revenue, only part of

Checking the land register

which we understood, as the instruction was imparted to us in Burmese by an elderly inspector. We were also shown how to do a chain survey and how to use a theodolite, accomplishments which I forgot very soon and which were never of the slightest use to me in later life. After this short introduction to land records work we were bundled out into the district with U Ba Thaw on a three week's tour. Though somewhat tiring, this tour was one of the most instructive that I ever did, for it brought me into touch for the first time with the Burmese people and their land, around which the rest of my service revolved.

The rice-cultivator's year begins with the first rains in mid-May. The ground, which has been baked hard by the blazing sun of March and April, suddenly becomes a sea of mud. The Burman yokes his bullocks, or it may be his buffaloes – in the dry zone the bullock is more commonly used – and proceeds to plough his land. The bullocks drag the plough and the farmer stands on top of it. The paddy seed is sown broadcast in small 'nurseries', and then there is nothing to be done for a month or six weeks. Early in August the plants in the nurseries have grown to a fair size, and they are then pulled up and transplanted in the main paddy fields by the women and children. Provided that all goes well climatically, there is little more to be done till the harvest. There are varieties of paddy which are harvested early or late, but the main crop is reaped in late November or December, and this work is carried out by the men, who cut off the ears with their sickles, leaving most of the straw behind, to be burnt later to act as a soil fertiliser.

The harvest was about to start when we set out on our tour. Our daily programme varied little. The Public Works Department maintained 'inspection bungalows' at convenient centres throughout the Burma districts. These were generally wooden buildings roofed with teak shingles. They had basic furniture – tables, chairs, bedsteads, meatsafes – and glass and crockery, and the caretaker would supply water, firewood and oil for lamps at a cost of four annas each per day (equivalent to 4½d.). The touring officer had to bring his own bedding, cutlery, cooking utensils and such food as he could not expect to obtain in the local bazaar.

Having established ourselves in an inspection bungalow, we would have an early light breakfast and set out at about 7 for an inspection. On all inspections we were accompanied by the revenue surveyor with the appropriate field maps and registers, and by the headman and a crowd of villagers, with whom we would check the accuracy of the surveyor's records by enquiring who was the owner of each plot of land that we passed and verifying that the crops

An inspection bungalow

planted on it were as shown in his maps. The villagers were all dressed in the Burmese *longyi* (or skirt), and most of them wore their hair long and tied up in a bun at the back; it took me some time to accustom myself to the fact that they were men and not women. Most carried the agricultural knife (or *dah*). Our inspection would last till the middle of the morning when, hot and dusty, we would return to the bungalow for a bath and our main breakfast. After breakfast the inspector and revenue surveyor would come to the bungalow with their maps and registers, and the reports of the inspection would be written up. In the afternoon, when the heat of the sun had somewhat decreased, we went out again for more inspections, getting back for tea at about 5.30.

Work was then over for the day, and we would go for a stroll in the neighbouring village, often conducted by the surveyor. On one occasion we persuaded the surveyor, a young man like ourselves, to teach us how to play the Burmese national game of *chinlon* (basket-ball). This is not really a game so much as an exhibition of proficiency. The players stand in a circle, gird up their *longyis* and kick a small cane ball from one to another. The ball is of wickerwork, the cane strips being so interwoven as to leave a number of small holes, and it is consequently very light. There is no scoring and the object is to keep the ball in the air as long as possible without touching it with the hands. The player who has the ball may either play it by himself, endeavouring to execute various stylish strokes – most of which have their own special names – or kick it on to one of the others; usually the last course is adopted only when the player is no longer able to keep it up himself. U Ba Thaw was a little concerned at our fraternising in this manner with such insignificant persons as revenue surveyors, and gave us some fatherly advice, certainly well meant and probably well founded, on the dangers of becoming too familiar with subordinates, who would in all likelihood try to take unfair advantage of the acquaintance. In our talks with him in the bungalow after dark we learnt a great deal about Burmese customs and ideas.

In the course of our tour we stayed at four or five inspection bungalows in different parts of the district, and we got to know by sight the other principal crops besides paddy. In the wet deltaic plains and in the Upper Burma wet zone paddy is almost the only crop, certainly the one of most importance. But in the dry zone a variety of other crops are grown: sessamum and groundnut (both used for vegetable oils), cotton, various types of beans and chillies. We also grew used to the village noises, especially after dark: the tinkling of the pagoda bells, the dull resonant sound of the gong from the monastery, the music of the bamboo pipe, and the sound of the villager returning home after dark and singing at the top of his voice to scare away the evil spirits.

At this time of the year Upper Burma was at its best. Some people have compared it with northern Italy. There were clear, crisp mornings which made thick clothing desirable. But before long it would grow hot and, by the time we had our breakfast, we were glad to be under a roof. The tops of the village pagodas glistened in the sun, and the villages were framed by palm trees. In Upper Burma the most common palms were the coconut and the toddy palm, from the latter of which was extracted the juice known as toddy or *tari*. Earthenware jars were tied high up underneath the palm leaves and into them the juice gradually seeped. In the early morning a drink of sweet toddy straight from the tree was most refreshing, but the liquid soon fermented and became sour and alcoholic.

Our period of attachment to the Land Records Department ended after about two months with a short practical test, and we were then free to concentrate on other aspects of our work. We had already from time to time sat on the bench beside a Burmese magistrate and listened to cases being tried. At this stage it was not easy to follow the evidence, which was all given in Burmese, but almost every magistrate had a typewriter on the bench on which he took down the evidence in English. If, therefore, anything was not intelligible to me, I had only to glance at the typewriter. Few magistrates typed with more than two fingers, but they managed to attain a very considerable speed.

Hall now decided that it was time for us to try some cases on our own. There were not many which could be passed to a Third Class Magistrate, for his powers were limited to a fine of fifty rupees and to one month's imprisonment. There were, however, a number of cases under the Excise Act, cases in which people were caught illegally manufacturing country spirit, for which a small fine was usually sufficient punishment; the magistrate then had personally to supervise the destruction of the illicit spirit, which was poured on to the ground somewhere near the court house. There were also municipal cases of a trivial nature. We had a clerk made available to us for our bench work, a Zerbadi (Burma Muslim) called Maung E, who had a long wisp of hair growing from a mole on his chin, of which he was presumably extremely proud, for he never made any attempt to cut it; and his teeth and lips were stained with betel juice. For my first few cases I merely typed out the charge in English and got Maung E to read it to the accused. After a time, however, I felt that, as I was supposed to be able to speak a certain amount of Burmese, I should make an effort to pronounce the charge myself. So, when my next case came up, I wrote out the charge in English, had it translated into Burmese by one of the magistrates, and duly took my seat on the bench prepared to recite it to the accused. The accused was an old woman, charged with using obscene language in a public place – to wit, the village street. I read the charge slowly, pausing at every possible stop and looking up at her; each time I looked she nodded, as if to indicate that she understood. Finally, when I asked her whether she pleaded guilty or not guilty, she completely deflated me by fixing me with a blank look and saying 'Paya?', the equivalent of 'I beg your pardon, sir'. In despair I handed the charge to Maung E and told him to read it again. When I came to know the Burmese better, I found that elderly people in particular would frequently regard a foreigner speaking their language with such astonishment that they would not attend to what he was saying.

We were very soon initiated into the practice of going on tour in the district, but, as Hall insisted that we should not go together, touring at this stage, with our comparative ignorance of Burmese, tended to be rather boring. We were provided with a young apprentice clerk called Maung Ba Toke, a cheerful little fellow with a mouth full of gold teeth, who always addressed us as 'Your Honour', somewhat to our embarrassment at first. His job was to accompany

The reception committee for a visiting officer

whichever of us was going on tour and to make all necessary arrangements with the headmen for the provision of transport within their areas, whether this was bullock-cart or horse. The district was fairly well provided with both roads and railway lines, and touring generally involved either a train journey or a drive in a rickety old bus to the inspection bungalow where one was to stay. In the latter event, the practice was to hire the entire bus, since in addition to the clerk there were the cook and the house boy to be accommodated, as well as the baggage and the cook's boxes. In fact an officer's equipage for touring his charge, especially when he rose to more senior positions, could be quite impressive, and at times might resemble a minor state procession. He would take, as well as the staff already mentioned, an office boy and – if he was in the frontier areas where he was in direct charge of the police – a constable or two. He might also be accompanied by a minor government official taking the opportunity of touring with his senior.

Soon after my arrival in Sagaing I had bought a horse from the bailiff of the District Court for two hundred rupees (£15). It was a Burma pony, smaller than the English horse but perfectly adequate, and had obviously been trained as a polo pony, though I am afraid that it had no opportunity of showing its capabilities in this field whilst in my possession. If I had a fair amount of outdoor work to do on tour, I would send the horse ahead the previous day with my *syce*, a tall Sikh, to wait for me at the inspection bungalow at which I intended to camp, and would follow myself with the rest of my staff by road or rail. There were many ponies in the villages of this district, and it was not unusual for the headman and some of his friends to accompany me on horseback when I rode out to my work. The Burmese saddle was made of upholstered cloth and rose both in front and behind; I had occasionally to use one, when I was lent a pony by a headman, and found it rather uncomfortable.

It was not easy for Hall to find jobs which we might be able to tackle by ourselves on tour. I was sent out on one or two occasions to inquire into complaints against headmen; these were frequent, whatever district one was in. Another job that fell to me was to check the measurement of 'tanks'. A Deputy Commissioner had a sum of money allocated to him each year, which was known as his 'discretionary fund', which he could use to assist villagers in minor works which would improve the amenities of the village. These might be roads, bridges, etc., and the villagers normally had to contribute something to the cost of the work, generally in the form of labour. Sagaing being in the dry zone, there was frequently a shortage of water in those villages which were not near a river. A number of grants were therefore made to enable villagers to dig large rectangular reservoirs in the ground, known as 'tanks', in which the rain water could be stored for use in time of drought. The government paid so much for each *kyin* dug (a *kyin* was a unit of volume), and my duty was to measure the number of *kyins* which had been dug and to authorise payment.

When there was no other particular work to be done in a village, one could always check the *thathameda* rolls. I have said earlier that one of the taxes collected by the district administration was the capitation tax. It was known by that name in Lower Burma, where each adult male had to pay it. In Upper Burma it was called *thathameda* and was assessed on the household. Under the Burmese kings the *thathameda* had been a tax on all property, but, with the introduction of land revenue under the British administration, it came to be simply a personal tax. The total amount payable by the village was calculated on the basis of a flat rate per household, but the actual sum to be paid by each individual household was fixed by local assessors (*thamadis*). Since it was not easy for them to compute the relative means of each household when agricultural land was not taken into account, the result was generally that each house paid much the same amount, except when there was no able-bodied male living in it. It was the headman's duty to compile the *thathameda* rolls, and inspecting officers would go round the village with him and check that no house had been omitted from the rolls. The *thathameda* and capitation taxes were considered objectionable by the Burmese politicians as being nothing but poll taxes, and in 1937 the first government under the new constitution had decided that they should be reduced by one-fifth annually till they were abolished. To make up for the revenue lost thereby, a state lottery was instituted, a form of raising money which appealed to the Burmese.

The most arduous tours that I did in Sagaing were in connection with remission work. The dry zone of Upper Burma was regarded as a 'precarious area', inasmuch as the rainfall was not regular and in some years there might be considerable failure of crops owing to inadequate or excessive rain. There was provision in the law that land revenue might be remitted in whole or in part on any holding where the actual crop outturn was less than one-third of that assumed at the last settlement to be the average outturn for the particular type of land. Not only lack or excess of rain, but attacks of insects and floods, were reasons for which remission might be given. In every case in which remission was applied for, an officer of the administration was required to make a personal visit to the land in question and either himself examine the crops or – if they had already been reaped, as was frequently the case – determine, by questioning the headman and neighbouring farmers, what had been the actual outturn. He would then submit a report, with his recommendation, to the Deputy Commissioner, who could authorise remission. As it often happened that the outturn normally obtained was a good deal higher than the assumed settlement outturn, and as remission was based on comparison with the latter, the applicant would generally find that the remission granted was less than he expected.

I spent two tours on remission duty, one in a paddy area while the weather was still quite pleasant, the other, when it was very much hotter, in wheat fields. On my first tour, as instructed by Hall, I visited every single plot for which remission had been asked, and this took several days of hard riding. On the second, which covered a much larger area, I asked advice from U Ba Thaw as to the best method of proceeding. He suggested that I should ride across the affected area in several directions, in order to get a general idea of the damage done – in this case by insects – and submit my report on that basis. John Hall was, however, not at all pleased when I returned to headquarters after only two days – he had apparently expected me to be away for at least a week – and submitted a report on the area as a whole instead of on each individual plot. He made some rather caustic remarks on my monthly diary; all officers had to submit these to show what they had done and what was happening in their area. I found it difficult to believe, however, that the Township and Assistant Township Officers, who were normally responsible for remission inspections, visited every plot. I had a shrewd suspicion that many of them simply sat in the village and made their reports and recommendations on the basis of discussions with the people. In a bad year applications for remission in some districts might be so numerous that the government had to post officers for a month or more on special remission duty.

Hall was of the opinion that neither Merrells nor I liked touring, and this was true up to a point. We had no authority, could solve no problems which the headmen might bring to us, and very often had to rack our brains to find enough to occupy our time. Once I had my own little kingdom, I thoroughly enjoyed getting away from the office and out into the villages.

CHAPTER FOUR

Under Training 1938-39: 2

SAGAING, though small, was an interesting district. It was cut in two by the Irrawaddy, which we normally crossed in a small rowing-boat. There was no government launch permanently in Sagaing, but the DC could always arrange with the Marine Department in Mandalay for one to be sent for his use if he wished to do a riverine tour. The district was generally undulating, and had a reddish soil, the only hills being the low and barren Sagaing Hills, covered with monasteries towards their southern end where they ran down to the river near Sagaing town. Agriculture, as I have said, was more diversified in the dry zone than in other parts of Burma and, instead of the acres and acres of flat paddy fields which made up most of the Lower Burma delta, the land was divided into fairly small holdings, on which paddy and the usual dry zone crops were grown.

There were a few sites of historical interest in the neighbourhood. Ava, for many years the capital of the Burmese kings, lay across the river opposite Sagaing town. It contained a few old monasteries, but was otherwise deserted. From a distance it looked picturesque, but at close quarters the pagodas and monasteries, like so many religious buildings in Burma, were seen to be shabby and frequently in a state of collapse. This was to a great extent a consequence of the Buddhist theory of merit (*kutho*). If a man built a pagoda or a monastery, he stored up merit for himself in the next life. If he merely repaired one that someone else had built, all the merit went to the original builder. If, therefore, you had the money to put up a religious building, it was obviously sound common sense to ensure that you got all the merit that you could. In the case of the great national pagodas, which were regarded as belonging to the community as a whole, this objection apparently did not apply, presumably because the merit created was shared by the community. They were usually under the control of a board of pagoda trustees which was responsible for raising the funds to carry out necessary repairs or additional adornments.

The most famous pagoda in the district was the Kaunghmudaw, which stood in the open plain near the foot of the Sagaing Hills and was visible from far and wide. It had been built by King Thalun

49

(1629–48) after he had moved his capital bank to Ava from Lower Burma. It is said that the pagoda was fashioned in the likeness of the breast of his favourite queen, but the pious Buddhist naturally regards this tale as blasphemous. Inside the Kaunghmudaw were enshrined a Buddha's tooth and a stone begging bowl of supernatural origin, both of which had been sent from Ceylon in 1576 to the Burmese king of the day. The tooth, reputed to be the famous Kandy tooth, had a remarkable history. Having reposed for many years in Kandy, it fell in 1560 into the hands of the Portuguese, who took it to their capital Goa. The King of Burma and other Buddhist kings offered huge sums of money and shiploads of goods for the return of the tooth, but, though the Portuguese civil authorities might have been willing enough to enter into a bargain of this nature, the pressure of the Catholic Church was such that they dared not. The tooth was therefore ground to powder and publicly burnt, and the ashes were cast into the river. It was not long, however, before it was miraculously restored to the temple in Kandy. Some years later the King of Burma, having been told that he was destined to wed a princess of Ceylon, sent an embassy to the island, which returned with a lady and a wedding present in the form of the Kandy tooth. Though it is said that the lady was not a princess and the tooth was not the Kandy tooth, King Bayinnaung was convinced that he had obtained possession of the authentic tooth of the Buddha. It was received with magnificent ceremony when it reached Burma and was deposited in the Mahazedi pagoda in Pegu in 1576; thence it journeyed to Ava in 1610, and was finally transferred to the Kaunghmudaw (which means literally 'the royal good deed').

Another interesting historical monument was the huge unfinished pagoda at Mingun, which lies on the Irrawaddy nearly opposite Mandalay. A later king, Bodawpaya (1782–1819) of the last Burmese dynasty, determined to build what was to be the largest pagoda in the world.

> This was to stagger humanity by its vastness. He himself frequently superintended the work (1790–97), camping on an island in the river and taking great pride in the leaden chambers which were his own idea. The height of the pagoda was to be 500 feet; but when it reached a third of this height, there arose a prophecy 'The pagoda is finished and the great country ruined!' Now there had been precisely the same prophecy about the Mingalazedi pagoda when the Tartars overthrew Pagan, so Bodawpaya abandoned the work ... The pagoda is the biggest pile of brick in existence. (G.E. Harvey, *Outline of Burmese History*.)

The bell which was to have been built into the pagoda was

completed, and is said to be the second largest in the world. It lies a little to one side of the pile of brick under a small roof, and I remember that I was able to stand inside it quite comfortably with only a little stooping.

Politically the district was as quiet as could be expected in those somewhat disturbed times, despite its proximity to Mandalay, where so many politically-minded monks were to be found. It had, I think, been virtually unaffected by the Burmese-Muslim riots of 1938. Elsewhere, especially in Mandalay, the monks were trying to whip up anti-foreign feeling. About this time they were waging a campaign against the wearing by Burmese women of jackets made of foreign cloth, and cases occurred of monks caning women in the open bazaar for wearing such jackets. It was difficult for the police to take any action, since the victims refused to report these assaults and, even if a case had been brought to court, would not have given evidence. Such was the reverence accorded to those who wore the yellow robe. I discussed this attitude of the people with intelligent Burmans, who knew as well as I did that large numbers of criminals had taken refuge in the monasteries and assumed the yellow robe. Their reply was that it was the robe that was respected, not the man wearing it; if in fact the wearer was not worthy to be a monk, he would be punished in his next existence for having worn it.

Though there were so many monks living in the monasteries on the Sagaing Hills, I do not remember that any of them gave any trouble; but perhaps, as a young officer under training, I might not have heard. There were undoubtedly some saintly men among them. I recall one, who was known as the Ye-u Sayadaw, who had to go to Mandalay for a minor operation; the DC had, I think, assisted in getting him into hospital, and he sent his car to fetch him back when he was discharged. I was returning myself from Mandalay shortly afterwards and, when I reached the Sagaing end of the Ava Bridge, I found crowds of people waiting to welcome back the Sayadaw. He was sitting beside the car, looking like a reverend archbishop and talking quietly to them. He then drove straight to Hall's bungalow to pay him a courtesy call.

School strikes were endemic in Burma at this period. Rangoon University was a hotbed of politics, and it had set the example of going on strike. The cause of the school strikes was frequently the alleged difficulty of the examination papers. During the early part of my time in Burma, students were on strike in most of the schools of the country for several weeks. Most Burmans attended government schools, though there were mission schools scattered about the country, generally in the larger centres of population, and other races, particularly the Chinese, ran their own schools. The strikers seemed to be blithely unconscious of the disastrous effect upon their own education which these frequent disturbances were likely to have, and Burmese parents in general had little control over their children, at all events in the towns. The village youngsters grew up in a more healthy atmosphere, but in the towns it was a common sight to see youths, often still at school over the age of twenty, ambling about in silk *longyis* and patent leather shoes, with hair heavily larded with scented pomade.

Mandalay, the centre of most of the Upper Burma troubles and the nearest large town to Sagaing, I used to visit from time to time, generally on shopping expeditions. The road lay through Amarapura, another old capital, and through the straggling suburbs of Mandalay itself. It was a cool and well-shaded road, but covered in the dry weather with dust, which the ubiquitous bullock-carts helped to swirl about. On the way we passed places where a considerable business was done in carving stone Buddhas; Buddhas of all sizes, seated or reclining in every recognised position, could be seen close to the roadside in workshops which had no walls but only corrugated iron roofs. On the outskirts of Mandalay the tram-lines began. Though not perhaps so romantic as its name might suggest to readers of Kipling, Mandalay was a town with a considerable attraction. The most interesting sight was the palace-city of the Kings of Burma.

Bridge across moat at Mandalay – gate tower in the rear

This was of no great antiquity, the capital having been transferred to Mandalay only in 1857, as a result of dreams and omens. The palace-city, outside which – at all events towards the end – the King had rarely ventured, was surrounded by a wall of pinkish brick one mile square, outside which was a moat. The moat was crossed at intervals by bridges leading to doorways in the wall which were crowned by the typical Burmese tiered and spire-like roofs called *pyathats*. Inside the walls lay King Thibaw's palace, which was later destroyed during the British reoccupation of Burma in 1945. It was built of wood and corrugated iron, the wood being covered with lacquer and tinsel. It was frequently described as tawdry by European visitors and so in a sense it was. But there was a certain splendour about it, particularly in the huge straight pillars of teak which supported the roofs. Under the British administration the palace area had been named Fort Dufferin, after the Viceroy under whom Upper Burma had been annexed, and other buildings, such as the Mandalay Club and the barracks of the British battalion quartered in the town, had been erected within the walls. But they did not in any way interfere with the palace.

The houses of the principal government officials lay facing the moat, some of them commanding a fine view of Mandalay Hill, from which the town took its name. This hill is a great rock which rises suddenly out of the plain, is covered with monasteries of white stone, and has literally hundreds of small pagodas clustered round its foot.

The shopping area of Mandalay was unattractive, consisting as it did of rows of stuccoed buildings of different shapes and sizes, occupied by Indian shop-keepers. But the big bazaar building in the centre of the town, though certainly a thing of no beauty, was full of interest. Here one could buy samples of most of the Burmese crafts: lacquerware, silver work, baskets (including the large square baskets known as *pas*, made of woven cane, which took the place of suitcases for many Burmese) and books, both modern works and copies of the Burmese classics. The bazaar was the centre of Burmese, as opposed to Indian, business in Mandalay, and I never came across any bazaar quite like it elsewhere in Burma.

Another place in which works of Burmese art could be bought was the house of Monsieur Martin, an old Frenchman or Belgian. It was said that he had at one time been a Catholic priest. From him one could buy articles which, though more costly than those obtainable in the bazaar, were of better quality and in greater variety. His lacquer furniture, for example, could be relied upon not to warp, for he employed his own lacquer workers and ensured that the wood was well seasoned before the lacquer was applied.

Mandalay was pleasantest during the cold weather. It became very hot in March and April, and at this time every year disease broke out: smallpox, plague and cholera.

Forty-two miles from Mandalay on top of the Shan plateau lay Maymyo, the former summer capital of Burma. One day Hall had to go up on business and took us with him. The road from Mandalay was very good, with some steep hairpin bends, and we soon felt the change in the atmosphere as we left the heat of the plains behind. Maymyo had an almost English appearance, so far as its flora was concerned. It possessed a Government House and a Secretariat, and prior to the introduction of ministerial government it had been the practice for the headquarters of government to move up there during the hot weather. The Burmese ministers, however, had no desire to follow this practice; they were used to the heat of Rangoon and the Shan plateau was almost foreign territory to them. The result was that, while the Governor and his entourage still spent part of the hot weather in Maymyo, and perhaps one or two of the Secretaries to Ministries did likewise, there was no longer any wholesale migration of the government to the hills. Many European wives used to go up to Maymyo for the worst of the hot weather.

Social life in Sagaing was somewhat restricted. I have already referred to the games of tennis and billiards in the small club. From time to time we Europeans would dine in each other's houses; if it were a large party to which one was invited, it was not uncommon to find on the table some of one's own cutlery and crockery. There was admirable liaison between the domestic staffs, and our servants always knew where we were going to dine without our telling them, since they had probably been already approached by our hosts' servants for the load of certain table appurtenances.

But the social occasions which I remember best were the entertainments given by the non-European communities. The Inspector of Schools, who was Chinese, once invited the senior officials – and this term would include all Europeans, even if they were only under training! – to a Chinese 'hot pot' dinner, the first of the many Chinese meals which I was to eat during my time in the East. A 'hot pot' dinner was in effect a dinner cooked on the table in the presence of the guests. On the table stood two or more large pots full of liquid, with a flame burning under each; there were also plates containing many types of Chinese food, uncooked or only partly cooked. The guests, using their chopsticks, picked up morsels of food from the plates and deposited them in the pots, from which they were later withdrawn and eaten. The richness of the soup which remained in the pots after this can well be imagined.

On another occasion the town gave a large tea party in the grounds of the Municipal Office in honour of the departure on transfer of Bradley, the Judge, and the arrival of his successor U Aung Tha Gyaw. At parties of this nature the Europeans were invariably served with what was known as 'English tea', which meant tea already mixed with large quantities of milk and sugar. Burmese tea was drunk weak, with neither sugar nor milk, in little bowls, after the Chinese fashion. Besides tea there was a variety of sweet cakes, usually of vivid shades of pink and green. Apart from the refreshments, however, parties of this nature could be quite enjoyable, and they did at all events give the officials some opportunity of mixing with the leading people of the town – an opportunity which was otherwise not often afforded them. But the local people rarely brought their wives with them, and the seating was so arranged that all the officials were together at one or two tables. U Aung Tha Gyaw, the Judge in part honour of whom this particular party was given, was an Arakanese, whom I was to meet on many occasions in my subsequent career; he came out to India after the Japanese invasion of Burma and, like me, was commissioned in the Civil Affairs Service. 'ATG', as we usually called him, was a very level-headed and upright man and, after Burma attained independence, he became a Judge of the High Court.

U Ba Thaw, the Superintendent of Land Records, invited us to a large tea party which he gave to celebrate his son's *shinbyu* ceremony and his daughter's ear-boring. The *shinbyu* (literally 'money-making') ceremony is to the Burmese Buddhist what baptism is to the Christian: his formal initiation into his religion. About the age of puberty, though frequently earlier and sometimes later, the Burmese youth becomes the central figure of a great family festival. His parents, who have probably been saving up for this for years, invite all their friends and many of the local monks to the house. The young boy, dressed in the costume of a Burmese prince, sits in state among the guests while they consume refreshments. When the reception is over, he mounts a white pony (or perhaps in these more modern times a decorated car) and is escorted slowly to the monastery where he is to be initiated. On arrival there, his head is shaved, his princely vestments exchanged for the yellow robe of the monk, and he enters the monastery. In the old days it was the practice for him to remain there for a complete Buddhist Lent (three months), but nowadays he probably stays for only a few days. Then he returns to the bosom of his family, a full member of the Buddhist faith. There is no similar ceremony for girls, for a female is an inferior being to a male, and her first aim is to amass so much merit in her present existence that she will be reborn a male in the next. Girls have their ears bored, but this has no religious significance and is of minor importance compared with the *shinbyu* ceremony, though, wherever possible, parents combine the two events to save expense. The *shinbyu* ceremony symbolises the youth's abandonment of the follies of this world, and recalls Prince Siddhartha's last appearance among his friends and courtiers before leaving them and his kingdom to become a homeless ascetic and ultimately to attain full enlightenment (Buddhahood). We were invited simply to the reception. The ceremony of escorting the youngster to the monastery is a more private, family affair.

Meanwhile, throughout my time in Sagaing I had been preparing for my first departmental examinations. These took place twice yearly, in May and November, and the subjects which I had to take were the Burmese language and papers in criminal, civil, revenue and treasury law. All had ultimately to be passed by the higher standard; for the Burmese examination there were separate papers for the lower and the higher standard, while for the rest there was but one paper and the standard attained depended entirely upon how well one did. An incentive to pass these examinations as early as possible was provided by the fact that one's first annual increment of salary became payable as soon as all subjects had been passed by the lower standard, and the second increment was granted when all had been passed by the higher.

A few days after our arrival in Sagaing, Hall had said he would arrange for his chief clerk to send over to our house the books which we should have to study for the examinations, and in due course three office boys arrived laden with books! These were the 'manuals' with which I was later to become so familiar. Each manual was divided into three parts: the first was the Act (say the Excise Act), the second the subsidiary legislation made under the Act, and the third contained a set of directions explaining how the Act was to be administered. One could naturally not be expected to carry all the details of these manuals in one's head; the important thing was to know where to find any particular rule or instruction when it was needed. I was told later that the Japanese, when they occupied Burma, were extremely scornful of our practice of reducing everything to the form of manuals. But though at first sight one might be appalled at the vast mass of paper with which the administration was wrapped up, these manuals proved great time-savers in the long run: on being presented with a problem, you turned up the appropriate manual and found either what you could do yourself or to whom you must refer the matter. Unfortunately from the point of view of the student preparing for his examinations, most of these manuals had a large wad of correction slips attached to the back cover, and one was continually having to refer from the original text to the corrections.

We endeavoured to improve our Burmese by taking lessons from a schoolmaster from the local Government High School, U Ba Toe, an unassuming little man in spectacles, from whom, looking back, I think I probably learnt a good deal. He used to come to our house in the evenings about twice a week. Some months later, after I had left Sagaing, he wrote to congratulate me on passing my higher standard Burmese, and I replied in my best Burmese, thanking him for what he had taught me. When I returned to Sagaing eight years afterwards as DC his widow came to see me and produced my letter, which had apparently been preserved as an important family document!

In due course the examinations were upon us, and we sat for all the papers except the higher Burmese, having been told that the examiners would never, on principle, allow a European to pass by the higher standard at his first examination. We did our papers in the Commissioner's office, together with a number of young Burmese officers from the neighbouring districts, and the Commissioner himself presided over the Burmese oral examination, assisted by Hall and a senior Burmese officer. The practice was to call in a villager, who was paid a small fee for his services, and to make the candidate converse with him.

Most of my training was now over and in a few months I could expect to be given charge of a subdivision. Meanwhile, it was decided that I might as well obtain some additional experience by moving to the neighbouring district of Lower Chindwin. The headquarters of the district was Monywa, and the Subdivisional Officer there was a European, George Cockburn, who was one year senior to me and was well thought of by the Commissioner. I think it was felt that in Sagaing my training as a future SDO had suffered somewhat from the fact that the SDO there, a Burman, had a great deal of semi-political work to do in headquarters and was rarely able to get out on tour for more than a night or two at a time. George Merrells was also moved on, being posted to Myinmu, a subdivisional headquarters in the Sagaing District, lying between Sagaing and Monywa, which also had a European SDO.

I duly set about my packing, which involved sending my house boy out to the bazaar to purchase a large bodkin, twine and quantities of gunny (hessian) sacking. In this sacking all my furniture was wrapped, and in about the middle of June I left Sagaing to travel the short rail journey of sixty-five miles to Monywa. The rains had broken a month before and the whole district looked green again after its parched appearance in April and May, when the temperatures went up to about 110 degrees. The paddy fields, baked hard by the heat of the sun, were now sufficiently saturated by the rain for ploughing to start, and the annual cycle of labour in the fields was beginning again.

Monywa was a more important, but less attractive, town than Sagaing. It was the principal port on the River Chindwin, from which it was protected by a long embankment (or *bund*, to use the Hindustani word by which such embankments were commonly known). The economy of the district was very similar to that of Sagaing, save that it had considerable areas of forest, worked by the Bombay Burmah Trading Corporation Ltd on lease from the Government. The district was, generally speaking, hotter than Sagaing, and its western portions, across the Chindwin, were very arid. Round Monywa itself the land was completely flat, except for some hillocks just over the river.

George Cockburn was at that time a bachelor like myself, and had arranged for me to share his bungalow. I had brought with me my house boy and cook, also my horse and syce, but there was room to accommodate them all. George, so far as I can remember, did not keep a horse, but he had an old car. He was a tall Scotsman, who occasionally used to wear a kilt. I recall one Burmese officer telling me that he saw George, shortly after his arrival in Monywa, walking down the road in his kilt, and his first reaction was to say to himself: 'What an enormous woman!' The DC was a Burman, U Maung Maung, a senior officer of the Class II Service, who in his younger days had seen service in France with the Burma Sappers and Miners. He was a cheerful fellow, able to hold his own socially with Europeans and, I should think, in normal times a good DC. He had, however, rather lost his head during the Burmese-Muslim riots of the previous year, even to the extent of telephoning to Rangoon and asking what he was to do next. The only European government officials, besides George Cockburn, were the doctor and the Superintendent of Police; the latter unfortunately despised the DC for his showing during the riots, and they were never on good terms. Other Europeans in the place were two Forest Managers of the Bombay Burmah; and junior members of their staff, who were working in the forests, would come into Monywa from time to time for a rest.

There was one other person in Monywa at that time of whom George and I saw a great deal. His name was Sao Kun Suik, and I christened him 'Suikers', by which name he was soon generally known. He was a Shan and a member of the ruling family of Kengtung, the largest and most easterly of the Shan States. His elder brother had been the Sawbwa (ruler) of Kengtung, and had been murdered as a result of a conspiracy in which certain members of the family were believed to be implicated. Suikers had been educated at the Shan Chiefs' School, and had now been sent to Burma to gain some experience of administrative practice, with the rank of Honorary Deputy Myook (under training)! Now a Deputy Myook was the lowest rank in the Subordinate Civil Service, and Suikers told us an entertaining story of his first dealings with the DC. He had arrived in Monywa one evening, knowing no one and having been told to report to the DC. He traced him to the circuit house (a type of inspection bungalow, occupied by the Judge when on circuit and by other officers when rooms were available), where he was having a drink or a meal. Suikers, who was very westernised, sent up his card with a note, in which he apologised for intruding, but said that he had just arrived and did not know where he was to stay. The DC evidently considered a Deputy Myook not worthy of his personal attention, and sent another note down to him. This exchange of notes apparently continued till Suikers had discovered where he was to be accommodated! I do not think that Suikers had at that time ever been outside Burma and the Shan States, but he had a far more Western outlook than many Burmese officials. We saw a good deal of him, both socially and in the course of our work, for both he and I were engaged in the same pursuit: learning from George Cockburn how to be administrative officers.

There was far more social life in Monywa than there had been in Sagaing. There was a golf course in the town and the club was a lively place. Every afternoon there was tennis, and this would be followed by a few rounds of drinks, and then perhaps by a number of games of billiards and slosh. This would lead sometimes to the reprehensible practice whereby a man would, late in the evening, accept a friend's invitation to 'pot luck' at his house, send no word to his servants that he would not be dining at home, and arrive back about midnight to tell his waiting servants that he had had his meal and was going to bed. I think we rarely got involved in one of these 'pot luck' invitations, but we made a point of sending word to our staff that they need not wait up for us. The club had members of all races, and visitors frequently dropped in, mainly skippers of the Irrawaddy Flotilla Company's steamers plying up the Chindwin from Mandalay. It was here that I first met Stanley White, one of these skippers, a tough little Scotsman, always bubbling over with energy. I ran into him on many occasions in later years; sometimes we were so rude to one another that we were barely on speaking terms, at other times we were good friends!

While in headquarters, I was occupied mainly in trying cases, still the petty cases which were all that a Third Class Magistrate could handle. But soon the results of the departmental examinations were published and, to my not inconsiderable surprise, I learnt that I had passed the lower standard Burmese 'with great credit' and the other papers by the higher standard. This meant that I had only the higher Burmese to take in November. As a result of my passing the law examinations, I was appointed a Second Class Magistrate, with powers of imprisonment up to six months and correspondingly greater powers of fining (up to two hundred rupees).

In Sagaing I had not yet done my period of attachment to the Police or Excise Departments, and this I did in Monywa. The Lower Chindwin District had an unenviable reputation for violent crime, such as murder and dacoity (gang robbery), and the Superintendent of Police had promised me that, when I was attached to him, he would send me out with the investigating officer to deal with the first such case that was reported. But it so happened that during my fortnight's attachment not a single case of violence was reported, and I spent most of my time on such mundane matters as learning about the various registers which were maintained in police stations.

The Superintendent of Excise, Arthur Po Saw, gave me an interesting week, taking me round to various opium dens and demonstrating the method of smoking. The distribution of opium was controlled by the government, which ran opium shops. Addicts were registered and given tickets which enabled them to purchase the permitted ration of opium at regular intervals from the shop. There was a considerable traffic in illicit opium, which was smuggled through Rangoon or over the China border, and the excise officers were continually bringing cases to court.

I was sent for a fortnight to a place called Salingyi, some ten miles away on the western side of the Chindwin, to learn how to run a sub-treasury. Salingyi was the headquarters of a Township Officer, who normally managed the sub-treasury in addition to his other work. I found that, apart from an hour in the morning and at most another hour before the close of business when I checked the books and counted the cash, I had no work to do, and I had to spend the hottest part of the day in the inspection bungalow, where I was staying, doing my best to keep cool. It was extremely hot at Salingyi, the heavy muggy heat that one gets during the rains when there has been no shower for several days, and the villagers were anxious for rain so that they could go ahead with their cultivation. It is customary in country places, when the farmers become concerned about the lack of rain, to organise a tug-of-war to arouse the *nats* (spirits) of the rain. I remember suggesting to the Township Officer that we should each raise a team for a tug-of-war, but nothing came of this; perhaps rain fell before we had time to arrange it.

About this time a very minor political incident took place in the district, which gives me an opportunity to say something about Burma politics. The House of Representatives under the new constitution had 132 seats, 41 of which were reserved for minority constituencies (Indians, Karens, Europeans, etc.) and for special constituencies (that it to say, commerce and industry). To the remaining general constituency seats (91) representatives of no fewer than seven different political parties had been elected, as well as a handful of members who belonged to no party. This shows how Burmese politics tended inevitably towards the multi-group system as in France rather than the strong party system of Great Britain. The largest single party when the constitution came into force in April 1937 was U Ba Pe's United GCBA (General Council of Buddhist Associations). This party, itself an amalgam of previously independent groups, had opposed separation from India. U Ba Pe was a moderate, but he was unable to raise sufficient support from other groups to form a ministry. Dr Ba Maw, who in 1936 had formed the *Sinyetha* (poor man's) party, though he had only sixteen members in the House, was able to form a ministry with the support of the minority groups, including the Karens, Indians and Europeans, and became the first Premier of Burma. His policy aimed principally at reform of the land tenure system and the general improvement of the cultivator's lot, but there never seemed to be very much difference between the aims of the different groups on the home front. He soon formed his own private army known as the Dahma Tat (Axe Force) and, in the view of some, began to exhibit dictatorial tendencies.

In 1938 a new party, the *Myochit* (our country) party, broke off from the United GCBA under U Saw, a loud-voiced and self-educated demagogue whom we shall meet again. He had no clear political programme, but was primarily opposed to Dr Ba Maw. He wielded considerable power through his control of one of the leading newspapers, and he too organised his own army, the Galon Tat (Eagle Force), from which he was often known as Galon Saw.

The *Thakins* were the ultra-nationalist and revolutionary party, and they had won only three seats in the House. The word *thakin* means 'master' and was always used in addressing a European. This is probably why the party adopted it, and each member placed the word in front of his name as though it were a title, Maung Hla Chit becoming Thakin Hla Chit. Though it had so small a representation in the House, the Thakin party had a great deal of influence throughout the country, and generally seemed better organised than the other groups. It consisted of the younger generation, and was very largely recruited from former students of Rangoon University which, as I have already said, was riddled with politics; and it maintained a close liaison with the students' union. The aim of the Thakins was complete independence for Burma; apart from this, they appeared to have no fixed political principles, though many inclined towards communist tenets. They took an active part in stirring up agrarian and labour disputes, and opposed every ministry. They insisted on addressing the House of Representatives in Burmese, though English was the official language for all who spoke it and most of their representatives could speak it well; and they would not associate with anyone opposed to their views. The Thakin party provided the first rulers of independent Burma, and their party song '*Doh Bama*' ('We Burmese') supplied the tune for the present national anthem. 'There is a fierce rhythm in the Doh Bama anthem which proclaims the rights of the people of Burma; the sound of it voiced by hundreds of enthusiasts is impressive.' (Foucar, *I Lived in Burma.*)

Dr Ba Maw's ministry fell in February 1939. The European group had kept him in power with their votes and enabled him to surmount several crises; not that they considered him to be necessarily any better than possible alternatives, but mainly to ensure some sort of stability in the government. The immediate cause of his fall was his government's handling of the Burmese-Muslim riots and of the strikes of students and schoolchildren which followed. It failed completely to take adequate measures to restore order, and the European and Indian groups supported a vote of no confidence, which was carried. Dr Ba Maw, it appears, was convinced that the Europeans had brought about his downfall. He later formed the 'Freedom Bloc', which hoped to use England's difficulties in the war with Hitler as a means of gaining independence. His utterances became anti-British, and he was sent to jail for sedition; he managed to escape in April 1942, just before the British withdrawal from Burma, and we shall see him as a leading figure in Burmese politics under the Japanese occupation.

The new Premier was U Pu, an elderly lawyer, dull, religious and pro-British, who led a new coalition containing both the U Ba Pe and the U Saw groups. He paid a visit to Monywa while I was away in Salingyi. He came by car and, while he was still some miles from the town, found the road blocked by numbers of young Thakins, who lay in front of his car and prevented it from proceeding till police had been called from Monywa to arrest the demonstrators! Lying down was a favourite Burmese method of obstruction, and it proved very effective, for the Burman considered it the greatest insult to touch another with his foot (even to point a foot at him was bad enough), and the person obstructed simply looked on helplessly till the representatives of law and order arrived to lift the obstructor out of the way. The demonstrators in the present case were duly brought before a magistrate, and I remember going and sitting in court one day while the case was in progress, and being impressed by the fact that hardly one of the accused had a really Burmese face; most of them looked at least partly Indian. Why this should have been so, I do not know, as no one could say that the Thakin party was composed largely of non-Burmese.

I did a few short tours with George Cockburn. On one occasion we went for a day-trip down the Chindwin, accompanied by Suikers, to investigate a complaint against a headman. The arrangement was that I should hold the inquiry, while George was there to assist me if necessary. Another day the two of us set out to hold a headman's election; supervision of these elections was normally the duty of the Subdivisional Officer. We drove out a certain distance in George's car, and then were met by a bullock-cart, which was to take us along a rough cart-track to our destination. George, who had had experience of bullock-carts, refused to ride in it, saying that it was more comfortable to trudge behind it; after a time I came to the same conclusion and joined him. There were certainly more comfortable methods of travel than sitting in a bullock-cart with no springs and no upholstery, while it jolted over bumps.

I was in Monywa for less than two months. Not long before I left I had gone on tour to the northern part of the district. About this time the paddy seedlings were springing up in the nurseries, which were patches of vivid green in the brown fields. After a few days I left by hired bus to return to Monywa, but on arrival at Alon – a place on the river about six miles short of Monywa – I found the waters of the Chindwin overflowing on to the road and was forced to abandon the bus for a pony gharry, in which I completed my journey. George Cockburn, who had been touring in another direction in his car and was returning at about the same time, had to have his car brought in by river. We found that, owing to unprecedented rains up in the north, the waters of the Chindwin had become so swollen that they had swept over the land north of the Monywa *bund* and had come pouring into the town. Though the depth of water on the roads was not such as to make it necessary to travel by boat, the low-lying compounds of many houses were well and truly flooded. Our activities during the next week or so seemed to centre entirely round the floods. As they subsided, and the water in the town was unable to escape back into the river because of the *bund,* a foul stench arose, and it was eventually necessary to breach the *bund* in order to let out the water.

But before the town was completely dry, I received orders posting me to Mogaung as Subdivisional Officer.

CHAPTER FIVE

First Charge 1939-40

MYITKYINA DISTRICT in the far north of Burma was the largest district in the country; it extended to the borders of Tibet and touched India and China on either side. It was also one of the most sparsely inhabited areas, having a population density of about fourteen to the square mile, and a total population of rather less than 300,000. It was extremely mountainous and it was only in the south, where the majority of the inhabitants were to be found, that there were fertile valleys in which the normal Burma crops could be grown. Elsewhere the people, Kachins and kindred races, practised shifting cultivation in their hills. Mogaung, to which I was now posted, lay in the southern part of the district, on the railway line from Rangoon and Mandalay, and some seventeen miles from Myitkyina, the district headquarters.

Though the Deputy Commissioner was generally a member of the Civil Service, the district was virtually the preserve of the Burma Frontier Service which, as I explained earlier, was formed after the First World War to administer the hill peoples. It was so subdivided administratively that the Burmese areas in the south were under the charge of three separate officers, each of whom was also responsible for the administration of a certain area of the Kachin Hills, with the title of Assistant Superintendent. Being more used to frontier peoples than to the Burmese, these officers generally preferred their work in the hills and they tended to leave much of the work in the Burmese plains to their Township Officers.

About the time that I went to Mogaung, however, a reorganisation had been decided upon, whereby two predominantly Burmese areas in the south were to be joined under one Subdivisional Officer at Mogaung, while the two hill areas which had formerly been attached to them were to be administered by an Assistant Superintendent of the Frontier Service with headquarters at Kamaing, which lay twenty-five miles north-west of Mogaung by road. This was obviously a much more satisfactory arrangement for the people of the area, for I found a very real feeling among the Burmese that their interests had been neglected by officers who put the hill tracts first. The reorganisation was not, however, to come into effect till the 1st October and, as I reached Mogaung in the middle of August, I had about six weeks in which I had to administer parts of the Kachin Hills with the Kachin title of *Bum Du Gaba* (Great Chief of the Hills).

I arrived in Mogaung by train in the small hours of the morning, and was met by Jaung Ba Than, who was to be my head clerk for the next year, and who conducted me to the inspection bungalow. My predecessor as SDO had been transferred elsewhere some two months before my arrival, and the Township Officer had been carrying on as best he could. He came to see me the next morning. U Sein Hman was a middle-aged, conscientious and hard-working officer, but he worked very slowly and his great defect was that he seemed unable to distinguish what was urgent from what was not. Every matter was dealt with in the order in which it reached him. I liked him, however, and we always got on very well together.

The inspection bungalow was next door to the SDO's house, into which I moved as soon as my furniture was unloaded from the goods waggon in which it had come from Monywa. It was a double-storeyed wooden building, but it had no electricity, for there was none in Mogaung, and I had to use paraffin-burning pressure lamps in the evenings. Both Sagaing and Monywa had had electricity during the hours of darkness, and pressure lamps seemed to attract the insects more than electric bulbs. I had only the bare minimum of furniture, just sufficient for my own use, and the house was therefore very sparsely furnished, the second bedroom being completely empty.

The small town of Mogaung lay beside the Mogaung River, which flowed into the Irrawaddy some miles away; it was regularly laid out, with streets running at right angles to each other. What I most enjoyed was the sight of hills, and real hills too, not the barren hillocks which had been almost all that Sagaing and Monywa could offer; towards the north they became higher and higher till they faded out on the horizon. The government buildings were most oddly sited. The railway station and the bungalows of the principal officials lay close together not far from the town. The hospital and the police station were at the extreme west of the town, on the road leading to Kamaing. And the government office and court house had been built almost in the forest, about a mile to the east of any part of the town, at the end of a road which led to nowhere. It was said that the person responsible for siting it had expected the town to develop in that direction, but he had been greatly mistaken. It was literally right out in the jungle, and once when the people had been complaining of a tiger which had been attacking their cattle, and I had issued cartridges to a retired Kachin policeman who had said he would try to shoot it, he did shoot it quite near to my office!

One of the first purchases which I had to make on my arrival in Mogaung was a bicycle to carry me to the office. I bought a sturdy and inexpensive make from the local branch of Messrs Rowe and Co Ltd – the department store which had branches all over Burma – refusing to be either impressed or deterred by the Karen manager telling me: 'All Your Honour's clerks have Raleigh bicycles.'

I suppose that one always looks with particular affection upon the area in which one held one's first independent charge. Moreover, mainly through the accident of war, Mogaung was the only place in Burma in which I spent as long as a year continuously, and I think that this was without any doubt the happiest time in my service.

I was the only European in the place, with the exception of a female missionary belonging to the Bible Churchmen's Missionary Society, who spent much of her time travelling, and whom I rarely met. But government officials frequently passed through Mogaung and stopped for a day or two at the inspection bungalow, and anyone going from the district headquarters at Myitkyina to Kamsing or to the Hukawng Valley, which lay north of Kamaing, had to break his journey at Mogaung.

The local officials were myself, the Township Officer, the Assistant Township Officer (a young fellow called U Ba Maung of about my own age), a Public Works officer, an Inspector of Police and a Public Health Inspector (all three Indians) and an Indian doctor, Dr Azim Khan, who ran the little hospital; there were also of course the subordinate police staff. The doctor was deservedly popular among the local people, and took a great pride in his hospital, which he would invite me to go round whenever I happened to be over there. He was a most unassuming man and a great after-tea walker (as I was myself), and we often met and walked together.

The office staff were the head clerk and four others, three peons (office boys) and four process-servers, who were away most of the time delivering notices or summonses. It was therefore small enough for me to know everyone, which I rarely found possible in subsequent stations. Among my staff I knew best my tour clerk, Maung Ba Thein. He had been educated at the Government English High School in Maymyo and had even been sent to Rangoon University for a while, but had, I think, failed to pass his first examinations. His knowledge of English was therefore better perhaps than that of his colleagues – though all were surprisingly good – but his written Burmese was correspondingly weaker. I remember reporting on him one year that, while his English was good, he wrote Burmese like an Englishman and spelt it like a cultivator! Indeed for a time, purely for the fun of it, I used to give him spelling tests in the office before work started; these generally consisted of rather difficult words derived from the classical Pali. Before long another clerk joined of his own accord, and soon the ATO, U Ba Maung, was asking if he might join the class!

I had brought my house boy and cook from Sagaing, but they grew homesick after a month or two in Mogaung and had asked to be allowed to go home. I well remember my extreme embarrassment when they came to make their final adieux and prostrated themselves before me on the ground in the Burmese *shikho* with the palms of their hands together. I was fortunately able to get two very much better replacements. Jangma La (always known as Ma La) was a smart little Kachin who had been a policeman for a time; he always wore loose black trousers instead of the Burmese *longyi*. He and his wife Ma Bauk, who used to do my darning for me, had no children of their own, but they had adopted a sweet little child called Ah Tut, who was about three years old when they came to me; he soon got into the habit of wandering into the house for a chat with me. The cook, Maung Mon, was a Burman, a much older man than Ma La, and a very good cook. These two remained with me till I sent them home during the Japanese invasion of Burma nearly three years later.

Mogaung town had been much more prosperous a few years before I went there, for it was the centre of the jade trade. Much of the famous Chinese jade came from the jade mines lying in the Kachin Hills some two days' journey to the north-west of Mogaung. These were in the jurisdiction of the Kansi *duwa* (chieftain), who received a certain amount of revenue from their working. It was, however, far less than he considered that he should have had as his share, and I fear that he was a somewhat disgruntled man. He was a rather Burmanised Kachin, who used to dress in the Burmese fashion. He had a house in Mogaung and I occasionally met him. All the jade had to be brought into Mogaung so that the royalty on it could be assessed. If the man who brought it argued that the valuation on which the royalty was based was too high, the Government would offer to buy the jade from him at that valuation.

The jade deposits are said to have been discovered and worked by the Chinese from about the thirteenth century, and the jade was exported to China in the early days by the overland trade route. I believe that none of the jade which the Chinese worked with such consummate craftsmanship came from China itself. Of the two varieties used, one (jadeite) came from Burma and the other (nephrite) from South Turkestan. I did not know till I went to Mogaung in what a variety of colours jade is found; the dark green, with which we are most familiar, was considered the most valuable.

Almost one in every two of the Burmese inhabitants of Mogaung described himself as a jade trader, but the Burmese traders did no more than buy the jade from those who had excavated it and sell it to the Chinese merchants, who exported it to China. So far as I know, no Burmese jade trader had ever been to China. The chief merchants in Mogaung were Lee San Cheik and his brother-in-law Ah Phan, both Chinese. San Cheik spoke good English, but his brother-in-law used to converse with me in Burmese, which he spoke with so pronounced a Chinese accent that I had at first the greatest difficulty in understanding him. It was San Cheik who used periodically to visit Shanghai to sell his jade, but after the Japanese invasion of China in 1937 the jade trade had fallen on evil days.

Mogaung lay in the northern wet zone, its rainfall being about the same as that in the Irrawaddy delta, about 90 inches a year. The Mogaung Township, which was the greater and more important part of my charge, was a valley lying between two ranges of hills. Down the middle of the valley ran the railway line. My jurisdiction extended for about eighty miles down the line, but, as the width of the valley was only five to ten miles, it was easy to reach any village within a short time by train and bicycle. The trains went only twice a day in each direction and were very slow, for they stopped at every station and had to take on produce; the obvious method of touring was therefore to halt at a convenient centre and to cycle to all the villages within easy reach. There were inspection bungalows at every other station on the line, and so touring could be undertaken in ease and comparative comfort.

The people of the area were predominantly Shan-Burmese, the Shans having at one time occupied much of northern Burma. But there were also small settlements dotted about the township where other peoples were to be found. There were Shan-Chinese, whose men wore trousers, Hkamti Shans from the far north, whose men were also trousered and whose women invariably smoked pipes (though I never saw their menfolk smoking them) and pure Shans (who were known as the 'big Shans' as distinct from the Shan-Burmese, who were the 'little Shans'). There were areas in which Gurkha ex-soldiers had been settled, and which were now peopled by their offspring, half Gurkha and half Indian; though these people were themselves most law-abiding, their huge herds of cattle and buffaloes were liable to damage other people's crops, and this sometimes resulted in cases being brought to court. Dark-skinned Uriyas from Orissa in India had established a number of villages. They would come over to Burma without their wives, but their families continued to increase in India. The Burmese considered it a huge joke when an Uriya who had not seen his wife for years would proudly announce that she had borne him another son. The practice, I was informed, was for the absent man's brother to take his place and ensure that his stock did not die out.

Agriculturally the cultivation of rice was the staple industry. There was, however, an important secondary crop, cane sugar. The Burma Sugar Company, a European-owned concern, had some years previously established itself in a large area of plain at Sahmaw, some twelve miles south of Mogaung. This area, so the story went, had been selected on the advice of the Government Agricultural Department as the most suitable in the district for growing sugar cane. The Company had taken a lease of land from the government and built a sugar refinery. They soon found that this was the one area in the district where sugar cane would not grow. All around, particularly on the foothills, the local people managed to grow it without any difficulty at all, and the Company decided in the end to abandon the attempt to grow their own cane. Instead they made advances of cash to the local Burmese and Kachins and bought their crop from them. This industry put a good deal of money into the local pockets. The Company had a staff of four Europeans, of whom the manager and chief engineer were permanently in Sahmaw, while the two others were generally travelling round the cane-growing areas, paying out advances to the growers and seeing that they were properly used. North of Mogaung there was another big cane centre, where a former European employee of the Company had established himself on his own and supplied the Company with cane.

Kamaing Township, the other half of my charge, lay to the west of Mogaung and was very different from it. It consisted of a number of Burmese islands in a sea of Kachin Hills. Kamaing itself, lying on the all-weather road which came from Mogaung, was not much more than a village, with a government office and hospital and a handful of shops. The Township officer for most of my time was a young fellow called U Than Nwe, who came from a family with a tradition of government service. His father U Ba Maung was a senior police officer, whom I was later to know and who in due course rose to be Inspector-General. The motor road continued for a short distance beyond Kamaing to the west and passed through two more small areas for which I was responsible. But the bulk of the Burmese population of the township was concentrated in small villages round the shores of the Indawgyi Lake, some thirty miles to the south of Kamaing; their principal occupation was fishing, though they did a certain amount of rice cultivation, sufficient for their own needs. The Indawgyi was a narrow lake, some fifteen to twenty miles long, and it was not easy to reach it from Kamaing: there was no road, and one had to go either by river in small country boats or overland along footpaths, and during the rains the overland route was always more or less flooded. The southern part of the lake could, however, be reached more easily from the Mogaung township. Apart from visits to Kamaing itself on routine office inspections, I was able to do little touring in the township. There was comparatively little work which required my personal attention, and I generally had as much as I could cope with in Mogaung.

Having just had some experience of floods in Monywa, I found that the first crisis with which I had to deal after my arrival in Mogaung was another flood. These generally occurred about once in three years, and so the local people knew what to do. Both the DC, Robin McGuire, and the Superintendent of Police, Neville Hill, came down from Myitkyina and spent a few days in Mogaung to help me, for, being entirely new to the place, I had as yet had no opportunity to meet the local people and to find my feet. We organised a rice-distribution centre on the platform of the railway station, one of the few places in the town that was not under water, and there we issued rations to last for three days at a time. The ground floor of my house was completely flooded, and I used to land by boat about half-way up the stairs. After about a week the floods subsided, the aftermath being extensive inspection of the paddy fields a few months later as a result of applications for remission of land revenue. Some miles down the railway line one of the small rivers changed its course – it had apparently a habit of doing this – and damaged a bridge. Through traffic came to a standstill and passengers and goods had to be transhipped. I was ordered down to assist in collecting porters and labour for the railway engineers engaged on repairing the bridge.

I had been less than three weeks in Mogaung when one morning the Public Health Inspector came to my house before breakfast to tell me that he had heard on his wireless the news that England and Germany were at war. This was confirmed by a telegram from the DC, which I found when I reached my office. Under the 1935 Government of Burma Act matters of defence and foreign affairs lay wholly within the Governor's competence, and so Burma became automatically at war with Germany without the Burmese Parliament being consulted. The outbreak of war made little immediate difference to us, though I was asked to investigate what stocks there were of various goods in the local shops and to watch that traders did not start raising their prices unreasonably. Little did I realise in 1939 that the war would lead ultimately to a hastening of Burma's independence.

When I was able to settle into my office seat, I found a very considerable backlog of files to be dealt with, for, as I have said, there had been an interval of some two months between my predecessor's departure and my arrival, and U Sein Hman had been unable to keep abreast of the work. Office and court work were both heavy. The morning would start with the hearing of petitions. Licensed petition-writers had their booths in the office compound, and persons wishing to present petitions would get them written for the prescribed fee, though of course they could write them themselves if they wished; an 8 annas revenue stamp had then to be affixed to the petition, which was presented either by the petitioner in person or by a lawyer on his behalf. In most cases no immediate answer or decision could be given, for the subject of the petition would generally require investigation. Having dealt with the petitions and some of my office work, I would take my seat on the bench at about midday and spend the greater part of the rest of the day in hearing cases.

My court work increased when, after about six months, I was appointed a First Class Magistrate with powers to try more important cases and to give sentences of imprisonment up to two years. Thefts were numerous, many being committed by Burmans from further south who had come up on a visit or to try to make money quickly. There was also a fair proportion of assault cases. The usual weapon of offence was the *dah* or agricultural knife. This invaluable implement was carried by every cultivator, who used it for slashing paths through jungle and for countless other purposes. Under the British administration it was made illegal for pointed *dahs* to be carried, and many Burmans regarded this prohibition as an insult. But the sharp cutting edge remained, and this alone made the *dah* a sufficiently lethal weapon. The Burman was quick-tempered and, if he had consumed a quantity of alcohol, he was quite liable to pick up his *dah* and slash his best friend over the head. There were generally one or two patients in the hospital who had been sent there by the police as the result of such incidents.

Of the cases of a more petty nature the majority were offences against the excise and opium laws. Mogaung being so near to the Chinese border and the Yunnan poppy fields, it was a comparatively easy matter for illicit opium to be smuggled in; a certain amount too was grown in the Kachin Hills. When a conviction was obtained, the court would order that both the opium and the implements associated with its use be confiscated. Some of the pipes were very well made of highly polished wood, with pieces of jade (of no value) inset in the wood, and for some time I had hanging on the wall of my sitting-room a couple of pipes which I had once confiscated. The Shans were addicted to distilling illicit liquor, and matters were made more difficult by the fact that in the Kachin Hills bordering on my jurisdiction it was not an offence for a man to distil his own country spirit, while in the plains, liquor could be legally obtained only from a liquor shop licensed by the government.

I do not remember that I tried any criminal case of unusual interest. On one occasion I had a young Hkamti Shan brought before me on a charge of adultery. He admitted the offence which, under the Indian Penal Code which was in force throughout Burma proper, was punishable with imprisonment for up to two years. During the short period of six weeks, however, in which I had administered a portion of the Kachin Hill tracts, I had been interested to find that the Indian Penal Code did not apply there. Most cases were tried by the tribal elders and their decision was confirmed by the Assistant Superintendent. Even the more serious cases did not go beyond the DC, with an appeal to the Commissioner in Sagaing. The Rangoon High Court had no authority in these areas. Penalties inflicted were almost invariably payable in kind: for instance, a convicted person would be ordered to pay so many gongs or so many cattle to the person whom he had wronged. I remember hearing even of a murder case in which the accused was sentenced to a punishment of this nature. When therefore my Hkamti Shan adulterer came before me for judgment, I felt that the penalty prescribed in the Indian Penal Code was quite inappropriate for a member of a backward hill tribe; many thought it unfortunate that it had been applied even to the Burmese. So I decided to call in a few elders of his race to give evidence as to the sort of punishment which would have been imposed on an adulterer under their own tribal customs. I assumed that it would have involved some restitution in kind to the injured husband. Somewhat to my consternation, however, witness after witness stood up and said that under Hkamti Shan custom both the guilty parties would have had their heads cut off. Reluctantly I sentenced the accused to imprisonment.

The local bar consisted of five 'pleaders', three Burmese and two Indian. Below those lawyers who had been admitted as Advocates of the High Court, there were two grades of pleader, the higher and the lower grade. The two Indians were far cleverer than the Burmans, and they practised both in Myitkyina and in Mogaung. Of the three Burmans, one spoke no English and one very little. The third, who spoke quite good English, unfortunately knew not quite enough to understand the law fully, and he was sometimes known to quote sections or rulings in support of his submissions which were in fact diametrically opposed to them! Prosecutions brought by the police were conducted by the Court Prosecuting Officer, who was generally either a sub-inspector or sometimes even a head constable; he was usually unable to hold his own against a clever Indian pleader for the defence, and on such occasions the court had to give him a certain amount of assistance.

The method of administering the oath to a witness depended on his race or religion. There were a few Christians in the area, mainly Kachins converted by the American Baptist Mission or the Bible Churchmen's Missionary Society, and they of course took their oath on the Bible. The Burmese Buddhist swore on the *kyansa*. This consisted of a number of thin strips of palm leaf, on which were inscribed the various calamities which would attend the giving of false evidence; they would be bound between two stout pieces of wood covered with red lacquer. The witness was required to hold the *kyansa* in his hands and to repeat the following words: 'To enable the court to decide this case I will give true evidence; if I do not give true evidence, may I suffer the punishments written in this *kyansa*.' Certain types of people were not allowed to take this oath, among them pregnant women. It was not uncommon for the official administering the oath to ask a female witness whether or not she was pregnant before handing her the *kyansa*. Once the prosecuting inspector was in the midst of administering the oath to a woman when he suddenly bethought himself that she might be pregnant and asked if she was; when she replied in the affirmative, he hurriedly snatched the *kyansa* from her hands.

A non-Christian Kachin witness was handed a *dah*, which he held over his head, with the cutting edge downwards; his oath consisted of the recital of a number of unpleasant things which he hoped might happen to him if he testified falsely: 'When I go into the jungle, may a tiger devour me; when I go into the water, may a sea-snake come and eat me; when I chop wood, may the head fly off my axe.' The person who administered the oath to a Chinese witness held up before him a paper on which Chinese characters were written and applied a lighted match to it; as it burnt, the witness was required to express a desire to be himself consumed in the same manner if he did not tell the truth. The Indian had simply to hold up his hands and make a plain declaration that he would tell the truth and would not give false evidence. I do not know whether it was due to the less picturesque nature of the oath, but in my experience more falsehoods were told in the witness box by Indians than by persons of other races. Especially at one time did I feel this to be so in the case of Muslims, and I remember being taken to task by the High Court for writing in one of my judgments: 'Examination of a number of Muslims has convinced me that in the Koran the Prophet omitted to stress the virtues of truth-telling.' A demi-official letter from the Registrar of the High Court told me (quite properly) that the Honourable Judges wished to draw my attention to the fact that for obvious reasons a remark of this nature should not appear in the judgment of a Court of Justice.

As the chief official in my subdivision, I had to keep a fatherly eye on the representatives of the other government departments who were working in my area. Most of them were Burmese, and they would generally look to me for assistance in any difficulty, for their immediate superiors were either in the district headquarters or perhaps even further away. The largest department was the police, which had three stations in my area; there were also members of the forest, public works, veterinary, medical, excise, education and railways departments, and an agricultural officer who used to visit us from time to time. All these were of comparatively subordinate status, but more senior officers of these departments would occasionally come on a tour of inspection, some from as far away as Mandalay and Sagaing.

In Lower Burma vast areas of agricultural land had passed into the hands of non-agriculturists to whom the former owners had mortgaged it in order to get money for the purchase of cattle, tools and sufficient food to last till the crop was ready for sale. The lesson had been learned by the time that Upper Burma was annexed, and there was provision in the law applicable to that part of the country that a non-agriculturist might not own agricultural land unless he worked it himself or with direct labour. In other words, there was to be no absentee landlordism as in Lower Burma. It was the duty of the land records staff to bring to the notice of the administration all cases of transfers of agricultural land between agriculturists and non-agriculturists, and on my arrival in Mogaung I found a large pile of such reports which had not yet been attended to. I took them with me on my first tours and gradually worked through the lot of them. The non-agriculturist who had acquired agricultural land either had to show to my satisfaction that he was working the land himself and not leasing it to a tenant, or was given a reasonable period in which to dispose of it to an agriculturist. In almost all cases he was an Indian, and most of them assured me that they had never before heard the rule which I was now enforcing, and suggested that it was a new law which the government had made. Possibly I took a more decided line in dealing with the problem than my predecessors had done; I certainly felt that it was my duty to ensure that the Burmese remained in possession of their own agricultural land, though naturally the Indian farmer who really worked his land was not disturbed.

Soon after my arrival in Mogaung I started a campaign against straying cattle. There were considerable areas of waste land dotted about the town, and certain cattle owners would turn their cattle loose on them in the daytime. The result was that these pieces of land, most of which were in close proximity to human dwellings, became fouled with droppings, which of course attracted flies. I therefore issued an order prohibiting owners from allowing their cattle to stray within the town area; in certain places they could let them graze, provided that they tied them up so that they could not wander at will. I found that most Burmese owners obeyed my instructions; they tied their cattle to the end of a long bamboo pole, pivoted on a post in the ground, and this gave the animals considerable freedom of movement. But the Indians made no attempt to comply with the order. I thereupon arranged with the Public Health Inspector for his gang of conservancy coolies to make occasional raids, seize straying cattle and put them in the cattle pound. This adjoined the police station, and in fact one of the police subordinates was in charge of it. When the owners came to pay the usual pound fee to bail out their cattle, the police took their names and reported them to me, and I had them brought to court. I was, however, unable to find any penalty prescribed in the Cattle Trespass Act or in any other likely enactment which exactly fitted this offence. I did, however, find an obscure section in the Police Act which made it an offence for anyone to keep cattle standing longer than was necessary for loading or unloading goods, and decided that charges should be made under that. All went well for a time; a considerable number of cases came before me, and in some quite substantial fines were imposed. Indeed the story went round Mogaung that I was trying to raise funds for the Burma War Donation by means of these fines. Eventually, however, a bullock belonging to one of the Indian pleaders was caught. He did not himself appear in court, the accused being one of his employees who was duly fined. The pleader, however, took the case up to Myitkyina on appeal, and the appellate court ruled that no offence had been committed under the section under which the case had been brought and that the fine must be refunded. I was extremely annoyed, for this meant that I could take no further action against straying cattle, but, as I realised only too well, the ruling was entirely correct. I gained some consolation from the fact that the person who had paid the fine had by this time left the pleader's employment and could not be traced; and therefore the fine was not refunded. But the pleader had gained his point.

Mention of the Burma War Donation reminds me of another incident. One morning before breakfast a deputation waited on me at my house, consisting of the Mogaung headman, Ah Phan the Chinese jade merchant, and a number of others. They had a proposition to put to me. They wanted, they said, to raise funds for the War Donation, and their suggestion was that a fair should be held for a week in Mogaung. This would afford entertainment to the local people, and the organisers would guarantee to hand over to me a fixed sum from the profits, which I would send to Rangoon as a contribution from Mogaung. I agreed, but drew their attention to the fact that gambling was contrary to the law, and stipulated that only games of skill should be permitted in the fair, and that there should be no games of chance or organised gambling. This was readily agreed to and, in my innocence, I never stopped to ask myself how so much money could be raised purely from games of skill. I do not think that any formal written permit was issued to the organisers, and certainly my stipulation regarding games of skill was not committed to writing.

Arrangements were duly put in train, and the fair opened. To show my support and interest, I went to the fair ground on the first night and was conducted round by Ah Phan. To my consternation, I found in progress games of *fantan*, '36 animals' and all the recognised gambling games. Having, evidently ill-advisedly, honoured the fair with my attendance, I felt that I could do no less than direct that these games be closed down forthwith. Ah Phan protested that he did not know that these games were going to be played and, as he was a fairly simple soul, it was not improbable that he was speaking the truth. He accompanied me as far as my house and, on the way, I thought over the matter and decided that I had been spoiling the people's fun, illegal though it may have been. So, having given Ah Phan a final warning that there was to be no more gambling for the rest of the week, I assured him that I should not myself turn up again. I left him to draw his own conclusions from that and, for all that I know, the gambling continued till the end.

I had, however, learned my lesson. Hearing of the profits made in Mogaung by the organisers, even after payment of the agreed sum to the War Donation, Chinese traders from the other small towns down the railway line came to me with requests that they too should be permitted to demonstrate their support for the war effort in the same manner. To all these worthy citizens I made it quite clear that no games of chance would be permitted, that this would be stipulated in the permit, and that police would be on duty to see that the fair was properly conducted. As a result, some of the applicants withdrew their requests, while others agreed to the terms, but considerably reduced the lump sum which they had proposed to pay to the War Donation.

Social pastimes in Mogaung were practically non-existent. There was no club and no cinema, though very occasionally a travelling cinema would arrive and show a Burmese film in one of the local buildings. In the compound of my house there was a tennis court, provided by government for the use of the subordinate government staff, and I used occasionally to play on it with the ATO and some of the clerks from the office. I also managed to arouse some enthusiasm for football, a game for which I personally had no great liking. I bought a ball and organised some games (Government versus Town), but I do not remember that we played very often. Occasionally the ATO or my clerk Maung Ba Thein would stroll over to my house in the evening to listen to the Burmese programme on my wireless set over a glass of beer. And that was about all. But I do not think that I ever felt bored or lonely. I did a great deal of reading, and frequently spent much of the evenings writing up judgments in the cases which I had been trying. I was once asked out to dinner by the doctor and once by one of the Indian pleaders, but I think those were probably the only occasions on which I dined away from home while I was in my headquarters. I had the doctor to my house, and once invited the ATO and most of the clerks to a meal: I gave them tinned haggis, which George Cockburn had recommended to me, but we all thought it overrated.

Though office and court work were heavy, I generally managed to go on tour for at least a week in every month. Most of my travelling was up and down the railway line, and I was able to visit every village and to know the more prominent men in each tolerably well. I rode from village to village on my bicycle, sometimes with my tour clerk Maung Ba Thein, sometimes on my own, and discussed with the headmen and villagers the crop prospects and other matters. The work was generally of a routine nature, which it would be of little interest to describe.

The Burmese village did not differ much from one end of Burma to the other. It was a mixture of orderliness and untidiness. There were neat rows of houses lining one or more parallel streets. Most of them were made of mat and thatch; that is to say, the walls were made of interwoven strips of bamboo, the floors were of split bamboo or

A headman's house

perhaps of timber, and the roofs were of thatch (or in Lower Burma, where it was not easy to obtain the proper kind of thatching grass, of the leaf of the nipah palm). The better houses were of timber construction throughout, and had galvanised iron roofs. Beside the house was generally a small store-house for paddy, and in the compound there might be one or two thatch shelters for cattle or for the womenfolk to winnow or pound their paddy. If the village was not built on the bank of a river, the compound might contain a well, though more usually there would be communal wells in the village. The compounds of the houses were bare of grass and flowers were rare, but there might be a mango tree or some coconut palms. The village streets were wide enough for a cart to pass, and were almost invariably unmetalled and very dusty. They would usually be littered with empty coconut shells and discarded mango stones, and everywhere were the village pie-dogs, living on such scraps of food as they could pick up, thin and often covered with sores. In the centre of the village there was often an open space, where a pagoda and the village rest-house (*zayat*) would be found. There would always be a monastery, generally in a secluded spot at one end of the village.

From time to time I had to hold a headman's election, and for this the village turned out in force. We provided each candidate with a ballot box from the office, covered with paper of the appropriate colour – which had been agreed beforehand with the candidates – and with each man's name written clearly in Burmese on the paper. The headman in temporary charge, who was usually the headman of a neighbouring tract, was responsible for making all arrangements in the village. Voting usually took place in the *zayat*, to which I have referred above, and which was a rest-house for travellers with a floor and roof but no sides; curtains would be arranged to make an enclosed polling booth. The supervising officer (myself) took his seat in the front part of the *zayat*, having in front of him the latest *thathameda* assessment roll, which constituted the electoral roll. All around were crowds of villagers waiting to vote and generally to watch the fun. Each candidate then took his box, with the lid off, and showed it to the throng standing or squatting in front of the *zayat*. The preliminaries over, I had the tops of the boxes screwed down in the presence of the candidates, and placed them on a table in the curtained-off enclosure. Voters came up one by one as their names were called, and I sometimes had to help the aged or the blind to deposit their votes in the right box. The voting counters were metal discs which, as a precaution, I initialled before handing them out. When all present entitled to vote had done so, I asked the candidates whether they wished me to wait any longer for those voters who had not appeared. When they all agreed to the closing of the poll, they were asked to sign a statement to that effect, to protect me against complaints later. The boxes were then opened and the votes counted in their presence, and the result declared. This was always subject to confirmation by the Deputy Commissioner, who might, before confirming it, have to deal with appeals from the unsuccessful candidates. The people in the Mogaung area were still sufficiently unsophisticated and honest to accept the result of an election, and I remember no case of appeal; further south an appeal was the rule rather than the exception.

On one tour I was wholly engaged in inquiring into the requirements of villagers living near the forests in respect of forest produce. There had been two types of forest in the area: the forest reserves, administered by the Forest Department, which exploited them under a proper system of control either themselves or through lessees or contractors; and the unclassified forests, in which the local people could extract their own requirements, subject only to a prohibition on the felling of certain species. Owing to the popularity of sugar cane cultivation and the money to be made from it, the greater part of the unclassified forests had been gradually cut down in order that cane might be planted, and representations had been made to the Minister of Forests that the people were finding great difficulty in obtaining forest products which they required for their everyday use. These were principally house-building materials (bamboo, cane and thatch) and firewood. It was therefore decided by the Minister that a system of permits should be instituted, whereby persons living near forest reserves might obtain their requirements to the extent specified in the permit; they were also permitted to graze a certain number of cattle in the reserves. The local forest officers held up their hands in horror at this act of sacrilege which was to be committed against their sacred reserves, and I had a great deal of work to do in calculating, by local inquiry, how much produce should be allowed for the different villages of the area. Ultimately the printed books of permits arrived and were issued, but I left Mogaung before the effect of this new policy could be assessed.

The only distinguished visitor who came to Mogaung in my time was the leader of the *Myochit* party, U Saw, who was now Minister of Forests, and I think that the purpose of his visit was to explain to the people the decision which I have described above. The Deputy Commissioner went down the line to meet him, and brought him up to Mogaung. The train arrived rather earlier than I had expected; I heard it, rushed out of my house and on to my bicycle, and was able to get on to the platform without the Minister noticing that I had not been there when the train came in; the DC noticed, however! The local worthies had arranged a breakfast party, and I sat at the same table with U Saw, his wife and small daughter, and the DC. U Saw came from Lower Burma and, as I have said before, was mainly self-educated. He was a coarse-grained ruffianly type, credited with more than one murder, but not without a sense of humour. He talked throughout the meal, while his wife sat looking very prim and proper and trying to control the small daughter. Not very long afterwards (September 1940) U Saw became Premier, promising increased Burmanisation of the government services and an honest, uncorrupt administration.

My only tours which were at all out of the ordinary were two to the area of the Indawgyi Lake. The first was in the 'open season', that is to say, in the cold and dry part of the year. I took myself, my entourage and my bicycle some way down the railway line, and then disembarked and headed westward for the Indawgyi. This involved a cycle journey along a rough road through a forest reserve, over a pass in the range of hills and then down to the little villages bordering on the great lake. My servants and kit followed, the former on foot and the latter on mules; there were a number of Yunnanese mule contractors who supplied mules for government officers touring in the hills during the dry weather. We spent the night at a small bungalow on the edge of the lake, where we could hear the water lapping on the shore. One of the principal objects of my visit was to be present at the annual Indawgyi pagoda festival, and to meet the various people who came to it, either to worship or to trade. The primary object of these festivals was to worship at the pagoda, but they afforded an opportunity for all the people from far around to get together and generally enjoy themselves. Stalls were set up, Indian merchants displayed their wares, and there were those dramatic performances so dear to the Burmese. There was certainly a gathering of the clans beside the Indawgyi: Burmese, Shans, Kachins, Shan-Chinese and Hkamti Shans, with a fair number of Indians from the towns on the railway line. Small huts of bamboo and palm-leaf were always erected for the principal guests, who on this occasion were myself, the Township Officer and a young European belonging to the firm of Steel Brothers, who worked forest concessions in the district. I took the opportunity of visiting a number of villages in the area and of discussing with the headmen the state of their crops, prospects for the coming year and the usual matters that were of mutual interest. I learnt too something of fishing operations in the lake. The fishing rights there were leased every year as the result of an auction to a single lessee, who paid a fixed fee to the government and had a monopoly of the catching of fish. There was, however, a curious physical phenomenon, in that at certain times of the year numbers of fish in the lake became stupefied by some sort of exhalation and floated on top of the water as if dead. These fish could be collected by any person who paid to government a licence fee known as the *ngabokkun*, which meant literally the 'rotten fish tax'. There were of course frequent disputes between the villagers and the fishery lessee on the question whether the fish gathered in by the former were genuinely fish stupefied by natural causes; on many occasions, I fear, their stupefaction was the result of their having been hit on the head!

My second visit to the lake area was in the middle of the rains of 1940. This was certainly not the ideal time to go, but there was a headman's election to be held and I did not want to put it off till the open season. As the village in question was north of the lake, the easiest way to reach it was from Kamaing. It was impossible to get to it on foot or bicycle, as the paths were deep in mud. I arranged therefore to borrow a couple of elephants from a headman who lived near Kamaing. This was without any doubt the most uncomfortable mode of travel which I ever employed. There were none of the upholstered *howdahs* on which Viceroys and their staff appear riding in pictures. Across the shoulders of each elephant were large

Bhamo bazaar

wicker baskets, into which was loaded our luggage; cross-legged on top of the luggage we sat, two persons to each elephant. The journey of some thirty miles took two days, the elephants moving at the rate of about two miles an hour. In some sections of the route their feet would sink about a foot into the mud. After six or seven hours on elephant-back, our legs would hardly support us when at last we dismounted. On arrival at our destination we found that it was pouring with rain, and this continued off and on during our stay, making things rather miserable. But the villagers did not think so. They were highly delighted, for there had apparently been a pro-longed drought prior to our arrival and they were beginning to fear for their crops. I was credited with bringing the rain. The nearest the Burmese could get to pronouncing my name was 'Mo', which meant 'rain', and 'Mogaung' in Burmese meant 'good rain' (though in fact the name of the town was said to be derived from two Shan words 'Möng Kawng', meaning the 'town of the drum'). I duly held the election, and decided that it would be more comfortable to return to Kamaing by boat than by elephant. This journey also took two days, and we spent a night on the way in a Kachin house. These were often larger than Burmese houses, and had separate apartments for the unmarried girls, known as the 'maidens' quarters'.

Among my other jobs, I was an honorary recruiter for the Burma Rifles. These were composed almost entirely of hill peoples (Chins, Kachins and Karens) and of Indians. The Burman was considered an unsatisfactory peace-time soldier; he quickly grew bored with the dull routine. But at about this time, presumably as a result of political pressure, there was a move to recruit more Burmese into the army. I was authorised to accept applications from potential recruits, to arrange for them to be medically examined and to forward their particulars. But it was impressed upon me that I must accept appli-cations from none but pure Burmese. So far as I can remember, the Shan-Burmese were regarded as eligible, but on several occasions, when young men who were only partly Burmese applied, I was put in the embarrassing position of having to tell them that, though they had lived all their lives in Burma, and were probably descended from Burma tribes on both sides, they could not be accepted in the Burma Rifles because they were not pure Burmese!

I had two European 'colonies' lying in my jurisdiction; they were the Sugar Company at Sahmaw and the Bible Churchmen's Missionary Society at Mohnyin. Mohnyin was a fairly import-ant place, and I had to visit it at least once a month on business, but I did not always meet the members of the mission. Some half a dozen of them – not all, however, stationed in Mohnyin – had been fellow-passengers of mine on the *Amarapoora*. Oddly enough, one of them, Colonel Middleton-West, had lived next door to me in England for many years, but I knew his family better than I knew him, as he had been abroad so much. He had spent his working life in the Indian medical service and, after his retirement and at a fairly advanced age, he had returned to Burma to run a hospital for the BCMS in the malaria-infested Hukawng Valley in the north, miles from any other Europeans. He was a man for whom I had a great admiration, as I had for another doctor belonging to the mission who ran a hospital in Mohnyin. The mission was, however, low-church Anglican by persuasion, and it was clear that some of the missionaries whom I met had started with the premise that Buddhism was wrong in any case and that there was therefore no point in their learning anything about it. They made no headway among the Burmese and confined their activities to the Kachins and Shans. Partial Christianisation of a village was apt to do more harm than good, for a man who became a Christian in a Buddhist village virtually cut himself off from many of the social activities of the village, which centred to a great extent round its religion; for example, there was the giving of alms to the monks and there were periodical contributions to the maintenance of the village pagoda.

Sahmaw consisted of the Sugar Company and its employees and a few shopkeepers. The occasions on which I had to go there for other than social reasons were therefore extremely limited; I was by virtue of my office an inspector of factories, but the Sahmaw Company observed all the regulations and this caused me no trouble. I was, however, once called down to deal with a strike of the Company's Burmese employees. Most factory workers in Burma were Indians, but it was accepted government policy that more and more Burmans should progressively be employed on this type of work. The European employer was inclined to grouse at this. He was used to dealing with Indians and spoke their language; moreover, Indians were accustomed to factory work. They had a lower standard of living than the Burmese and were content to do a dull, monotonous job for hours on end, frequently involving heavy manual work. The Burman did not take so easily to this, and was no more inclined than the British workman to work like a slave for little pay. Hence the employer frequently found that he could not get as much work out of his Burmese labour as he got from his Indians, and would complain about the incurable laziness of the Burman. The following passage, from a *Report on Indian Immigration* by Mr James Baxter, the government's financial adviser, published in 1940, is, however, interesting:

The opinion of employers of labour, whether European, Burmese or Indian, is unanimous that Burmese labourers are not as efficient as Indian in dull, monotonous work involving heavy manual labour, such as cutting earth or carrying heavy loads, but it is equally unanimous that 'when the work is intricate the Burmans understand it better than the Indians' and that the 'Burman is more anxious to occupy the skilled artisan positions than to take up the unskilled work'. It is found generally that Burmans can compete successfully with any Indian in work of a skilled or semi-skilled nature.

I do not remember the precise cause of the strike at Sahmaw. It was led by a young man who had come from Lower Burma, who was probably out to cause trouble, and it soon died down. But I recollect that my inquiries led me to the conclusion that it might never have occurred if the management had been in closer touch with their Burmese staff and had been able to speak to them direct instead of through interpreters.

Of politics in Mogaung there was very little. The Thakin party had its adherents in some of the larger villages, but generally speaking the people were too unsophisticated to take much interest in politics. One of the leading Thakins in the area, whom I got to know fairly well, was an elderly cultivator with weak eyes. He would invariably address me by my official designation, while most people would address me as Thakin (master) or Thakingyi (big master). I used therefore always to speak to him as Thakingyi, much to the amusement of any bystanders. He took it in good part, however, and was perhaps even flattered to be so addressed!

There were few outstanding characters in my first charge. U Ngwe, the headman of Mohnyin, was a grand old man who, despite his age, invariably insisted on accompanying me whenever I had work to do in Mohnyin town. His great friend, a man considerably younger than him, was Sao La Nan, the Kachin Taungok, who also lived in Mohnyin. A Taungok was a government official in the hill tracts, who stood midway between the Assistant Superintendent and the Kachin chiefs or *duwas*. Sao La Nan was not strictly speaking accountable to me in any way, as I held no jurisdiction in the hill tracts, but he always made a point of coming to see me when I visited Mohnyin.

In Mogaung town, apart from government officials, I remember best two monks, men of entirely different character one from the other. U Arsaya looked like a rather worldly prelate of the Middle Ages, and he dabbled a good deal in politics, making fairly frequent visits to Mandalay. The police used to keep an eye on his activities, but in my time he never overstepped the mark. He used to visit me in my house from time to time, and I used to be a little irritated – though I hope I never showed it – at what I thought the rather patronising way in which he conversed with me, as if he thought me an inexperienced and slightly ridiculous youngster, as no doubt I was. The other monk was a little wizened old man, whose name I never learned. He was a monk of the old school, and he would talk with regret of the way in which nowadays monks were interesting themselves in politics, which was entirely contrary to the rules of the Order. Every three months prizes were drawn in the Burma state lottery, which had been started in 1938/39 and yielded revenue to the extent of nearly two million rupees out of total revenue receipts of about 170 million rupees. On the evening on which the results of the draw were to be broadcast, I could be certain that my monkish friend would present himself in my house with a little novice as his attendant. He would sit quietly in a chair, saying not a word, till the broadcast was over, and then, after a brief farewell, return to his monastery. I could offer him nothing either to eat or to drink, for monks are forbidden to drink strong liquor and to consume any food after midday. He would, however, accept a Burma cheroot, which had to be conveyed to him through his acolyte. I was very much touched, when I left Mogaung for good by a train which departed at about 11 p.m., to find this old monk standing aloof from the rest of the people on the platform and waiting to speed me on my way.

Towards the end of my time in Mogaung I was busy making the preliminary arrangements for the conduct of the census, which was due to take place in March 1941. I was responsible for ensuring that all the instructions issued by the Superintendent of Census Operations were understood and in due course carried out, and had already held a few meetings with my headmen to explain to them in general terms what their particular responsibilities would be. But I had left the district before the census activities were very far advanced.

I rarely went outside my subdivision. In the November after my arrival I had to go to Myitkyina to sit for my higher Burmese examination, and I then took a few days' leave to go with the Superintendent of Police up into the Kachin Hills on a fishing trip. On this occasion I visited the confluence of the two rivers called the Nmai Hka and the Mali Hka, which unite to form the great Irrawaddy. At Christmas 1939 the DC invited me to stay with him for a few days, and I was making tentative arrangements to spend the Christmas of 1940 at a place called Sima on the Chinese border, and to do a tour during the cold weather which would take me through the jade mines. Having been over a year in Mogaung, I suppose I was beginning to look upon myself as a permanency, and I had even planted a number of vegetables in my garden in late October; I was soon to learn that to do this was a sure way to invite a transfer.

It was therefore as something of a bolt from the blue that early in November 1940 I received a telegram from Rangoon to say that certain junior European members of the Civil Service including myself were to be released to undergo a three months' militia course in Maymyo. I was unable to take anything with me but a few suitcases, and of course I could take no servants, as we were to live in barracks. I had to leave them behind in Mogaung, but, as I learnt that the Township Officer, U Sein Hman, was to take over from me as Subdivisional Officer, I was able to arrange with him to house both my servants and my property till I knew what was to become of me after the course was over.

In the middle of November I left Mogaung for Mandalay. At Sagaing station my friend Ohn Maung met me. He was now married and had a small child, and he was Subdivisional Officer in Amarapura, which, as I have already mentioned, lay between Sagaing and Mandalay. He had arranged that I should stay with him for the night, and the following morning he drove me up to Maymyo, where I reported for duty at the Alexandra Barracks.

CHAPTER SIX

In the Irrawaddy Delta 1941

IN OUR MILITIA COURSE we were instructed by officers and non-commissioned officers of the King's Own Yorkshire Light Infantry, the British battalion at that time stationed in Maymyo. I think that the majority of us began the course with a certain amount of enthusiasm. There were, I supposed, a hundred or more of us, Europeans and Anglo-Burmans, of whom about twenty were government servants like myself, and I found both George Cockburn and George Merrells in my platoon. But the lack of imagination with which the course was conducted rapidly cooled my ardour and that of some of my colleagues. No distinction was drawn between those who, like myself, had spent five years in an Officers' Training Corps at school and those who had never handled a rifle or had any military training in their lives. All of us spent hours on elementary foot and arms drill and, when at last we came to rather more advanced work, we found that this centred round the Lewis gun, which was admitted by our instructors to be almost obsolete. We suggested that it might be more use if we were taught to use a Bren gun, but we were told that there were only two in Burma, one of which was in pieces for demonstration purposes. The lack of modern weapons can be gauged from the fact that, when one of the battalion's sergeants was once seen in the barracks carrying a tommy-gun under his arm, crowds of regulars gathered round him to look at it! Though it seemed fairly obvious that, if we had to meet any enemy, it would be the Japanese, our instructors seemed to have no information about their tactics or armament. It was assumed that any enemy would behave in the orthodox manner of the First World War.

We had Saturdays and Sundays free, and I often drove down on the Saturday with Merrells, who had his own car with him, to Mandalay. Maymyo was so un-Burmese that it was with a feeling akin to relief that we reached the foot of the Shan hills and emerged into the heat of the Burma plains. We were given about a week's holiday at Christmas 1940 and Merrells and I motored to Taunggyi, the capital of the Shan States, having arranged for our houseboys

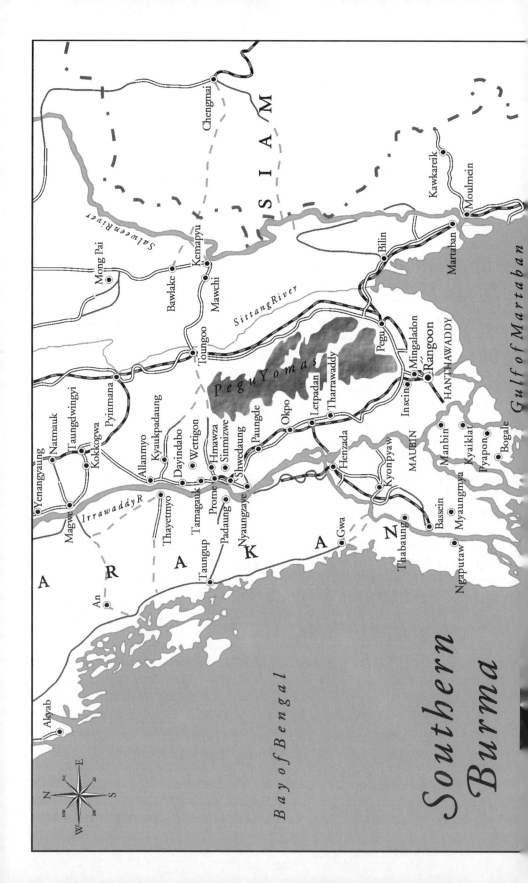

to join us. Here we had a pleasant few days, during which we did a trip to the Inle Lake, where the boatmen stand upright on their boats and propel them by twisting one leg round the oar. We returned to Maymyo via the small state of Hsipaw, and saw the quaint little palace of the local chief, standing among lawns and English flowers.

The militia course ended in late February, and a considerable number of those who attended it were notified that they had been selected to take an Officers' Training Course. I was not so selected, and was returned to the Government of Burma for civilian duty. I was later sent a copy of my report, which stated that I was considered unlikely to make a good officer, but that I might be suitable for clerical work (I had been seen using a typewriter in the barracks!).

I returned to Mogaung, where I had left my possessions and my servants, and stayed in the inspection bungalow awaiting my posting orders. I hoped that I might be re-posted to Mogaung, where I had after all spent not much more than a year. But a few days later I received a telegram from the Home Department in Rangoon informing me that I was to go to Bassein as Subdivisional Officer.

I was not at all pleased at this. Bassein was in Lower Burma, the chief town of the Irrawaddy Delta and the seat of the Commissioner of the Irrawaddy Division. My short service had hitherto been in Upper Burma, which I had been taught to regard as the true Burma. It still retained much of the social organisation and way of life of pre-British Burma, having been annexed as it stood only fifty-five years before. Lower Burma, on the other hand, which had been British for nearly ninety years, had been largely depopulated when it was annexed, and had been subsequently settled by a mixture of people, some from southern India and some from independent Burma, many of whom had been attracted by the hope of making money from the rich rice fields of the delta. Another reason why I viewed with mixed feelings the prospect of going to Bassein was that in Mogaung I had been in my own little kingdom, while in Bassein there would be not only a DC, but a Commissioner as well, in the same station. Those who have lived in small and comparatively solitary stations come in time to look with aversion on the prospect of moving into a more social atmosphere. I heard of cases, when I was in Mogaung, in which the DC found great difficulty in persuading an officer in an isolated post in the hills to come into headquarters for a few days to see some different faces and get a change of environment. These officers had grown so much accustomed to living among their own particular native peoples and rarely seeing a white face that they had no inclination for a change. I remember thinking myself how irksome I should find living in a station like Bassein where, I understood, there would be no fewer than twenty Europeans! But I got used to it very soon, and was able to enjoy life as much – or nearly as much – as when I was on my own.

Both my cook Maung Mon and my houseboy Ma La announced that they were coming with me to Bassein, and I was particularly flattered that Ma La, a Kachin, should feel like this, especially as he had refused to follow his former employer to a station in the south. At the end of the first week in March we left Mogaung for good and travelled the six hundred-odd miles by train to Rangoon, a journey which took a day and two nights. We arrived in the early morning and, after breakfasting at Rangoon station, I set out to pay some calls in the Secretariat. The only necessary official call was on the Home Secretary (now MacDougall who had been my Commissioner when I first went to Sagaing). He told me that I was being posted to the delta in order to gain experience of a different part of the country. I went to Government House to sign the Governor's visiting book and left Rangoon the same evening for Bassein in one of the Irrawaddy Flotilla Company's steamers. This Company ran a large number of services along the vast network of creeks in the delta, as well as operating big paddle steamers up and down the main Irrawaddy and its tributary the Chindwin.

The steamer was due to sail at 7 in the evening, and there was a rather noisy party of Burmans and Indians on board who were seeing off one of the passengers; among the party was the Finance Minister. My fellow-passengers in the first-class saloon were a European of the firm of Steel Brothers, who was paying a routine visit to Bassein with his wife, and a young Burman, very self-assured and speaking English with a strong American accent, who disembarked before we reached Bassein; he came, I believe, of a family which had made a good deal of money out of the rice trade, and I assume that he had been sent to the United States for his education. We should have reached our destination early the following morning, but, when we awoke, we found the steamer stationary, and a thick fog all around us. At this time of the year fog frequently arose over the delta creeks in the early morning. We were unable to get under way again till the fog lifted, and we reached Bassein in the afternoon.

Bassein (which the English pronounce Bass-een, with the accent on the first syllable) lies on one of the largest creeks of the Irrawaddy Delta, and the town presented an attractive appearance as we sailed up in brilliant sunshine. It had for centuries been an important port, long before Rangoon was founded. Ralph Fitch, the first recorded Englishman to visit Burma, landed there in 1587 from Bengal. Its

A river steamer on the Irrawaddy

English name was derived from the Portuguese; the Burmese called it Pathein, rhyming with 'inane' and with the accent on the second syllable. The foreshore, with its sweep of white stucco buildings, was faintly reminiscent of some southern European town. There were a number of rice mills on the water front, both above and below the town, ugly buildings constructed, as was usual in Burma, of corrugated iron sheeting. Bassein's principal pagoda, the Shwe-moktaw, was glittering in the sunshine, though it had not the advantage of Rangoon's Shwe Dagon of standing on an eminence. On the opposite bank of the river was a poorer suburb, more like a village than a part of a town, with a mass of coconut palms rising above mat and thatch houses.

I arrived to find Bassein in the midst of festivities designed to raise money for the Burma War Donation, and my predecessor, who was the chief organiser, was in no hurry to leave. There was little work done for some days, for most of the population, official and unofficial, were preoccupied. The various events included boat races on the river, in which long boats of about twenty men each competed, and the side-betting provided the greatest attraction to the Burmese spectators; Burmese boxing, which consisted largely of posturing and leaping into the air; and side-shows of various sorts. During this period I lived in the circuit house, which was down near the foreshore. Government did not provide a house in Bassein for the SDO, but I arranged to take over my predecessor's rented house, which belonged to a Burmese police officer. This was situated at Kanthonsint (Three Lakes), some two miles out of the town, overlooking the golf course and some small lakes; most of the senior government officers were housed in this area. The position was pleasant, but the house had no electric light. I wrote to the landlord, offering to contribute half the cost of installing it, but never received any reply.

Bassein town straggled for a long distance along the river and extended up to two miles inland. The shopping centre consisted of two long streets running parallel to each other, with short streets connecting them. Rowe and Company, the department store, had a shop, but all the rest were managed by Indians or Burmese. In the residential areas buildings were mainly of plastered brick or of timber with corrugated iron roofs.

I soon met the principal officials and the European non-officials. My new Commissioner, Bennison, and his wife were kind enough to send a message over to the circuit house, as soon as they heard of my arrival, asking me to dinner. The doctor, a portly Scotsman, called on me within the first day or two and carried me across the road to a drinks session (*tête-à-tête*) in the club, which he advised me not to join. It had been the old government club of Bassein, its membership being almost entirely official, and it had lost ground heavily in recent years to the golf club at Kanthonsint, which was a non-official club and to which most of the Europeans and many Burmese belonged. In fact the old club was kept going only by members making a point of meeting there one evening a week. I never did join, though I soon became a member of the golf club, having bought a bag of clubs for twenty-five rupees in an auction!

Among the other Europeans in Bassein were Freddy Wemyss, the Police Superintendent, and Hanson, the Inspector of Boilers, who shared a house with him; they were both grass widowers, and I saw a good deal of them at that time, and came across them later after I left Bassein. There were the Judge, the Port Officer, four pilots who spent much of their time away down the river, and five men engaged in business. Altogether, including children, the European community numbered about twenty-five.

My immediate superior, the DC, was a Burman, U Hla Pe, a senior member of the Class II Civil Service, who had been promoted. I did not have much direct dealing with him, but my recollection of him is that he was a forthright type of man who believed in saying what he thought. He was, however, transferred a few months later and succeeded by another Burmese officer, U Thein Nyunt, a quiet and

rather colourless man. The Burmese officer who had the most character was the Akunwun (or Chief Revenue Officer) U Aung Pe, a
fat and cheerful person with little eyes, who after the war served
under me in two districts.

There was some social intercourse between the races, but it had
its limitations. In the golf club the Burmese members might stay for
one drink after finishing their game, but the fact that all Burmese
families ate their evening meal much earlier than Europeans did
generally prevented them from staying any longer and so we did
not see very much of them. There was some formal entertaining by
both European and Burmese officers to which members of the other
race would be invited, but the difficulty was always the women. As
I have explained earlier, it was extremely rare for a Burmese officer's
wife to speak English, while the Burmese vocabulary of the European
wife was generally only sufficient to enable her to converse with
her servants. Once the Bennisons invited the DC and his wife to
dinner, and I was warned that I was to sit next to Mrs DC so that
I could talk to her in Burmese!

My charge, as Subdivisional Officer, was the south-western – and
larger – half of the district, including the whole of the sea coast. It
was divided into four townships, the headquarters of two of them
being Bassein itself; of the others, Thabaung was some three hours
upstream from Bassein, while Ngaputaw was about the same distance downstream. My office was a small building, only a few yards
from the DC's office, and it housed my own staff and the staff of
the two Township Officers. My head clerk spoke little English and
preferred to talk in Burmese; he continually chewed betel-nut and
was certainly no live wire, but he did his best. The judicial clerk,
who was also my tour clerk, used to annoy me intensely by his
wanting to translate everything that was said to me into English.
Whether he thought my ignorance of Burmese was so abysmal that
this was necessary or merely wished to show off his English, I never
discovered; but when I returned to Bassein as DC after the war and
met him again, he spoke nothing but Burmese to me! (It was a
curious trait among Burmese officials of the lower grades that they
felt very uncomfortable when speaking English to a senior European,
though they had no inhibitions about speaking it to a more junior
man.)

In headquarters a great deal of my time was spent on the bench.
Bassein, unlike an unsophisticated place like Mogaung, had a large
number of magistrates – not only administrative officers like myself
working part-time in a magisterial capacity, but also full-time magistrates of the Judicial Service. We administrative officers had no civil

cases to try, and the criminal cases allocated to us by the District Magistrate (the DC) were mainly thefts and the less serious cases of assault. But the SDO's time on the bench was very largely occupied in hearing cases brought under the preventive sections of the Criminal Procedure Code. If the police were unable to prove a case against a suspected criminal (it was generally theft of which he was suspected), they could bring evidence against him of general bad character. The standard procedure was for the prosecution to call the suspect's headman and three respectable elders of the village, who would depose in respect of him: that they had known him for so many years; that he had no ostensible means of livelihood; that he associated with certain named bad characters; that he had been suspected in certain cases of theft; and that, unless he were called on to execute a bond to be of good behaviour, he would be a menace to the public. The upshot was that the magistrate would generally call upon the respondent to enter into a bond with two sureties in the sum of two hundred rupees to be of good behaviour for a period of one year. If, as usually happened, he was unable to find the sureties, he was committed to jail for a year. In other words, a man who in the eyes of the law was innocent was sentenced to imprisonment for a year.

Many magistrates regarded this type of case with extreme distaste; since, however, it was invariably an administrative officer who was the trying magistrate, he was torn between his desire to help the police to preserve law and order within his jurisdiction and his concern that justice should be done to the man in the dock. There was undoubtedly much to be said both for and against these preventive sections of the law. The inhabitants of a Burmese village, especially in Upper Burma where the village was a more closely-knit unit, generally had a pretty shrewd idea who was responsible for crimes in the area and, if no case could be pinned on him, would frequently themselves ask the police to take action to have him bound down; and an obvious inference could be drawn from the fact that no one in the village would stand surety for him. On the other hand, this interference with the liberty of the subject was repugnant to our own British ideas of justice. That it was not so repugnant to the Burmese themselves was brought home to me when I returned to Bassein after the war and in the course of my tours made solicitous inquiries as to the welfare of various persons whom I had once bound down or imprisoned in this way. The usual reply was that they were no longer alive; when at last I expressed my surprise that so many should have died in so short a space of time, my informants told me with a smile that most of the 'bad hats' had died under the Japanese-sponsored Burmese administration. Indeed I heard it said after our return that now that the British were back the people would again go in fear of the criminals among them. We liked to praise our standards of justice and our courts which had no respect for race or person; but the frequency with which our courts threw out cases on a technicality produced in the minds of the ordinary people a bewilderment at the strange processes of British justice, which would allow a man whom all his neighbours knew to be guilty to return home free to plague them again.

In my early months land tenancy cases occupied much of my time. I have already referred to the fact that very large areas of agricultural land had passed, by process of mortgage and foreclosure, from their original owners into the hands of non-agriculturists. The latter belonged mainly to the south Indian caste of Chettyars, who were money-lenders by profession, and who used to let their lands on annual tenancy agreements. This alienation of the land of Lower Burma to non-agriculturists was perhaps the biggest economic problem of the country, and one which we were never able to solve. The Burmese cultivator needed access to capital. The government attempted to meet his need by setting aside each year a large sum of money for the payment of advances to cultivators for the purchase of cattle, seed and implements. But the amounts which could be advanced to each individual were so small, and the procedure for obtaining an advance so lengthy, that the Burman found it much easier to turn to the Chettyar and obtain as much as he wanted on the security of his land. The government's agricultural loans were issued by the Township Officers and, since they might be held responsible if the loan was not recovered, they were naturally reluctant to sanction any advance unless they were satisfied that the security was more than enough to cover it. Moreover, some Township Officers were not above withholding part of the advance and putting it into their own pockets.

Over large areas of the delta, then, the rice lands were worked by men who were only the tenants of some non-agriculturist. The main defects in the tenancy system were that rents were unduly high, that leases were made for a year at a time only and so gave no security of tenure, that the lease sometimes contained unfair clauses such as giving the landlord first option on purchase of part of the crop, that many tenants relet the land to subtenants, and that in bad years the landlord would allow little remission of rent.

A Tenancy Act was passed in 1939, which attempted to remedy these defects, but which soon proved unworkable owing to the physical inability of officers in the districts to make the thousands of investigations which would have been required. Among other things, however, the Act made it incumbent on a landlord to renew a lease, provided that the tenant had not treated him unfairly during the past year. A date was fixed by which the tenant must submit his claim to government for the renewal of a tenancy in cases in which the landlord had indicated his unwillingness to renew. In the vast majority of cases tenancies were renewed without the tenant having to approach the government, but I had to hold many lengthy inquiries into cases in which the landlord had refused a renewal. When the closing date arrived, I declined to entertain any more applications, and the government gave implicit support to my action by rebuking an officer in a neighbouring district who had continued to accept applications after the prescribed date. Nevertheless, it appears that I was criticised by the politicians of the Bassein District, for when shortly afterwards the Minister for Labour, U Ba On, who had formerly been a lower-grade pleader in Bassein, visited the town in the course of a tour of the delta in the launch *The Lady Innes* (which was generally used by the Governor as his official launch), he told the DC that he would like to see me to discuss tenancy applications.

I duly called upon him one morning, and he proceeded to tell me that, though he did not dispute the legality of my action in turning down time-barred applications from tenants, he would like me to bear in mind the fact that the Indian landowners were wily and deceitful men, while the poor Burmese cultivator was a simple soul who needed all the protection that government officers could give him. I had some pleasure in telling him that in no single case which had been presented to me after the time had expired was an Indian landlord concerned. I explained that the Chettyars always gave their tenants a proper written form of tenancy lease; the tenant knew therefore that, if he did not get this by a certain date, he should apply to government for redress. The Burmese landlord, on the other hand, gave leases by word of mouth; having told the last year's tenant that his tenancy would be renewed for another year, he would suddenly change his mind when it was too late for the old tenant to do anything about it, and lease the land to someone else who would offer a higher rent. This rather took the wind out of the Minister's sails, and our interview came to a speedy conclusion.

It has been the practice to vilify the Chettyars, and certainly their rates of interest were not low. But I came to have a considerable respect for them. Their offices looked most business-like; even in the village offices one would find *dhoti*-clad Indians squatting on the floor and making entries in large ledgers lying on low tables; and the ledgers were beautifully kept in Tamil characters. Had it not been for the Chettyars, it is difficult to know who would have financed the rice-growing industry of Burma; the government could certainly not have done so. And it must be remembered that the Chettyars did not want all the land that had passed into their hands; they would much rather have had their money back, and there were numerous examples of a Chettyar helping his debtor, by reducing rates of interest, to go on repaying his loan rather than foreclose and be saddled with the land. And it is generally agreed that Burmese money-lenders charged even higher rates of interest than the Chettyars.

One of the duties that fell to me as SDO was the fixing of the ground rents to be charged on leasehold plots in urban areas when the current leases expired, as they appeared to do with great frequency. Most of this work arose in Bassein town, and my habit was to let cases accumulate till I had a fair number, and then go down to town one Sunday morning with my head clerk and the revenue surveyor, visit all the plots, value them and assess the rents. The valuation was arrived at in a somewhat rough and ready manner. The surveyor would supply me with details of the prices at which land in the vicinity had recently changed hands and, by modifying these figures to take account of differences in the situation and size of the plots which I had to value, I reached what seemed a fairly equitable valuation.

When I arrived in Bassein I still had no car, and my friend Hanson used to lend me his car and driver for these Sunday excursions. In September 1941, however, I decided to buy my own car, a small Morris, for which I had to pay what then seemed the large sum of four thousand rupees (£300); four months later I had to abandon it during the Japanese invasion. For my car I engaged a driver, a Karen called Saw Hla Tin. ('Saw' was the male prefix used by many Karens in place of the Burmese 'U' or 'Maung'.) Christians frequently gave the surname of some missionary to their children, and thus one found such names as Saw Brown and Saw Judson. There was a well-known footballer in Rangoon called Saw Belly. The local newspaper once reported that a team had been severely handicapped by the absence of Saw Belly; *Punch* got hold of this report, and printed it with the obvious comment that he was absent 'for the reason stated'.

The population of my new subdivision was principally Burmese and Karen. The latter, with whom I had not as yet had any dealings, were, like the Burmese, a Mongol race. Originally a hill people from Karenni, south of the Shan States, they had spread over considerable areas of the delta. In the main, they were a quiet and likeable people who gave very little trouble, but they were not very intelligent and were far outclassed by the Burmese, who had oppressed them in the past and against whom they still harboured a latent animosity. They made good soldiers, no doubt for the same reason as the Gurkhas: they were slow-witted but, once they grasped what they had to do, they went at it with a single-minded determination which left them no time to think of anything else. They were able to endure the monotony of peace-time soldiering, unlike the Burmese who would frequently desert. The Karens have received high praise from British officials (especially military officers) who have worked with them, and particularly from those who had little time for the Burmese.

They were divided in the delta areas into two main branches, the Sgaw Karens and the Pwo Karens. Most of the Sgaws were Christians, either Catholics or American Baptists, while the Pwos were mainly Buddhists. The spread of Christianity among them is ascribed to a tradition of theirs. Y'wa, the creator of the world (so the story goes), had three sons; the eldest was the Karen, the second was the Burman and the youngest was the white man. When Y'wa was on his deathbed, his two elder sons were away on a journey. So he gave his youngest son three books: a gold book was to be given to the Karen, a silver book to the Burman, while the white man was to keep the third book, which was of brass. The white man, however, cheated his eldest brother and kept the gold book for himself; this book has been identified by many Karens with the Bible. The American Baptist Mission ran two good high schools in Bassein, one for Sgaws and one for Pwos, each under the management of an American. There was also a Catholic Mission, with a school, in Bassein, and I occasionally met a Father Bouche, who lived all alone some miles from Bassein on a small hillock overlooking one of the larger creeks; he was a cheerful old man with a true appreciation of a Burma cheroot.

Sir San C. Po was the veteran leader of the Karens or, at all events, of the Sgaws, a white-headed old man with a neat white beard, who spoke excellent English. He seemed, however, unable to concentrate on general principles, and was continually coming to see me on rather petty personal matters. He would tell me that one of the candidates in a headman's election which I was shortly to hold was the son of an old friend of his, and would try to urge his case, though I repeatedly explained to him that I never made any attempt to influence the electors. In the same way, he would try to persuade me to grant a gun licence to some particular protégé of his. When I first met him, he presented me with a book which he had written years before on *The Karens of Burma*. Later he asked me what I thought of it, and I said I considered it unfortunate that he had written as though the Karens and Burmese could never work together, for one day the British would presumably leave Burma and the two races would have to make the best of things. But he insisted that it was impossible for them to live together in peaceful co-operation. There is a story to account for this too. When Y'wa created the world, he took three handfuls of earth and threw them around him. From one sprang the Burmans, from another the Karens and from the third the foreigners. The Karens talked too much and Y'wa thought there were too many of them, so he threw another half handful to the Burmese. This gave the Burmese a supremacy over the Karens, whom they have oppressed ever since.

I must admit that at times I found the Karens very tiresome. I had once arranged to hold a headman's election in a Sgaw Karen village. I duly arrived on the appointed day, to find no one present but the two candidates; normally the whole village turned out in force when an election was to take place. Mystified, I enquired what was the matter and was told that, as it was a Sunday, no one could take part in the election; this was apparently tantamount to working on the Sabbath Day. I had to postpone the election and come back the next month. Some months later I was on my way to hold an election in another Karen village and the day before it was to take place I suddenly realised that I had fixed it for another Sunday; when one was on tour days of the week meant nothing. I arrived, quite prepared again to find a nearly deserted village, but it turned out that this was a Buddhist village, and the election took place as arranged. But even this did not go smoothly, for the defeated candidate made a false report to the DC on my conduct of the election. I never heard the result of this, for I was transferred soon afterwards.

The Karens were a very musical race. On my visits to their villages it was customary for a quartet or sextet of young men and women to be lined up to give an impromptu recital of songs, sung in parts. It was perhaps unfortunate that these songs were almost invariably Baptist hymns – or at all events sounded as if they were – and very rarely did I hear anything which appeared to be a native secular song. I was particularly impressed by the musical tastes of the Karens once when I was on tour. I had been walking across the paddy fields to visit the headman of a Karen village, who during the cultivating season was living in his temporary hut in the fields. I went up into this hut of bamboo matting and thatch, and found an old and very rustic-looking headman sitting at a table and copying out music written in the western notation!

Apart from the Burmese and the Karens, the only indigenous people in my charge were the Arakanese – who were found along the west coast and in some villages near the mouth of the Bassein River – and a few villages of Chins, who tattooed the faces of their womenfolk after marriage to ensure that they should not attract other men! Neither of these peoples played much part in the life of the district. There was also the usual Indian trading class in the towns and in some of the larger villages, and a strong Chinese element, especially in Bassein town, where some of the richest merchants were Chinese or Sino-Burmese. There was a village consisting entirely of Chinese which had grown up on the main creek from Bassein to Myaungmya (the headquarters of the adjoining district). It had steadily grown bigger, almost unnoticed by the Administration, till it had reached a considerable size. I decided to take a census of the population in order that some check might be kept on the growth of the place; but I do not suppose that anything was ever done about this.

The principal occupation of the people in my subdivision was the growing of rice. Save in the hill areas of the Arakan Yoma which ran down the district from north to south parallel with the coastline of the Bay of Bengal, almost all the cultivable land was planted with paddy. Scattered about the subdivision at convenient places were rice mills, generally owned by Indians or Chinese, and rice for export eventually found its way to Bassein, which was the port for most of the delta. Ocean-going ships under various national flags were always to be seen tied up alongside the main rice wharves and the prosperity of the merchants and the cultivators was founded on rice.

Subsidiary occupations were timber-felling and fishing. The Arakan Yoma contained some forests, and there was teak in the northern parts of the district. In my charge, however, which was generally low-lying and swampy, the main forest produce was firewood from the mangrove forests. Fishing was the principal industry of the villages near the mouth of the Bassein River, where fences of split cane and traps of various shapes and sizes could be seen in the water as one came alongside. Diamond Island, some miles off the mouth of the river, which I never succeeded in visiting, was the centre of the turtle fishery, and it produced large quantities of turtles' eggs, considered by those who like them to be a great delicacy, though I must admit that I never really acquired a taste for them. They are round, with soft shells, and have a strong flavour. Later in Sarawak I learnt to eat them raw with a dash of Worcestershire sauce, and I think they are probably most palatable in this form of 'prairie oyster'.

Touring in the delta was monotonous, as it was done almost entirely by launch; if the launch was unable to reach a particular village, the villagers sent a sampan to meet it and I would be rowed up narrow streams to my destination. As may be imagined, there was little opportunity on this sort of tour to stretch one's legs. The only overland tour which I might have done would have been across the Arakan Yoma to the coast of the Bay of Bengal, and I hoped to do this in the cold weather of 1941–42; but I was no longer in Bassein then, and I had to defer the trip till 1946. A curse of the delta creeks was the water-hyacinth (known in Burma as *beda*), which from time to time came down in great masses and choked the smaller streams. It had purple flowers and looked very pretty when it was in bloom. Legend had it that the wife of a British official had introduced it from Bengal on account of its pretty flowers, but I cannot vouch for the truth of this tale. I have been in streams where it has taken a motor launch an hour to turn round because it has been surrounded by *beda*, and one can easily imagine the hindrance it proved to native unpowered craft. Sandbanks were another nuisance. The Indian crews of the government launches were pretty knowledgeable as a rule about the snags to be met in the various creeks, but I remember visiting one village a long way up a narrow river and the launch getting stuck on a sandbank as we were leaving. Numbers of young men waded out from the village and succeeded in pushing us off, thoroughly enjoying themselves. I found that this incident was remembered when I went back to the same village five years later as DC: they could even tell me how much money I had given them as a reward for their assistance, though I had forgotten myself.

The most interesting area in my subdivision was Ngaputaw (the southernmost township), not only for its variety of races, but because the villages near the mouth of the Bassein River, whose inhabitants lived mainly on the proceeds of their fishing, were so very different from those in the predominantly rice-growing areas. Especially was this so on Hainggyi Island, which lay just inside the river mouth. The islanders were mostly fishermen, and the village of Hainggyi always reeked of the salt sea. It was untidy and smelly, but it had a certain charm, and was reminiscent in some ways of a Breton fishing village. During my time the community was split in two as the result of disagreement between rival monasteries. I did not attempt to intervene, thinking it better that the solution should be left to the Burmese Deputy Commissioner and the Burmese Township Officer.

Hainggyi Island, formerly known to the English as Negrais, had been one of the earliest English trading posts in Burma. The post had been established in 1753 and a fort had been built. Four years later the Burmese king Alaungpaya ceded it to the English in perpetuity. But in 1759, as the result of a false report that the traders in Negrais were supplying his enemies, the Mons, with cannon, Alaungpaya gave orders that their post was to be destroyed. Eight of the twelve Englishmen there and a hundred Indians were killed, and the fort was burnt. Its remains were still to be seen out in the paddy fields, and they bore an inscription recording the history of the fort. When, however, I returned to Hainggyi after the war, I was told by the headman that the Japanese had ordered the ruins to be pulled down.

From time to time, when I was on tour, I would be invited to witness a Burmese *pwè* or theatrical performance. It has been said that 'there is no nation on the face of the earth so fond of theatrical representations as the Burmese', and a *pwè* will be part of every important celebration. At a birth or a *shinbyu* ceremony, at an ear-boring or a marriage, at the building of a bridge or a water tank, at the dedication of a pagoda or a monastery, and on countless other occasions there is a *pwè*. The performance takes place in the open air, in the village street or some other convenient space, a small roofed enclosure being constructed for the actors. From the roof hang a number of pressure lamps, for the *pwè* does not begin till after dark and goes on all night. Since brawls occasionally arose during the performance, it was necessary for anyone wishing to organise a *pwè* to apply for permission to the local government officials, and arrangements would then be made for police to be on the scene to prevent trouble.

The spectators begin to arrive in the late afternoon, bringing with them mats and blankets, and settle themselves on the ground. Stalls are set up round the perimeter, at which refreshments and cheroots are available. No admission fee is charged, except in the big towns like Rangoon, where the *pwè* might be held in a large hall.

Long before the *pwè* is due to start the orchestra assembles on the ground in front of the stage, tunes up and begins to play. The principal instrument is the *saing-waing*, a circular frame on which hang drums of different sizes; the performer sits in the middle and strikes them with his hands. There is a similar instrument, the *kyi-waing*, consisting of gongs of graduated sizes. The instrument most prominent for its noise is the *hnè*, a sort of clarinet; this is a reed instrument, with a metal horn loosely attached to the end; I acquired one soon after I arrived in Burma, but never attained much skill in playing it. There are also crude flutes, cymbals large and small, and percussion instruments made of lengths of bamboo split down the centre and operated as clappers.

As the stage has no wings and there are no dressing rooms, the performers' 'off-stage' activities are carried out at the sides of the stage in full view of the audience. Before the *pwè* starts they arrive, dress themselves and make themselves up. The fact that they are 'on stage' is indicated merely by their standing up. When they are not on, they sit down again and smoke, chew betel or spit through the interstices in the floor.

The stock characters in the *pwès* are the princess with her maids of honour, the prince, and the ministers, who are generally the clowns. The princess's part is to dance and to sing in the high-pitched nasal voice which the Burmese consider attractive. Her face is smeared with powder and is completely expressionless. The prince likewise sings and dances and betrays no emotions in his features. The dancing is in effect posturing. The princess is somewhat hampered in her movements by her tight skirt, and much of her effort is directed to manoeuvring her hands and arms and moving her body in graceful attitudes. The prince is less restricted by his dress, and some of his dances which I have seen appear to be derived from the dance of the male bird round the female. The ministers' dancing is confined to buffoonery, and their role is principally to talk to one another. Their humour can be extremely broad, and it requires a very good knowledge of colloquial Burmese to be able to understand much of it. I personally always found it very difficult to concentrate on the dialogue at a *pwè* because of the noise round about; members of the audience seemed to be constantly moving, and in the background was the hum of conversation at the refreshment stalls.

There are different varieties of *pwè*, but the main drama of the *zat-pwè*, the highest type of *pwè*, is founded on the tales of the Buddha's previous existences, which are themselves borrowed from India. Generally the main drama is not reached until the early hours of the morning, and I doubt if I ever saw the beginning of one, for I usually left the *pwè* for my bed by about 1.30 a.m. The rest of the audience would remain till dawn, perhaps taking an occasional nap.

The Bassein headmen do not stand out in my memory as the Mogaung headmen did. There were far more of them and therefore I did not meet individuals so often; but there were also, I think, few outstanding personalities. Here I met my only woman headman. There were others in Burma, but they were only a handful. Daw Soe Chon had an air of quiet competence; her house was far better furnished than mine, and her son was, I believe, a lawyer in Rangoon. I was surprised at the number of village tracts which had no headman and were being administered by a neighbouring headman. When I enquired the reason, I was told that elections for a new headman had been held, but that appeals against the results had been lodged by the unsuccessful candidates with the Commissioner, who had not yet reached a decision on them. Most of the cases were still with him when I left Bassein eight months later!

Very occasionally I came across a headman with two wives, and this tended to hinder him in his work, for he would normally maintain a separate establishment for each of them and would divide his time between the two houses. Polygamy is permitted by Burmese custom, but in practice it is very rare to find a man with more than one wife, and it is regarded as something of a joke among his neighbours. On the other hand, divorce is comparatively easy. The essence of marriage is publicity, the fact being usually established by means of a feast or a ceremonial tea-drinking, to which the headman and prominent men of the village are invited, and at which they are notified that henceforth Maung Hla Maung and Ma Tin Shwe are man and wife. In the same way, a husband and wife can call together the village elders and announce that their marriage is ended. According to the Burmese customary laws, a woman may divorce her husband if he cannot support her, if he is always ill, if he leads an idle life or if he becomes a cripple; a man may divorce his wife if she bears him no male children, does not love him, or persists in going to a house which he has forbidden her to visit. But, despite the ease of divorce, it is not as common as one might suppose.

One day I arrived in my launch at a village very much off the beaten track, and found the headman, an old man, obviously very ill. I was told that he had eaten nothing for several days, and I managed to persuade his relations to let me take him to Bassein hospital. We were not very far from Bassein as the crow flies, but it took us several hours to reach it along the winding creeks, and the headman was at once admitted to the hospital. I am afraid that I was too late, and he died a few days afterwards.

The Burmese are always extremely reluctant to enter a hospital. They say that, once you are admitted, you are almost certain to die; and this was to a great extent true, because they would go to hospital only in the last resort when it was often too late to cure them. On the other hand, there is never any lack of out-patients at hospitals who come to get medicines for their various ailments. Every village, however, has its *sesayas* or physicians, who may perhaps be called herbalists rather than medicine men, and their services are much in demand. Their medicines are compounded of barks, leaves, flowers, seeds, roots and a few simple minerals. I once found one of the doctors in the Bassein hospital giving a course to some of the local *sesayas*; he was taking them from bed to bed and asking them to question each patient and to diagnose his complaint. I should have thought that this practice might well have borne fruit, but I never met it elsewhere, and of course the *sesayas* would in any case not have had access to modern drugs. In addition to the *sesaya's* prescriptions, the Burmese use shampooing (or massaging) for almost every ailment, and all Burmans seem to have a knowledge of this. Often after a long day's walking I have had the aches removed from my body by the skilful massaging of my servant or some other person.

It was in Bassein that I first met an unusual death custom. I had received the news that one of my headmen had died, and a few hours later a letter was placed before me in my office for signature, addressed to this same man, in which he was informed that, having discharged his duties faithfully, he was released from any further obligation to perform them. I drew the attention of my clerks to the fact that the addressee of the letter was dead and that there seemed therefore little object in writing to him, but I was informed that it was customary to write a letter of this nature to a deceased official. It would be read out at his funeral and would serve as a full and honourable discharge from his earthly functions.

I had little to do with local politics and intrigue in Bassein town, though there was plenty of both, due to a large extent to the influential Chinese community. The leading Burmese politician was U Mya Bu, a pleader and President of the Municipal Committee, and son of a retired Deputy Commissioner. He belonged to the extremist Thakin party, and was a pleasant enough fellow to all outward appearance. I learned later that he lost a good deal of his influence by his behaviour during the Japanese occupation, and I did not meet him after the war. There were two prominent Japanese: Kimura, a doctor, and Kongo, who was a photographer. Kimura left for Japan shortly after my arrival and I never met him. Kongo was a member of the golf club and was still in Bassein when I left, but he took care to get out of Burma before Japan invaded the country. Both these gentlemen returned to Bassein with the victorious Japanese forces. The leading Karen of the younger generation was Saw Ba U Gyi. He was an advocate, but I never remember seeing him in court. He was also a wealthy landowner and was occupied mainly in superintending his estates, and no doubt also in politics. He was married to an English wife, but they did not mix with European society, and I met them only in the golf club, and even then infrequently. I fear that she, poor girl, must have led a lonely life, and I believe she later left her husband. After Burma was granted independence, Saw Ba U Gyi was mainly responsible for instigating the Karens to armed opposition against the new government, and he was eventually killed.

I do not remember any particular political difficulties with the members of the priesthood. The Burma Police were endeavouring to enlist the support of some of the better monks in their campaign to suppress crime. An Anti-Crime Association had been formed, and one of the leading lights was a Bassein monk called U Narada, who lived in a monastery just beyond the golf course. He was a sharp-witted little man, who wore spectacles with metal frames. Freddy Wemyss, while he was Superintendent of Police, had a great deal to do with U Narada and I soon met him. There was of course always a considerable element of risk involved in giving official support to such a movement, for one could never be certain that its leaders were not playing a double game. It was, however, a risk that had to be taken. There were those who said that U Narada was not to be trusted; I can only say that, so far as my acquaintance with him went – and I had more to do with him after the war – I had no ground for distrusting him. With Wemyss's active support, both moral and financial, a Boys' Home was started, under U Narada's supervision, in his monastery. It was intended primarily for boys who lacked any proper parental care and who might otherwise have drifted into crime. I often visited the monastery and the boys certainly seemed happy enough; they earned a little pocket-money by acting as caddies for golfers.

As far as national politics were concerned, I have already mentioned that U Saw, leader of the Myochit party, had become Premier towards the end of 1940. Five years earlier he had visited Japan on a journalistic mission, and had met some of the leading persons in the country. He had been given a great reception and on his return had written a number of newspaper articles in praise of Japan, which was said to be now financing his newspaper. In May 1941 Sir Reginald Dorman-Smith became Governor of Burma in succession to Sir Archibald Cochrane. He was an Irishman, aged only forty-two, and had already held office as Minister of Agriculture in England. On the face of it, he appeared to have had greater political experience than his predecessor.

U Saw, a man of unbounded ambition, to whom his own personal interests came before those of his country, saw himself as the man destined to achieve independence for Burma and consequently a supreme position for himself. By the time that Dorman-Smith arrived, he had few rivals. Dr Ba Maw had been imprisoned for sedition, and U Saw had invoked the war-time Defence of Burma Rules to put his other leading opponents in jail. U Ba Pe, U Ba Thi,

U Ba U, U Ba Win and U Ba Hlaing, the first three being former ministers, went one by one into detention, lending point to the comment that all members of the House with a 'Ba' to their names would soon find themselves in prison. A local newspaper published a cartoon depicting six black sheep in a pen and U Saw with a shepherd's crook in his hand exclaiming, 'Ba, Ba, black sheep.' The way was therefore open for him to acquire all the credit for leading Burma to independence, and a promise of this at some early date in the future would enable him to maintain himself in power against any other party or combination. His policy was to offer Burma's full co-operation in the war in return for a promise of independence immediately it had ended. The Governor tried to persuade the British Government to give some such assurance, for after all it had always been the declared aim of British policy that dominion status should one day be granted to India and Burma. But the British Government declined to make any pronouncement in the middle of the war on the date when Burma would achieve this status, and, though they agreed to invite U Saw to visit England for talks, they made it clear that there was no question of their discussing self-government for Burma.

At the end of September U Saw left for England. Before his departure he decided to pay his respects to the Shwe Dagon Pagoda, but it was characteristic of him that he should choose a novel manner in which to do so. He had bought an old aircraft for his Myochit party, and he and his wife went up in it and circled over the pagoda. It was considered by Buddhists to be most disrespectful for any human being to have a sacred object below his feet, and his offence was magnified by his allowing a female to be placed in that position. He left Burma, accompanied by U Tin Tut, the most senior Burmese officer in the Civil Service, who was Secretary to the Defence Council, and he did not return till the war was over, for reasons which will appear in due course.

Meanwhile the war went on and its shadows were approaching nearer to Burma. A skeleton Air Raid Precautions organisation was set up in Bassein with the Port Officer in charge, and from time to time practice blackouts were held; some amusement was caused in the European community when the Manager of the Imperial Bank (a European) was prosecuted and sentenced to a small fine for inadequately blacking out his house. Once the government held a 'Defence Exercise' throughout Burma, which lasted for two or three days; telegrams prefixed 'Defence Exercise' flew through the districts telling of the landing of enemy troops on the coast, the holding of seditious meetings, and so forth. It was alleged that in one or two cases the originator of the telegram forgot to use the prefix 'Defence Exercise' and the recipient took it at its face value! A Home Guard was started in Rangoon, and Wemyss was transferred there to organise it. Towards the end of the year 1941 we began to feel that a Japanese attack on Burma might not be long delayed.

CHAPTER SEVEN

The Japanese Invade
1941-42

*I*N NOVEMBER I was posted to Mergui as Headquarters Assistant. Mergui was the most southerly district in Burma, at the end of the long Tenasserim Division, the leg of Burma which lies between Siam and the Andaman Sea and reaches down towards the Malay Peninsula. The possibility of war with Japan was increasing, and the Government was strengthening the European element in the administration of the eastern districts. The Headquarters Assistant, as I have explained earlier, was the Deputy Commissioner's principal officer at the district headquarters, and deputised for him in his absence. He was generally a Burmese officer, but he might be a European who was not yet ripe for the charge of a district. My predecessor, Freddie Yarnold, who was some three years my senior, was to be promoted to Deputy Commissioner and to remain in the district. I looked forward to the transfer, for in Mergui I should find a more equatorial type of climate, blue seas and many little islands, and strange fruit such as the mangosteen and the foul-smelling, but very rich, durian.

A few days before my departure from Bassein I sent off to Rangoon my car with my driver and my heavy luggage. Wishing, as usual, to spend no longer in Rangoon than was absolutely necessary, I had arranged to have merely the inside of a day there. I was met at the wharf by my car and paid my official call at the Secretariat on the Home Secretary, who was still MacDougall. He told me that my ultimate destination would probably be Victoria Point in the extreme south of Mergui District, and that Naiff, who was Subdivisional Officer there and slightly senior to me, would take my place in Mergui as Headquarters Assistant; it was, however, undesirable to make too many changes in the present unsettled conditions. Much of the rest of the day I spent with my friend Ohn Maung, now working in the Secretariat, who came down to the station in the evening to see me off and commissioned me to send him some durian preserve from Mergui.

The overland journey to Mergui involved travelling overnight by train to Martaban on the Salween River, crossing the river by ferry to Moulmein, headquarters of the Tenasserim Division, making another train journey to Ye, where the railway line ended, and finally driving some 150 miles to Mergui.

The following morning the train reached Martaban, and on the ferry I met Archdeacon Higginbottom (whom I already knew slightly), who was accompanying the Chinese Bishop of Kunming on a tour of Burma. Higginbottom was later to meet his death at the hands of the Japanese while trying to protect the property of refugees. I had booked accommodation for one night in the Circuit House and, as soon as I had settled in, I went to call on the Commissioner and the Deputy Commissioner. I had met neither before, and both invited me to their houses for drinks in the evening. Pelly, the Commissioner, was a former Indian Army officer now on the verge of retirement. Ian Wallace, the Deputy Commissioner, then in his late thirties, was one of the most outstanding men in the Service of the younger generation, an able administrator and a very good Burmese speaker.

I had little opportunity to see anything of Moulmein, which had been the first capital of British Burma, for the following morning I left for Ye. I had already booked accommodation for my car on the train, but I found that the Inspector-General of the Military Police had possessed himself of my truck and taken it down the line. I was told that no other truck was available, and that I should have to wait a day or two till this one returned. I decided therefore to leave the car behind with my driver, while I proceeded to Ye with the rest of my staff. We arrived in the late afternoon and thence went by bus over a well-rutted road to Tavoy, headquarters of the district immediately to the north of Mergui. For some time I was under the impression that the driver and his mate were Chinese, as I could not understand a word that they said, but I later realised that they were Tavoyans, speaking with the peculiar accent of the district. The Burmese kings are said to have settled in Tavoy large numbers of Arakanese prisoners, who imported the Arakanese dialect. When later I was working in Arakan, I seemed to find little difficulty in picking up their tongue; no doubt the Tavoy accent could be mastered with a little experience, but it is likely that it had been influenced by Siamese. We reached Tavoy at a late hour and found accommodation in the Government Rest House. George Merrells was in Tavoy on military service, and next day he called on me and took me to the Club. Owing to the roughness of the road from Ye, I decided to go back to meet my car and drive it up myself rather than leave it to the driver's tender mercies. I took the return journey fairly slowly, and spent a night on the way in a Rest House.

I had arranged in Tavoy to hire a bus to take my staff and my kit to Mergui, and I drove behind it in my car. The road was good, but there were some seven ferries to be crossed, and sometimes we were held up for a considerable time. We drove all day and spent the night at Palaw, a township headquarters in the Mergui district. In the afternoon of the following day, the 1st December, we reached Mergui, some eight days after our departure from Bassein. I installed myself in the Rest House and went to call on Freddie Yarnold, whom I had met once for a few minutes in the Secretariat in Rangoon. He was a bachelor like myself, and invited me to share the Deputy Commissioner's house with him till such time as my heavy baggage, which was coming by sea from Rangoon, had arrived and I had rented a house for myself.

The Tenasserim coastal strip, of which Mergui formed a part, had been subject to the Burmese kings of the Pagan dynasty (1044–1287), but, on the fall of that dynasty, had for many years been ruled by Siam. In the latter part of the seventeenth century it had been used as a base by a number of English 'interlopers', persons who were not members of the East India Company and who interfered very considerably with the Company's lawful activities. The most famous of these was Samuel White ('Siamese White'), whose wife is buried in Mergui. The Tenasserim area was reconquered by Burma towards the end of the eighteenth century and was ceded to Britain after the First Burmese War of 1824–26.

Mergui lay on the shores of the Andaman Sea, which is in effect a part of the Bay of Bengal; off the coast, from a little north of Mergui town to the southern limit of the District, were the numerous islets of the Mergui Archipelago. The bazaar area of the town lay down by the harbour, and on the high ground overlooking it were the Deputy Commissioner's house, his office, the Government Rest House and the principal pagoda. Those on the heights could hear the echo of footsteps and voices from beneath, especially at the time of the early morning shopping, and I remember the din to which I used to awake. There was a pleasant view across the harbour to the islands of Pataw and Patet and, beyond them, to King Island, the largest in the Archipelago, all a vivid green broken only by the whiteness of the pagodas.

The principal government officials besides the Deputy Commissioner and myself were the Superintendent of Police, the Civil Surgeon, the Public Works Department Engineer and the Port Officer, the last working directly under the Deputy Commissioner. As garrison we had a battalion of the Burma Rifles, Karen troops under British officers. There were also based on Mergui two motor launches of the Burma Navy. Apart from the officials, there were a number of other Europeans scattered about the District: some were rubber planters, some were tin miners, and some were little more than beachcombers.

The local population, the Merguians, were a Burmese people with, I should imagine, a strong Siamese and Malay admixture. Their accent differed from the pure Burmese, and at first I had to have an interpreter standing by me in case of need; moreover they used a number of words which were not normally used in Burmese. For example, the principal weapon of offence in the District was not the *dah* (or agricultural knife), but the axe, which they called *kappa*; this was not the usual Burmese word for an axe, and I later learned that it was Malay. Besides the Merguians, there was in the town a colony of Goanese, clustered round the Catholic Church, bearing such familiar names as De Silva, De Souza, Rodriguez, Pereira and so forth. There was also a curious race which I never came across in my short stay in Mergui: the Salons, sometimes referred to as the 'Water Gipsies'. These people lived principally in the islands of the Archipelago, moving round from island to island in their boats, wearing little or no clothing and taking to flight when any other boat approached. Some of them did, however, make an appearance on the mainland from time to time, having overcome their fear of other people, and I was told that they were almost uniformly filthy.

The motor road from Ye ended at Mergui. Our sea communications were maintained by the British India services to Rangoon, and the Straits Steamship vessels sailing between Moulmein and Penang. Imperial Airways flying boats used to touch down in the harbour, and there was also an airfield. We had a landline telegraph link with Tavoy, Moulmein and Rangoon, and there was direct wireless communication between Rangoon and Victoria Point, where Burma's extreme tip looked across the water at Siam. Touring within the District was done northwards by road and southwards by sea. There were two government launches, the *Kimhwa* and the *Curtana*, the latter bearing the same name as the ship in which Samuel White had once to escape from Mergui. I never saw the *Curtana*, and believe that she was in Rangoon for refitting.

My first and most important task in Mergui was to set up a Civil Defence organisation. It seemed that very little had yet been done. When the war started, the Burma Government had established a rather amateur 'ARP' organisation under an ICS officer, but the new Governor, Sir Reginald Dorman-Smith, who had arrived in Burma a few months earlier, had recently imported an expert from England, who had revised the whole scheme and rechristened it 'Civil Defence' in accordance with the latest thinking on the subject. A considerable amount of literature had arrived from Rangoon, but nothing at all had been done outside Mergui Town to organise any Civil Defence measures, and not very much had been done in the town. My work consisted mainly in discussing the problem with the municipal officials and the ward headmen of the town, appointing wardens and instructing them in their duties, and generally running about the town in my car supervising practice alarms. We had an air raid siren supplied from Rangoon, which we installed on top of the power station, and we provided the wardens with whistles to signal the beginning and end of an alarm. My ordinary office work at this time was mainly the dull task of renewing gun licences which were due to expire at the end of the year; this meant checking each weapon with the description in the licence, ensuring that renewal fees had been paid, and seeing that the renewal was noted both on the licence and on the counterfoil kept in the office.

On the morning of the 8th December, exactly a week after my arrival, Edwards, the Superintendent of Police, came to our house and told us that someone – I think it was one of his Burmese police officers – had heard a report over the wireless of the Japanese attacks on Pearl Harbour and Malaya. Edwards had himself listened at the first possible opportunity, and was able to confirm what he had been told. As yet there was no word from Rangoon instructing us what action to take, so we decided to go ahead and arrest all Japanese nationals in the district; they were mainly pearl-fishers and the police had them listed. They were sent to Rangoon by the first available ship. During the course of the morning an Imperial Airways flying boat touched down in the harbour; on board was a senior officer of the Royal Air Force, who confirmed that we were at war with Japan. Before long Rangoon told us to arrange for the demolition of a small airstrip some miles to the south of Mergui. Doubtless there was good reason for this order, but the airstrip had only recently been completed, and there was naturally considerable local criticism of the fact that an airstrip constructed presumably for defence purposes was put out of action as soon as war drew near. Field-Marshal Sir William Slim, in his *Defeat into Victory*, considers the siting of the Burma airfields to have been completely wrong, in that nearly all of them lay on a long north-south line facing the Siamese frontier; their proximity to the frontier meant that no adequate warning of enemy raids could be given.

Meanwhile my Civil Defence organisation was slowly taking

shape. We thought that there might well be Japanese air raids, and probably an attempt at invasion. But most of us, I think, imagined in our ignorance that any invasion would be repulsed without much difficulty. Had not General McLeod, the GOC, Burma, recently toured the frontier defences and announced, on his return to Rangoon, that he was satisfied that Burma was prepared to meet any attack? On Japan's entry into the war he issued an Order of the Day: 'In the air, on the sea, and on the lands, Burma is ready to repulse any foe. It is with every confidence that I call on the soldiers to face the enemy with calmness and courage. We shall throw back the invaders and free Burma for ever from the threat which has dawned to-day.' We were not to know that General Wavell, on a visit to Burma two months earlier, had expressed his concern at the extent of unpreparedness in Burma's defences.

And so I went on with my own local defence measures. I arranged a number of practice blackouts, but it was difficult to persuade the people to cooperate. The ordinary townsman went about the streets after dark carrying an unshaded torch in his hand, the night-time food sellers kept glowing braziers beside their stalls, and they looked upon our instructions to show no lights as an unnecessary interference with the liberty of the subject. After innumerable admonitions had been given in the first few days of practices, we started taking offenders to court. In the event, these blackout practices proved to be quite unnecessary, for the Japanese found nothing to stop them from bombing Mergui by day. During this time a senior Arakanese police officer, seconded as Staff Officer to the Civil Defence Controller, came down and stayed in our house, and gave a public address to the citizens of Mergui on the importance of Civil Defence work.

But the Japanese air raid of the 13th December on Mergui put an end to my organisation, which was after all less than a fortnight old. Twenty-seven aircraft in three rows of nine appeared in the morning flying very high over the town; they looked rather a fine sight, and many of the citizens came out from their houses to look at them. And then they dropped their bombs; some fell on the airfield and caused a few casualties; a stick just missed the Burmah Oil Company's store and jetty and fell into the harbour. The wardens' organisation collapsed at once. Most of the wardens left Mergui, ostensibly to move their families to safety on the islands, and never returned. It was perhaps hard to blame them. The Burmese had never experienced the horrors of modern warfare; the only fighting which had taken place in their country during the preceding century had been during the Second Burmese War of 1852, the pacification of Upper Burma (1886-90) and Saya San's rebellion of 1930. Throughout the country, as the Japanese invasion proceeded, Civil Defence arrangements broke down for precisely the same reason; only the Europeans and Anglo-Burmans could be counted on to remain at their posts.

Soon after this all the rest of my kit, furniture, refrigerator and other household goods, arrived from Rangoon and was placed in a house which I had arranged to rent. Freddie Yarnold, however, asked me to stay on with him till the situation improved. We were frequently receiving and despatching telegrams in the government code and, as he and I were the only officials of the administration who possessed the key, it was convenient that we should continue to live together. As a result, the bulk of my household goods were never unpacked and were left still in their crates when we had later to withdraw from Mergui.

The defence of Burma had for the past year been the responsibility of Far East Command under Sir Robert Brooke-Popham, whose headquarters was at Singapore. As a result of representations by General Wavell, Burma was transferred to the India Command a few days after Pearl Harbour, but before the end of December it passed to a new South-West Pacific Command under Wavell, with headquarters in Java. Wavell, it is now known, considered that there were compelling military reasons why Burma should remain under India, but he was overruled on political grounds to satisfy the Chinese. Burma remained, however, under the South-West Pacific Command only for five weeks.

It was now becoming clear to us that the Japanese invasion of Burma could not be long delayed. Their troops were already in Siam, and they were advancing down the Malay Peninsula towards Singapore. It was also clear that, when they entered Burma, they would meet little opposition, at all events in the Tenasserim Division. From the military point of view this long coastal strip was regarded as indefensible with the forces available. And in any case the British Government's view was that the defence of Singapore took priority over that of Burma. We heard it rumoured that all troops in Tenasserim would be withdrawn.

It was interesting to see the effect of the imminent likelihood of an enemy invasion on some of the senior government officials. The majority realised that they had a job to do and did it to the best of their ability; these were much too busy to give undue thought to what might happen when the Japanese arrived. Those, however, whose normal work was interrupted probably had more time for thought. One asked permission to move his office on to a launch in the harbour; it was not granted. The Burmese Judge from Tavoy, who was in Mergui holding sessions when the air raid took place, instructed the two senior judicial officials to come and sleep with him in the Rest House, which somewhat amused us. One of our Burmese administrative officers disappeared for a few days after the raid, and we considered taking disciplinary action against him till more important things put that out of our heads. But some Burmese officers did extremely well, in particular the Deputy Superintendent of Police, an elderly man named U Po Saing, who had a considerable burden of responsibility laid upon his shoulders owing to the necessity for the Superintendent to be frequently on tour.

There was an astonishing lack of military intelligence as to what was happening on our frontier. Slim says that we had been prevented from setting up any intelligence organisation in Siam for fear of offending the neutral susceptibilities of the Siamese. All that we civilians knew – and the military appeared to know even less – about the situation in Siam came from reports sent to us by Naiff, the Subdivisional Officer at Victoria Point. The general impression which these gave was that the Siamese would make no attempt to resist the Japanese and would be quite prepared to collaborate with them. The British Minister in Bangkok, I was informed, when he learnt the substance of these reports, indignantly repudiated them, but their accuracy was born out by events.

All Deputy Commissioners held a sealed envelope, which was to be opened only when the word was given. The envelope contained the 'invasion instructions'. These were, in brief, that, in the event of an enemy invasion, technical officers of the government should be evacuated, but that officers of the administration and the police should remain behind and carry on the administration under enemy occupation. These instructions had of course been framed with a comparatively gentlemanly enemy in view.

Meanwhile, we learned from Naiff that the Japanese were advancing through Siam towards Victoria Point. It appeared that their attack was two-pronged, the southern prong aimed at Victoria Point and the northern at the mountain range which divided Tavoy District from Siam. These mountains were uninhabited and thickly covered with jungle, and only a few little-used tracks crossed them. Many people who claimed to know the area asserted confidently that it would be impossible to get artillery or other heavy equipment over the mountains. But we were soon to learn that the Japanese could frequently accomplish the seemingly impossible. As their southern column of invasion approached Victoria Point, we grew increasingly anxious for the safety of Naiff and of Achard, his Anglo-Burmese

Police Inspector, who of course knew of the invasion instructions. But, at what seemed almost the eleventh hour, we learned from Rangoon that a wireless message had been sent to Naiff, telling him that, after ensuring that all civilians who were unable to mix with the local population had been safely evacuated, he could leave himself. It was said afterwards that this alteration of the original invasion instructions, which applied thereafter throughout the Burma campaign, had been authorised as the result of what had happened in Penang and northern Malaya, where the Japanese had either killed or imprisoned the officials of the British administration.

Victoria Point was occupied by the Japanese on the 15th December. A few days after we had received the message from Rangoon, the police arrived from Victoria Point, but without Achard; they told us that he had ordered them to leave. We assumed therefore that Naiff had received the altered instructions, and that he and Achard would reach Mergui shortly. But soon afterwards the wireless staff from Victoria Point arrived, and told us that the message from Rangoon had not been received before they dismantled their set. As both Naiff and Achard knew the original invasion instructions, the suspicion naturally arose that the police had deserted. I recorded a mass of evidence from successive waves of evacuees from Victoria Point, both Burmese and European, but Freddie Yarnold destroyed it shortly before he left Burma in order to lighten his luggage. My inquiry made it pretty clear that the police had left without permission, and this was confirmed by Achard when I met him after the war. Naiff and Achard were among the very few Burma government officials who fell into the hands of the Japanese, and both survived their internment.

The next event of interest was the Japanese 'invasion' of Bokpyin. Bokpyin was a small township headquarters on the coast, the only government administrative station between Mergui and Victoria Point. One morning, just as we had finished breakfast, Edwards, the Superintendent of Police, came around to our house with a Burmese police officer who brought news that the Japanese were in Bokpyin. This officer had come from Bokpyin to Mergui on business and was returning to Bokpyin. While the launch in which he travelled was lying off Bokpyin waiting for the tide to rise so that it could enter, small boats full of people came out from the town with the information that Japanese troops were in possession of it. The vessel's *serang* (the Indian in charge of her) at once turned about and returned to Mergui. We lost no time in passing on this news to the Battalion Commander. He was generally inclined to be sceptical of the truth of any information received through civilian sources, despite the lack of military intelligence. In this case he adopted the attitude that the report was probably without foundation, but that, to make quite certain, he would arrange for the Royal Air Force to fly over Bokpyin and see what was happening. He later told us that, as he had expected, the information was quite untrue, for the RAF had reported that everything seemed perfectly quiet. It was not until a few days later, when the young Township Officer, U Pa Aung, and some of his staff arrived in Mergui, having escaped from the Japanese with nothing but the clothes which they were wearing, that the Battalion Commander would concede that the Japanese had in fact entered Bokpyin. U Pa Aung had himself been captured, but had apparently had little difficulty in making his escape.

Some of our troops were now sent down to Bokpyin. Though their commanding officer was killed in the ensuing fighting, it appeared that the Japanese were little more than a reconnaissance party, and they withdrew. The station being again in our hands, we had of course to send back the Township Officer and re-establish the administration. U Pa Aung was a good young officer and made no difficulties about returning after his unpleasant experience. Freddie Yarnold asked me to go down with him and report on what had happened. We went in the government launch *Kimhwa* and had a pleasant trip through the Archipelago. We found everything looking quiet in Bokpyin; the only unusual thing that I can remember was that the Japanese troops had torn up the records in the township office, and there were pages from the register of criminal cases lying scattered in the road outside the office. I returned to Mergui the following day and reported on my visit. Bokpyin was the only place which I entered *after* the Japanese had left during the first Burma campaign.

Meanwhile the enemy, having already reached the sea to the south of us (at Victoria Point), were pushing ahead to our north over the mountains separating Siam from Tavoy District. Accompanying them (though of course we did not know this) were a number of young Burmans, members of the extreme Thakin party, who had fled from Burma some eighteen months before to escape arrest by U Saw, and had made their way to Japan. They later became known, from their number, as the Thirty, and among them was a Thakin Aung San, whose name as yet was unknown, but who was to be the chief architect of Burma's independence.

One morning, at about 4 a.m., Freddie Yarnold awoke me with a code telegram to be deciphered. It told us that Tavoy would probably be occupied by the Japanese that morning; after ensuring that all essential personnel in our district, and others who could not easily mix with the local population, were evacuated, we could leave ourselves. A few hours later Tavoy fell and the telegraph link between Rangoon and ourselves was cut. The Deputy Commissioner and the Superintendent of Police were both captured and interned for the rest of the war. The local Thakins joined Aung San and the Thirty, to form the nucleus of the Burma Independence Army. When the Battalion Commander heard the news, he told us that he expected now to receive orders to withdraw his troops. Though some of his junior officers, in speaking to us, were critical of any such move, the fact remained that Mergui now lay in an isolated pocket, with Japanese to north and south, mountains to the east and the sea to the west, and it would have been senseless to tie up a battalion of troops there. The Japanese could walk in whenever they wished, and the troops could be far more usefully employed elsewhere.

Our only means of withdrawal was now by sea. There was naturally considerable speculation as to how soon the Japanese would turn in our direction. I could not help feeling that, had I been in their position, I should have pushed on to Moulmein after capturing Tavoy, leaving Mergui to be mopped up at leisure. This is in fact what the Japanese did, and we learned later that their troops did not enter Mergui till several days after we had left.

We were informed by Rangoon – I think that messages must at this time have been passed through Army wireless channels – that a ship called the *Harvey Adamson* would be coming to Mergui to take off all but the 'last ditchers'. There was some argument with the Battalion Commander on the amount of accommodation to be allocated to military and civilian passengers, but, after referring back to Rangoon, we eventually came to an agreement. We sent messages to the various isolated European planters and tin miners and to the Burmese officials in the district, telling them to come to Mergui in time to leave on the *Harvey Adamson*, and most managed to get in before she sailed. In one case a European had withdrawn so far inland after the air raid that we were unable to get a message to him in time; his son, who was living elsewhere in the district, duly arrived, but refused to leave without his father and went off to look for him; both eventually reached Rangoon, and the last that I heard of them was that the father was breathing fire and slaughter against 'that young DC'. Two Europeans came in from one of the islands to catch the ship, and had tea in our house, but, after discussion between themselves, they told us that they had decided not to travel to Rangoon in a ship which was so large that it was likely to invite attention from enemy aircraft. They talked of trying to make their own way to Rangoon in due course in a Chinese fishing junk, but said that meanwhile they would return to their island. I was told that they had Burmese families there, and I never heard what happened to them.

I issued free tickets to civilians for passages on the *Harvey Adamson*, and Yarnold and I decided to send our servants on her. I gave mine a letter to Freddy Wemyss, asking him to put them up for a stated number of days and, if I did not appear within that time, to send them to their homes. I had only males with me now, having sent off Ma La's wife and child some time earlier. I also made a will and enclosed it in a letter home, which I sent with Ma La, asking Wemyss to post it if I did not turn up. The ship was due to berth in the middle of the night and to sail at about 3 a.m. The following morning I was surprised to see an Anglo-Indian family who had been given tickets for the *Harvey Adamson* approach our house. Their sad story was that they had done all their packing the previous night and settled down for a short nap; when they awoke, it was nearly dawn and they had missed the ship. As there was likely to be little accommodation available for civilians among the 'last ditchers', I was somewhat reluctant to allow them a second chance, but the women turned on the tears, and Freddie Yarnold agreed to find room for them.

The next few days were spent in carrying out such civilian 'denial' measures as were necessary. These concerned chiefly the contents of the Treasury and the stocks of government petrol. We dug a shallow trench not far from the Deputy Commissioner's bungalow, brought over the bulk of the currency notes from the Treasury and placed them in the trench. They were well soaked with kerosene oil and ignited by means of a flaming one hundred rupees note. This was the first of a number of such operations in which I was to assist during the next few months. The Burmese clerks and Treasury staff who helped me thoroughly enjoyed this novel pastime, but the burning took much longer than I had expected, as we were constantly finding whole bundles of notes beneath the ashes which had hardly been touched by the fire. While I was engaged in supervising the burning, Freddie Yarnold was doing some other work down in the town. I was just finishing when I heard ominous sounds of a disturbance from below. I looked down, and could see Freddie standing near the doors of the government rice stores, while large crowds of Indians were gathered round them. Fearing that a riot was starting, I jumped into my car and raced down. I think that an ugly situation could have developed: the Indians were short of food and were demanding a share of the rice stocks in the stores. As we were hoping to leave Mergui shortly, there seemed no point in refusing their request, and Freddie had already decided to let them have the rice. The crowd was soon persuaded that, if they would sit down in an orderly fashion and wait their turn, they would receive their quota. We managed to form them into some sort of a queue (a Western habit entirely foreign to the East), though Freddie caused some little confusion by trying to arrange a separate queue for the women, an act of chivalry which the Indian coolie did not really appreciate.

We had, I think, three days after the departure of the *Harvey Adamson*, and gradually our preparations were complete. One morning we went out in the harbour launch, which we had loaded with bags of silver rupees and smaller coin; in the peaceful harbour, surrounded by the green islets, and beneath the tropical sun, we emptied these bags one by one into the water. We removed and burnt all the secret files in the office. I collected a pile of dull files dealing with land matters which had been lying on Freddie's desk for weeks, as he had had no time to deal with them; having tied them together and marked them 'Most Secret', I put them into the safe, locked it and threw away the key. I often wonder whether the Japanese ever found these files and, if so, whether they spent hours poring over them in the hope of discovering something interesting. Edwards meanwhile went down the coast in the *Kimhwa* to collect the government staff from Bokpyin, and his deputy U Po Saing did very good work in the destruction of police stocks of fuel and in many other ways.

We were told that a ship, the *Henrik Jessen*, would be sent from Rangoon to fetch the remaining troops and civilians. We were to meet her at Tenasserim Island in the Archipelago, whither we were to make our way in such small craft as were available in Mergui. So far as I can remember, the Army had a few launches, we had the *Kimhwa* and the harbour launch *Jelinga* (though the latter was hardly a sea-going craft), and there were one or two more. Unfortunately we again had some disagreement with the Battalion Commander, who said that he would require all the launches for his troops, but who in the end was kind enough to allow us the use of our own *Kimhwa*. The result was that we had very drastically to restrict the numbers of civilians who could leave with us. Our instructions were to evacuate such of the government staff as could not mingle with the local population. Most of our subordinate clerical and police staff were local men who did not want to leave Mergui. But we also had now to leave behind some of the subordinate Indian staff, clerks of the Public Works Department, prison warders, etc., whom we had intended to take with us. This we did with extreme reluctance, and only because the Army demanded practically all the available transport. At the time we were extremely bitter about the Army's attitude, but, taking the long view, it was probably right that preference in evacuation should be given to trained soldiers over civilians whose immediate usefulness to the government was problematical. Subsequently I met in Calcutta some of the Indians who had been left behind in Mergui. They had come overland to Moulmein, and so I suppose that probably most of the Indian staff got away. On the question whether Indian civilians should have been left behind rather than Europeans or Anglo-Burmans, I think our decision was undoubtedly right, distasteful though it was at the time: the Japanese would have taken little notice of an Indian moving through the areas held by them, but a white man would have had no chance at all; the Indian had probably more to fear from the Burmese than from the Japanese.

The main body of the troops, under the Battalion Commander, set out in their launches for the rendezvous the day before us. They left behind a small demolition party to blow up the jetties and oil storage installations. In the early hours of our last morning (23rd January) in Mergui I made several trips to the *Kimhwa* with provisions and personal possessions. We each took as much of the latter as we could carry; I remember that I had one suitcase and a bedding roll. We had a rather luxurious early morning tea, at which we consumed several delicacies from our private store which we should otherwise have left behind. It was served by our Indian *pani-wallah* (water-carrier), who had been locked up by the police some days previously for expressing anti-British sentiments while under the influence of liquor. He alone of our domestic staff remained with us to the end. He was a local man, so we did not take him with us.

Day dawned, and silent and rather sullen crowds of local people began to gather in groups at the street corners, staring at us whenever we passed by. Most of the troops had gone, and the local police had been paid off and had departed for their homes. We did not know whether any attempt would be made to prevent our departure – an uncomfortable feeling which made me, at any rate, resolve that in future I would keep on the right side of the Army in an evacuation. But in the event nothing happened. Meanwhile the noise of explosions arose periodically from the jetties. Members of one demolition group, which was trying to blow up the Oil Company's petrol storage depot, suffered from severe burns. There was still one of the Burma Navy's motor launches in the harbour and, as there were no doctors left in Mergui, she took over one man who was very badly burned; I believe that he later died. One of the last things that Freddy

Yarnold and I did was to go to the jail to order the release of the prisoners. I was amused to see some of them prostrate themselves before the Burmese Jail Superintendent when they took leave of him, while he, in a fatherly way, told them to go home and behave themselves. Arriving back at the main jetty, where our launch was waiting, I had a personal 'denial' measure to carry out. I opened the bonnet of my car, cut every wire that I could find, and then called on a soldier (I think he was a Gurkha) on duty at the jetty to fix his bayonet and go round stabbing all my tyres. He thought this was great fun.

At last at about midday we left, to the sound of explosions from the jetties, some of which the demolition squads were evidently finding it difficult to blow up; and I had one of the largest and stiffest gins that I have ever had. We were a mixed collection: the Europeans were Yarnold, Edwards, myself and a man from one of the tin mines who had just reached Mergui; the rest were Burmans, Indians and Anglo-Burmans. We had arranged to anchor at night off a small island in the Archipelago. On our way thither Yarnold and I went down to the engine-room to burn the last packet of currency notes which we had kept against any emergency. The Indian *serang* was almost in tears at seeing good money burning, and asked us to give it to him if we had no use for it ourselves; but I fear that his pleas were in vain. We reached our island – an uninhabited one – about an hour before sunset; most of us went ashore to walk along the beach, and a few bathed. U Po Saing wanted to bathe, but he was wearing his police uniform and had no *longyi* immediately to hand. Seeing, however, one of his subordinates in mufti, and wearing a *longyi*, he shouted to him: 'Hey, you! have you any pants under your *longyi*?' 'Yes, sir,' replied the man, 'I have, but they are only very short ones.' 'Give me your *longyi*, then', said U Po Saing and went into the sea with it, while his unfortunate subordinate, wearing the briefest of cotton pants, hid himself as best he could from the view of the few women in the party. This peaceful bathing scene on a desert island was rather an anticlimax after the events of the morning.

Later in the night we weighed anchor for Tenasserim Island, our rendezvous with the troops and with the *Henrik Jessen*, which appeared soon after our arrival, under the command of a bearded Dane. In the early hours of the morning (24th January), while it was still dark, we sailed for Rangoon and had an uneventful journey, though we passed through an area where a ship had hit a mine only a few days earlier. On the second day, the 25th January 1942, we tied up in the Rangoon River, the heads of the first district administration in Burma to withdraw before the Japanese approach.

What were our feelings at this moment? I had no particular attachment to Mergui District, for I had been there less than eight weeks and had only once been outside the town. But we all felt that we had let the people down. We had been their rulers and guides whom they trusted, but at the first sign of real danger we ran away and left them to look after themselves. It is true that we had been ordered to leave, and we knew very well that, had we stayed, we should have been put into a Japanese prison camp, where we should have been of no more use to the people than if we had not been there at all. But would they have respected us more if we had remained and been taken prisoners? This was a question which agitated one throughout the Burma campaign, and to which no final answer can be given. It is, however, worth noting that it was frequently the policy of the Japanese to lower their European prisoners in the eyes of the local population by ill-treatment and public humiliation, and this must have had on many people the effect which they desired. Perhaps, then, we should not have achieved anything by staying. Be this as it may, I registered the hope that, when the Japanese had finally been expelled from Burma, I should not be sent back to Mergui, which I had left so ignominiously.

CHAPTER EIGHT

The Retreat to India 1942

EFORE THE WAR Rangoon had been a city with a population of 400,000 – Indians, Burmese, Chinese and Europeans. On the 23rd December 1941, and again on Christmas Day the Japanese bombed the city in the daytime, concentrating on the docks and the Mingaladon airport eleven miles away. Rangoon had only two squadrons of fighters: a Royal Air Force squadron of old-fashioned Buffaloes and the American Volunteer Group's squadron of far superior Tomahawks. The AVG, as its name implied, was a group of American volunteers, employed by Chiang Kai-Shek to help him in his war against the Japanese in China; it had been in Burma before the attack on Pearl Harbour, its job being to ferry to China the American aircraft which were being supplied through Rangoon. This small Allied force went out to meet the enemy raiders and proved more than a match for the greatly superior Japanese numbers so far as casualties were concerned; thereafter the Japanese confined their air attacks to the hours of darkness.

But the raids, particularly the first one which caught the people of Rangoon unawares, caused a great number of civilian casualties. It is estimated that on the 23rd December, 2,000 people were killed, while 750 died later. The immediate result was a mass exodus of the Indian labouring population. Most of the essential labour of Rangoon, employed by the Corporation and the Port Authority, was Indian, and their first instinct was to get back to their own country as quickly as possible. A horde of refugees, on foot and in bullock carts, streamed northwards out of Rangoon on their way to India. There was no road linking Burma with India, and their immediate destination was the Taungup pass, a track leading over the Arakan hills to the coast of the Bay of Bengal, where they hoped to board ships bound for India. Work in the port came to a standstill; ships could not be unloaded and military supplies and reinforcements, if they came, could not therefore be landed. The health and transport services depended mainly on Indians, and so did trade; many of those who fled were shopkeepers, who simply closed their shops and went. Burmese also left the city, but they generally camped in nearby villages and monasteries, and in any case they did not constitute Rangoon's essential labour force. Strong measures were needed to restore the city to life and, by means of persuasion, promises, warnings and threats, the government managed to bring back the bulk of the refugees within a week. They were settled in camps on the outskirts of Rangoon, where they were provided with free food, and the port was reopened. All went well for about a fortnight, but in the middle of January there was another sudden exodus of Indians. A rumour had apparently spread – in which they believed implicitly – that Rangoon was to be bombed for fifteen days continuously. From then onwards the flow of refugees did not cease. As many as could get away from Rangoon by sea did so, but the demands for accommodation in ships were far greater than could possibly be met.

When we arrived in Rangoon, Yarnold and I went to the house of a friend of his, Rennick of the Rangoon Corporation, who very kindly took us in. His wife was in Maymyo, and I stayed with him till I left Rangoon. The next day we reported at the Secretariat, now dispersed among a number of buildings in the residential area. Yarnold, who had worked in the Secretariat before, was given a job there almost at once; he had an interview with the Governor that day and gave him an account of our evacuation from Mergui. The Home Secretary – no longer MacDougall, who had become one of the Governor's Counsellors – gave me to understand that I should receive my posting orders within a few days. I called on a number of my friends, including Hall, my former Deputy Commissioner in Sagaing, who was now Secretary to the Judicial Department and doing two other jobs at the same time. Ohn Maung's department had moved from Rangoon and I did not meet him. I collected my servants from Wemyss's house and returned to Rennick's to wait for orders. I waited for three weeks.

The effect of the air raids on business in the city was only too apparent. Many shops were closed because their owners had departed for India. The big European banks had withdrawn, for the greater protection of their customers, to Upper Burma. As the moon waxed and the nights became lighter, Japanese bombers came every evening. One learned to distinguish the peculiar booming sound of the Japanese aircraft. Rennick was Civil Defence Officer for the Rangoon town area and, as soon as the alarm was sounded, he was up and dressed, and watching to see whether the bombs fell in his area or outside. On almost every night the raiders passed over the city and dropped their bombs in the vicinity of Mingaladon, where the Rangoon airport and the military cantonment were. One night I saw a Japanese aircraft come down in flames and next day crowds of people, including ourselves, went to look at the wreck. The Royal Air Force now had some more modern fighters – Hurricanes – but the maximum number available at any time did not exceed the equivalent of two squadrons.

After a few days I went back to the Home Secretary to enquire when I might expect my posting orders. He told me that I should probably be sent either to Maymyo or to Kyukhok, a customs post on the Chinese frontier, which had assumed a new importance with the outbreak of war with Japan and our consequent alliance with the Chinese. Chiang Kai-Shek had offered a month previously to send two of his armies – each equivalent roughly to a British division – into Burma, but his offer was not at once accepted, partly for political reasons, and partly because of the difficulty of providing his troops with supplies and transport. Certain units were at once accepted, but it was not until the end of January that it was agreed to accept larger numbers. Even so, it took an unconscionable time for the Chinese troops to get moving. There were Chinese in Rangoon while I was there, presumably connected with the American Volunteer Group, and they used to drive their military lorries at breakneck speed through the centre of the city.

I went again to the Home Secretary and said that, even if it was not yet decided where I was to be posted, I should like something to do while I was waiting in Rangoon. He made a note of this, but, though I was forced to stay in Rangoon for over three weeks, the only work which could be found for me was occasionally to sleep at night beside the telephone in the house of the Inspector-General of Police. That a young and able-bodied male with a reasonably good knowledge of the Burmese language could be found no more useful employment at a time like this is some indication of the state of affairs in government circles.

Meanwhile the news from the front grew more depressing. The Japanese took Moulmein on the 31st January, and crossed the Salween; it was little more than two months since I had passed over it peacefully. The general air of gloom was heightened by the news that a British army had surrendered to the Japanese in Singapore on the 15th February. It seemed inevitable that Rangoon would fall, and that a general evacuation would soon be ordered. Arrangements had been made to move the government departments from Rangoon to Maymyo and some had already gone. Essential civilian personnel had been issued with 'E' labels, which were to be affixed to the windscreens of their cars when the general evacuation was ordered. These labels would protect the vehicles from being requisitioned and would ensure that their owners – or such of them as were not to leave Rangoon in the last ship for India – had means of transport to take them up-country.

I continued to live in enforced idleness, restricted in my movements except when I had the use of Rennick's car, and occupied myself with reading, visiting the Secretariat to enquire about my posting, or doing some shopping. I bought the minimum of essential kit to enable me to live wherever I might be posted: cheap Japanese crockery and so forth. At last one day, when I went to the Secretariat on my usual errand, I was told that I was to go as Subdivisional Officer to Zigon in the Tharrawaddy district. Tharrawaddy had always been a district with a rather bad name. Saya San's rebellion of 1930 had started there, and it was inclined to be unsettled politically. Zigon was the northern of its two subdivisions, about 115 miles from Rangoon on the railway line to Prome; it lay on the route taken by the Indian refugees to the Taungup pass. I was informed that the Burmese Subdivisional Officer there was suffering from 'despondency and alarm', and was instructed to proceed to relieve him with all speed. I lost no time in arranging my departure. It was not easy to get seats in trains at this time, but by producing my written posting orders I was able to book seats for myself and my servants for the following day.

Rangoon was now a dying city. It was estimated that the population had dropped by nearly two-thirds, fewer shops were open, there was less transport, released lunatics roamed the streets by day and gangs of looters by night; the stream of Indian refugees leaving the city increased, partly through fear of the Burmese criminal element. My train left in the late afternoon of the 22nd February, and on the following day the signal was given to put up the 'E' labels, and the general evacuation of Rangoon was ordered. Only the troops and civilians engaged on the most essential work remained.

My first-class compartment was crowded, all the other passengers being Indians bound for Prome and thence for the Arakan coast. The train reached Zigon in the middle of the night, and I was taken to the Government Rest House by a Burmese official from Zigon who happened to be on the train. The next morning I made myself known to U Ba Ohn, the Subdivisional Officer, who, far from being in a state of despondency and alarm, was unwilling to hand over his subdivision to me, as he had received no orders to do so. He rang the Deputy Commissioner in Tharrawaddy, who had also had no information from Rangoon of my posting. For the next week I stayed in Zigon, kicking my heels and writing to the Deputy Commissioner to ask him to requisition a car for my use. U Ba Ohn, though he did not make way for me, was very hospitable and invited me to his house, where I met his family. He had a young son of about sixteen and a small daughter, a very sharp and lively young person of, I suppose, about twelve.

Meanwhile train-loads of Indian refugees were passing every day through Zigon on their way to Prome, while many others came on foot. There must obviously be plenty of work to be done and, hearing that John Hall had just been sent to Prome as Deputy Commissioner, I thought that I would go and offer my services to him, as I was doing nothing in Zigon. But the next day, when I was walking along the main road, I met Swithinbank, Commissioner of the Pegu Division, driving up to Prome. He stopped and told me that he had just had news that Hall had shot himself. The real reason for this I never knew. As Secretary to the Judicial Department, he had given orders for the release of the convicts from the Rangoon jail. The appearance of these people on the streets added to the chaos, and his action aroused a storm of criticism, which seems to have preyed on his mind. In retrospect, however, it seems that, if he had made any error at all, it was only in ordering the release perhaps twenty-four hours earlier than was necessary. It had presumably been already decided that no attempt would be made to move the convicts up-country under guard; they could only have been an embarrassment to an administration which already had so much on its hands in the districts. But another reason for Hall's taking his life may have lain in his own history. As I have said earlier, his father had a deep love of the Burmese, which he had inherited. Now he saw collapsing around him all that he, his father and their colleagues had spent their lives in building, an administration in which the ordinary Burman could go without fear about his lawful pursuits.

Soon afterwards I received instructions that I was to proceed to Tharrawaddy, the district headquarters, on transfer, and on the 1st March I was driven there in U Ba Ohn's car. The Deputy Commissioner, U Khin Maung Pyu, was a Shan member of the Indian Civil Service. He was not at his best in an office chair dealing with files, but he was a first-class administrative officer, quick in decision and full of energy. I think that he was the only non-European Deputy Commissioner who was left in sole charge of his district during our withdrawal before the Japanese. Others were either replaced or were given European officers as Additional Deputy Commissioners who did most of the work connected with the Army and the evacuation of civilians.

Khin Maung Pyu's wife and children had gone back to the Shan States, and he had only his two younger brothers, Khin Maung Hla and Khin Maung Lay, living with him. He had arranged for me too to live in his house. He asked me to make myself responsible for the requisitioning of transport, a fitting reward for my importunity in the matter of a car for myself. Every day I went out with a

Sub-Inspector of the Police Traffic Department and a number of drivers to search for suitable vehicles. Car-owners naturally did all they could to prevent us from requisitioning their cars. First we found the rotor arms removed, and dealt with this by carrying a few spares. Then we found that cars were being cleverly camouflaged; one was hidden inside what appeared to be a paddy store. We were somewhat exercised about payment for the cars which we requisitioned. In nearly all cases they were taken for military use; receipts were given, but it was some time before arrangements were made with the Army which enabled us to make immediate payment on their behalf. I was also responsible for moving supplies of petrol up the road and dumping them in the various government stations for use by official vehicles. When I passed through Zigon, I generally stopped for a little refreshment at U Ba Ohn's house. His young daughter would run out to welcome me and then make a beeline for my truck to see if I had any petrol with me. If I had, she generally managed to wheedle some out of me.

I was then appointed by Khin Maung Pyu to be his unofficial Headquarters Assistant. The official holder of the post was an elderly Burman, and Khin Maung Pyu now decided to send up-country those of his officials who were unlikely to be of any further assistance to him, and whose presence would soon be more of an embarrassment than a help. The ordinary routine work of government was virtually at a standstill, and our principal functions now were to help the Army and to see that refugees passed through the district as quickly as possible and without impeding military operations. The Superintendent of Police, U Ba Maung, was an elderly and charming person. He was the father of U Than Nwe, who had been my Township Officer in Kamaing, but he was hardly a man of sufficient forcefulness for the emergency conditions in which we were now living.

Evacuation arrangements now occupied much of my time. Special trains for evacuees had to be arranged with the Burma Railways, whose officials were most co-operative. Some of those who travelled on these trains were Indians in the government service, such as the Rangoon police, who had been moved first from Rangoon to Tharrawaddy, and who now must move on further. On one train went the staff of the Census Department. In writing of Mogaung I have referred to the preliminary arrangements for the census, which was held in March 1941. The officer in charge of the census operations was U Ka Si, a senior member of the Indian Civil Service, who was to be my Commissioner after the war, and later Burmese Ambassador in London. He had moved from Rangoon to Tharrawaddy with his staff and their enormous collection of statistics. Whether they arrived with their records intact, I do not know. But I do know that for several days after they had left Tharrawaddy there were census papers littering the station. I did not hear what happened subsequently to their records, but I understand that they were never recovered after the end of the Japanese occupation. All that remained were two pages, summarising the total population of each Division.

I made my closest acquaintance with a Japanese bomb one day when I had gone to the station at Letpadan, some ten miles north of Tharrawaddy, to make arrangements for an evacuation train. I had parked my requisitioned car just outside the station building and was talking to the railway officials inside, when we heard the familiar throb of Japanese aircraft engines and then a succession of explosions, one of which sounded as though it was just outside the building. We flung ourselves under tables till the aircraft had passed and, when I went outside, I found my car had dents in the roof from clods of earth thrown up by the bombs. They must have been fairly small bombs, for there was a crater only a few yards from the car. Some damage was done to the railway lines. So far as I can recall, there was only one fatal casualty, but a number of people, including two children, were buried by loose earth and had to be taken to the hospital suffering from shock, after they had been brought to the surface. Khin Maung Pyu, who knew that I had gone to Letpadan, drove there as soon as he heard of the bombing, and was relieved to find me unhurt.

I now return to the front. On the 23rd February the British forces withdrew behind the Sittang River, the last natural obstacle between the Japanese and Rangoon. Three days later it was learned that an Australian division on its way home from the Middle East, which Churchill had hoped to divert to Burma, would not be coming, as the Australian Government would not agree. There were no other troops which could reach Rangoon in time, and the city was doomed.

The Governor remained in Rangoon, but most of his Government was now in Maymyo. Sir Paw Tun had become Premier since the disappearance of U Saw from the political scene. We last saw U Saw circling round the Shwe Dagon pagoda in his aircraft before leaving for England with U Tin Tut. He had an interview with Churchill, in which he asked for a promise that Burma would be granted self-government immediately after the war. But Churchill refused to discuss constitutional matters in the middle of a war, and U Saw left England in November 1941 with no assurances regarding the date of self-government. He set off home through the United States, where he tried to enlist the support of President Roosevelt. He and

U Tin Tut reached Hawaii on the day after the Japanese attack on Pearl Harbour. Passenger flights westwards had been suspended, and they had to turn eastwards. While they were waiting in Lisbon for a connection, U Saw called on the Japanese Ambassador and informed him that, if the Japanese invaded Burma, the Burmese would rise against the British. This became known to British Intelligence and, when U Saw's aircraft landed at Haifa, he and U Tin Tut were arrested and transferred to Uganda, where U Saw was detained till the end of the war. No evidence was ever produced to incriminate U Tin Tut who, after the evacuation of the Burma Government to India, was recalled to duty.

It was decided that all essential workers in Rangoon except the demolition squads were to leave on the 28th February, and after that date only the Governor, Army Headquarters and the garrison, the demolition squads and some of the population remained. Demolitions were to start early on the 1st March, the day on which the Governor planned to leave for Maymyo. He left according to plan, although on Wavell's order the demolitions were postponed.

On the 6th March an official of the Reserve Bank arrived in Tharrawaddy from Maymyo with a friend, and they had lunch in our house. They were on their way to Rangoon to draw more cash from the Reserve Bank vaults, and were in good spirits. A couple of days later they passed through again at high speed, refusing to stop for a meal; they said that they had been caught in a Japanese road block and were now going northwards as fast as they could. It later transpired that the decision had been made that Army Headquarters and the Rangoon garrison should withdraw from the city in the morning of the 7th March, leaving behind the demolition squads, which consisted of some six hundred Europeans, Indians and Anglo-Burmans (or Anglo-Indians). The withdrawal took place, but on arrival at the village of Taukkyan, some twenty-one miles north of Rangoon, where the roads to Prome and Mandalay diverged, our troops found their way blocked by the Japanese. This was the only road out of Rangoon, and for a moment it looked as though the British headquarters had been cut off. Orders were sent recalling some troops who had already passed through Taukkyan, and they tried in vain to open the road. But the next morning, when preparations had been made for a full-scale assault on the road block, it was found to have vanished, and the garrison continued on its way. Why the Japanese removed the road block, when they appeared to have the British force in their power, has never been officially explained. It is generally supposed that the Japanese commander had been given orders to by-pass Rangoon on the north and to make a surprise attack from the west. To cover his flank from surprise, he placed a block on the road at Taukkyan. Having completed his task, and got his main force over the road, he removed the block, and rigid Japanese adherence to orders allowed the headquarters of the British army to escape.

Meanwhile the retreating troops were arriving in force in Tharrawaddy. There were only two British divisions in Burma, the 17th Indian Division and the 1st Burma Division, and the former now established its headquarters in Tharrawaddy. I met General Cowan, its commander, who was, I think, the only Divisional Commander to command the same division throughout the two Burma campaigns. I remember well how critical we civilians were of the fact that our troops seemed to be completely tied to the roads with their heavy motor transport, while the Japanese were constantly infiltrating through jungle tracks. The same criticism has since been voiced by both civilian and military historians. The 17th Indian Division, which had not long arrived in Burma, had been trained and equipped for desert warfare in the Middle East, while the 1st Burma Division had had little or no training in jungle tactics, and many of its units had been hastily raised at the last minute. Field-Marshal Slim regards this lack of proper training as one of the main factors contributing to the speed of the British defeat. He writes:

> To our men, British or Indian, the jungle was a strange, fearsome place; moving and fighting in it was a nightmare. We were too ready to classify jungle as 'impenetrable', as indeed it was to us with our motor transport, bulky supplies, and inexperience. To us it appeared only as an obstacle to movement and to vision; to the Japanese it was a welcome means of concealed manoeuvre and surprise. The Japanese used formations specially trained and equipped for a country of jungle and rivers, while we used troops whose training and equipment, as far as they had been completed, were for the open desert. The Japanese reaped the deserved reward for their foresight and thorough preparation; we paid the penalty for our lack of both.

It now became clear that there was no longer anything useful that we civilians could do in Tharrawaddy, and Khin Maung Pyu suggested to the Army that we should leave the town and establish our headquarters further north. This was agreed. We sent the contents of the Treasury, save what cash we were likely to require in the district, under armed guard to Prome, and handed over charge of the jail to the Army who, I believe, released the prisoners the following day. We made our headquarters at Gyobingauk, forty-four miles north of Tharrawaddy and seven miles south of Zigon. But after four or five days further military withdrawals caused us to move again sixteen miles north to Nattalin, the last government station in the district. Our party consisted of Khin Maung Pyu and his brothers, U Ba Maung, a young Burmese officer who was undergoing training, the Madrassi stenographer from the District Office, and myself. During these days most of the Indian clerical staff had but one idea in their heads, to get to India as quickly as possible; and who shall blame them? This little Madrassi, Sekaran, deserves all praise for staying with us of his own free will and remaining cheerful throughout.

During our short stay in Gyobingauk and Nattalin we occupied ourselves mainly in driving round the villages, showing ourselves and generally trying to encourage the people. To the average Burman the war was a private matter between the British and the Japanese, which they had unfortunately decided to stage in his country. He did not much mind whether the British or the Japanese occupied his district. What did worry him was whether his village and his fields would be fought over. Time and again we were asked the question: 'Will the fighting pass by us?' As we withdrew northwards, we did what we could to provide the people of the larger villages with the means of protecting themselves against criminals, who were appearing as law and order broke down. The local police were allowed to return home with their arms and instructed to use them for the protection of their villages. U Sein Hman, my friend from Mogaung days, had settled in Minhal, a small town on the railway line, where with a few of the local elders he had established a committee of administration. We drove there one morning with a number of rifles, which we handed over to him with our good wishes.

At this time we had little work to do in connection with the Army. Complaints were made to us that local villagers were charging the troops exorbitant prices for vegetables in the bazaars and I drove up and down the road, stopping at the bazaars and warning the sellers to charge fair prices. Occasionally there were complaints made by civilians of misconduct on the part of Indian soldiers, which we took up with their officers to the best of our ability. They naturally had far more important problems to exercise them than complaints against their men, but I remember one occasion on which an officer of the Jats to whom I brought some Burmese villagers with an allegation of robbery by one of his sepoys, having found one item of stolen property on the culprit, promptly paid up in cash the value of the articles which were not recovered. This type of summary justice certainly had a very good effect on the average villager.

I have little recollection of seeing aircraft during this period, but, if one did see them, they were generally Japanese. The Royal Air Force squadrons were now based on Akyab and Magwe, and on the 21st March they made a very successful raid on enemy aircraft at Mingaladon. But the same afternoon the Japanese delivered a smashing blow on our aircraft at Magwe. Most of them were caught on the ground and, though our men put up as good a fight as they could, most of their aircraft were destroyed; the few that could still fly left for Akyab. Twice in the next week the Japanese launched attacks on Akyab, which was also abandoned. The American Volunteer Group had withdrawn to China after the bombing of Magwe, and there were now no Allied aircraft left in Burma. Henceforth all the aircraft which we saw were Japanese, and they met with no opposition.

The time now came when we could do no more for the civil population in Tharrawaddy District. British and Japanese troops were fighting only a few miles down the road, and early on the 26th March we left Nattalin for Prome, forty miles to the north. The Commissioner, Swithinbank, was now there, and we found him living with George Webster, the Deputy Commissioner. We reported to Swithinbank for orders. He told the others that they could proceed northwards to join their families, but directed me to stay in Prome. I bade them farewell, and saw none of them again till the war was over.

I was in the middle of a late breakfast in Webster's house when I heard aircraft overhead. We all dashed for the trenches which had been dug in the garden and waited till the raid was over. Webster and I then went into the town. Some buildings had been set on fire by the raid and there was a strong wind blowing. It soon became obvious that, if something was not done very soon, the fire would spread. The local fire brigade was no longer to be found; I do not know whether they had disappeared on this day or some time previously. The Superintendent of Police got hold of the fire engine and drove it to the scene of the conflagration, but we were unable to get it working, and we had to watch helplessly while Prome burned. The Deputy Commissioner's house was not far from the town and the area of the fire and, as it seemed possible that the flames might reach it, Swithinbank, Webster and I removed ourselves to 'the hill' on the other side of the town, where a number of Europeans lived. Here we spent the next three days, during which the town continued to smoulder. Seen from the hill, the partially consumed buildings, with oddly shaped unburnt pieces standing up here and there, reminded me strangely of a distant view of the spires and towers of Oxford.

Another occupant of Webster's house who moved with us was Archdeacon Higginbottom, whom I had last met while on my way to Mergui. He had somehow acquired a number of large mail-bags full of letters and he spent his days sorting them into pigeon-holes according to destination – a work of supererogation, for I doubt if he ever took them out of Prome.

It was while I was in Prome that I first heard the name of General Slim. The two British divisions in Burma (the 17th Indian Division and the 1st Burma Division) had now been combined into a corps known as 1st Burcorps, and Slim had come to command it. His connection with Burma was to last until, as commander of the 14th Army, he reconquered it from the Japanese in 1945. He was now serving under General Alexander, who had recently been appointed to the Burma Command and had, I think, arrived at his headquarters in Rangoon only two days before the garrison marched out. Wavell's South-West Pacific Command had been closed down after the fall of Singapore, and he had returned to the India Command. Operational control of the Burma front also passed back to India, and so in the space of less than three months which had elapsed since the Japanese entry into the war, four different headquarters had been responsible for the defence of Burma: Far Eastern Command in Singapore, India Command, South-West Pacific Command in Java, and again India Command.

In Burma proper the fighting was now on two fronts, as we withdrew northwards from Rangoon: the Irrawaddy front on the west and, separated from it by the range of hills known as the Pegu Yomas, what may be called the Sittang front on the east. Until recently these two fronts had been defended by the two British divisions, but now at last the Chinese 5th Army, promised for so long, arrived and took over the Sittang front, leaving the 1st Burma Division free to cross the Irrawaddy front and to join the 17th Indian Division under Slim's command. My own line of withdrawal was along the Irrawaddy, and consequently I had no direct dealings with the Chinese. A number of my colleagues were, however, posted as liaison officers with Chinese troops, and stories filtered through to us of the summary justice meted out by the officers to their men. If a complaint was made of looting or other misbehaviour by Chinese soldiers and the soldiers were identified, the officers were as likely as not to draw their revolvers and shoot the culprits out of hand. The 5th Army, on first taking up its position on the Sittang front, had some small successes against the enemy, which naturally evoked from us some criticism of our own troops, who seemed to do nothing but withdraw. But the Chinese had had several years' experience of fighting the Japanese. On our own front we had a Colonel Gordon Chu, who called himself the Chinese Liaison Officer, and whom I came across from time to time; he was a sprightly little man with a moustache and a marked American accent.

I stayed in Prome for only four days. Apart from work arising from the fire, and liaising with various military units, the only job of which I have any clear recollection is that of spending hours in the Treasury vault counting currency notes which were to be sent up-country. Meanwhile the enemy advanced towards Prome, and one day we could hear clearly the noise of a battle being fought at Shwedaung some nine miles to the south. According to Slim, several units of Burmese took part in this battle on the Japanese side, wearing the blue uniforms of the Burma Independence Army. I had previously heard a story, whose source I was never able to trace, that, as the last of the demolition squads were leaving Mergui in January, they saw men in blue uniforms lining the shore.

Swithinbank now decided that no useful purpose would be served by civil officers remaining in Prome, and on the 30th March he, Webster and I drove north to Magwe, 150 miles away, to report to the Commissioner of the Magwe Division and to wait for orders. The Deputy Commissioner (Lindop) had his wife still with him; she was the first European woman whom I had seen for some weeks, but she was leaving the next day. The Commissioner (McCracken) was also living with him, but Lindop cheerfully took in the three of us, while McCracken wired to the Government in Maymyo to ask what we were to do next. On the following day Lindop received a message from the local military formation that Generals Wavell and Alexander were arriving on a flying visit, and was asked if he would give them dinner and beds for the night. Alexander's name at this time I hardly knew, but Wavell was already famous. Mrs Lindop had left, and arrangements were made for the accommodation of the distinguished visitors. Wavell was clearly a tired and worried man, with little time to waste on civilians, and his conversation at dinner was mainly military 'shop' with Alexander, unrelated to the Burma campaign. Alexander must have been just as worried as Wavell, but he showed no sign of it. He seemed a friendly person with great charm, and one felt that in normal times he must have been very good company.

Next day Swithinbank and I received orders to proceed to Maymyo. We left Magwe on the 2nd April, each in our own cars and with our servants. We drove through the oilfields area of Yenangyaung, looking very brown and dry, and in due course turned east to Meiktila and the main road from Rangoon to Mandalay. Just beyond

Meiktila, while I was travelling at some forty miles an hour, my requisitioned car developed a puncture in one of the front tyres. It slewed round, making, as it seemed, straight for a large tree, and came to rest on its side. My servants were somewhat shaken, but no one was hurt. At that moment a lorry-load of Chin troops, under the command of an officer whom I had known on the militia course, came down the road. They put the car on its wheels and changed the punctured tyre, and I was able to proceed on my way with the loss only of my spectacles, which must have been pocketed by one of the civilian bystanders. Meanwhile Swithinbank who had gone ahead, realising that I was no longer following him, came back to see what was happening. As it was growing late, we decided to stop for the night at the nearest Rest House, some twenty miles beyond Meiktila. That evening we found that we had a classical education in common, and we sat on the verandah quoting Greek verse to each other. I had hitherto regarded Swithinbank as a somewhat formidable character. He was tall and gaunt and some thirty years older than I was, but from that evening, though I met him but rarely afterwards, I saw him as the likeable person that he was reputed to be. He was much loved by the Burmese, and used to say that his happiest days were those when he was a Subdivisional Officer and had more time to move among the people than he had later in more

A Chin funeral party

senior posts. Even as a Commissioner, he preferred to do his travelling on foot, with an old bag slung over his shoulder.

The next day, Good Friday, we set out for Maymyo. Some thirty miles south of Mandalay we saw Japanese aircraft returning from a raid on Mandalay. We stopped and scrambled into the nearest ditch, but they took no notice of us. Ten miles short of Mandalay, at the bridge over the Myitnge River, my car had another puncture. I had now no spare tyre, and Swithinbank suggested that I should go with him to Maymyo, and then take his car and come back for my servants and luggage. As we drew near to Mandalay, we met buses full of frightened Burmese fleeing the town. The air raid had been a severe one. The Japanese, it seems, took a particular pleasure in making their heaviest raids on Christian festival days; it will be recalled that Rangoon had been bombed on Christmas Day. On this day they had given the greater part of their attention to the riverside, where the wharves were, but the town too suffered considerable damage, which was aggravated by the fires which broke out after the raid. We drove straight through Mandalay without stopping, passing a number of dead bodies, both human and cattle, and reached Maymyo in the afternoon.

Having arranged accommodation there with Freddy Wemyss, I took Swithinbank's car and went back to fetch my staff. They had evidently been having a serious talk in my absence, and the first thing that Ma La said to me was that he thought it would be best if I let them return to their homes in Myitkyina District. I had sent his wife and little Ah Tut back while we were still in Mergui, and he had hitherto seemed quite content to stay with me. The cook had received a telegram in Mergui in the customary form, 'Mother hopeless come quick', but in his case it was the wife who was 'hopeless'. I suspected that he had himself arranged for the telegram to be sent, especially as I had always understood him to be a widower; I told him that I could not at that time let him go, and he accepted this without demur. But now that it seemed obvious that nothing short of a miracle was going to stop the Japanese from advancing into Upper Burma, there seemed no point in my keeping my servants with me any longer. It was clearly my duty to ensure that they were able to get to their homes before it was too late, and I agreed that, when we reached Maymyo, I would discharge them.

I had a week of comparative idleness in Maymyo, and even this short period in a fairly cool atmosphere, after the heat of the plains, was very beneficial. Much of my time I spent in looking for another car, and I was eventually able to persuade the government to requisition one for me. I sent off my servants by train, and hoped that they reached their destination safely. I never heard of them again and, though I tried to make enquiries after the war, I was never posted anywhere near Myitkyina District. In their place I engaged a man called Maung Nyunt, who had once been employed as a driver by a police officer.

I was posted to Ye-u in the Shwebo District as Subdivisional Officer, and left Maymyo on the 11th April, taking Maung Nyunt and his wife with me. I had to stop in Mandalay to get a pass to cross the Ava Bridge to Sagaing. Freddie Yarnold was now Deputy Commissioner there; he did a very good job in Mandalay after the bombing, for which he was awarded the MBE, and was a man who possessed the great virtue of never becoming flustered. There were crowds of people waiting to see him and, when I sent in my name, I described myself as an 'Evacuation Expert'. I thought that, having had to withdraw from three districts in succession, I was in a fair way to becoming an expert. Bodies of Chinese troops were arriving in Mandalay; some were youngsters with fresh pink cheeks, who looked as though they were in their early 'teens.

In Sagaing I reported to the Commissioner, Reynolds, whom I had not met before. He was, I think, the most senior officer in the Service, and had a reputation for rudeness. He told me that he had never asked for me to be posted to Ye-u; there was a Burmese Subdivisional Officer there called U Hla Pe with whom he was perfectly satisfied. He hastened to assure me, however, that he was pleased to have me, and said that he wanted me to concern myself with the evacuation of Indian refugees and liaison with the Army; the routine business of administration was to be left to U Hla Pe, who would remain in Ye-u as an Additional Subdivisional Officer. I spent the night in Sagaing and went on my way the next morning.

Ye-u lay on the Mu River and on a road which ran south-west from Shwebo to Monywa. Each year during the dry season a temporary bridge was built over the river; at other times of the year passengers and vehicles crossed by ferry. In peacetime it was a quiet little place, but now it was a hive of activity. A refugees' transit camp had been established there to accommodate the steady flow of Indians making their way overland to India, and from here they set out on the next stage of their journey, to the River Chindwin. Prome was now in the hands of the Japanese and the Taungup pass route was therefore no longer in use; and in any case for those Indians who lived in Upper Burma the Chindwin route was the nearest. Ye-u was also now the headquarters of a number of senior officers of the Public Works Department, who were trying in desperate haste to improve the road from there to Shwegyin on the banks of the Chindwin, in order that it might be used by military transport during the Army's retreat. For some twenty miles it was already a good road, but for the remaining seventy miles it was a mere track through largely waterless forests, which crossed the sandy beds of innumerable streams.

U Hla Pe was living in the Subdivisional Officer's official house and, as he had his family with him, I naturally had no wish to turn him out. I made arrangements therefore to rent a house. It was a typical Burmese house, and I attempted to beautify it a little by spreading over the earth floor of the main room a number of coarse cane mats, such as were generally used in paddy stores.

My first task was to examine the arrangements for dealing with refugees. The running of the camp was not my concern; my job was to see that refugees were passed through it as quickly as possible. Our main object was to ensure that the Army's operations were not hampered by the presence of hordes of these unfortunate people. We could not therefore send them along the road to Shwegyin and in any case, as I have said, about seventy miles of that road had no water. The camp was under the general supervision of one Butcher who had been in civil life, I believe, an undertaker in Rangoon; he was a pleasant enough fellow, but to my mind too gentle in dealing with Indian crowds. I must emphasise that there was no lack of understanding on our part of their plight, but at times the heavy hand was essential if anything was to be accomplished. Butcher was assisted by a little American padre called Clare, who belonged to a Methodist mission. He was by no means a youngster, he was doing this job of his own choice, he was living in comparative discomfort and was on the move all day, and yet I never saw him anything but cheerful. He required no alcoholic stimulus to keep up his spirits and, when offered a drink, would always refuse it and reply, with a twinkle in his eye: 'Strong drink is a mocker.' His unfailing good humour was a great asset to us in those days.

The refugees were in the main being left to make their own way onwards from Ye-u, though I think that some arrangements had been made for the supply of a limited number of bullock carts. The result was that the turnover in the camp was not fast enough. I arranged for special evacuee trains to run from Ye-u to a station called Kanbya some twenty miles down the line towards Monywa; this reduced the length of the overland journey to the Chindwin. The Burmese head-man of the Kanbya area was extremely co-operative, and collected as many bullock-carts as he could raise to meet the trains. The intention was that the women, small children and old men should ride in these carts, for the refugees were supposed to bring with them no more property than they could carry. But naturally the desire to cling for as long as possible to all that remained of their worldly goods was strong, and we had endless arguments over the amount of their luggage. We tried to reduce it in the first instance by providing a very limited number of carts for transport from the camp to Ye-u station, and then by holding up at the station as much heavy baggage – such as chairs and tables – as we could. Even so, when they arrived at Kanbya many refugees preferred to make their old men and women walk, while they piled the carts high with their gramophones, tables, chairs, carpets and other non-essentials. I frequently travelled down on the train, accompanied by Padre Clare or Butcher, to see that the arrangements were working smoothly. The train always went in the afternoon, and a certain amount of forceful persuasion was needed at Kanbya, to make the refugees transfer themselves from the train to the carts with the minimum of confusion and delay, so that the party could get well on its way before dark.

I was not altogether happy about the arrangements for receiving the refugees once they reached the Chindwin, and sending them on the next stage of their journey. The Chindwin was outside my jurisdiction, so I discussed the matter over the telephone with the Deputy Commissioner responsible, and arranged to drive to Monwya and talk things over with him. An Indian police officer named Bhattacharjee offered to drive Butcher and me there in his car, and we set out early in the morning. As we were leaving, I asked Bhattacharjee if he had a spare tyre; he said he had not, but that his car never gave any trouble. The upshot was that after some thirty miles we had a puncture and could go no further. Fortunately the road to Monywa ran very close to the railway line, and we made our way to the nearest station, where I telephoned the Deputy Commissioner and told him that we should not be coming after all. We were only a few miles from Kanbya and, as an evacuee train would be coming down in the afternoon, we could return in it to Ye-u. We spent the interval in visiting some villages and talking to the people, and consumed a few glasses of coconut water, our only sustenance that day. In due course we reached Kanbya, to find that the train was already in and that the refugees had organised a sit-down strike, on the ground that insufficient carts had been provided. I told them that, if they were not ready to move in fifteen minutes, the carts would be sent back to the village and they would be left to make their way on foot to the Chindwin; the 'strike' ended at once. I cannot recall how many thousands we passed through Ye-u on their way to India in the three weeks that I spent there, but almost till our last day we were sending trains down to Kanbya.

Towards the end we could not trust the Indian engine-drivers by themselves. It was rumoured that they wanted to get to Monywa and thence to India and that they would not stop the trains at Kanbya. I had to put armed police in the driver's van to see that he carried out his instructions, and on at least one occasion I travelled in the van myself.

Meanwhile work was going ahead on the road from Ye-u to the Chindwin at Shwegyin. I had little to do with the Public Works Department, for they had their own labour force and it seemed to be working satisfactorily. Much of it came from the Catholic villages in the area. The inhabitants of these villages were descendants of the Portuguese followers of Felipe de Brito, an adventurer nominally in the service of the King of Arakan, who in the early years of the seventeenth century had established himself at Syriam, near the present Rangoon, and made himself virtually independent. The stranglehold which he imposed on foreign trade by forcing it all to pass through Syriam, and his pillaging of Buddhist pagodas and shrines, eventually drew down upon him the wrath of the King of Burma, who in 1613 besieged and took Syriam. De Brito himself was impaled. His followers, who numbered (with Eurasians, women and children) some four hundred, were enslaved, sent up-country and eventually settled in villages between the Chindwin and Mu Rivers. They were known locally as *bayingyi* (from the term *feringhi*, which used to be applied to the Portuguese freebooters), and they had remained distinct communities, speaking Burmese but retaining their Catholic faith, with their little village churches and priests from their community. Facially they did not look Burmese, but in the colour of their skin and their hair they differed in no way from the Burmese.

One of the Public Works Department officers was living in a house near to mine, and I occasionally dropped in on him of an evening. I always found him sitting in front of a bottle of whisky. Most evenings he would become maudlin drunk, and would before long utter the pronouncement: 'We are in a state of siege.' And so in a sense we were. The Japanese held the coastline, and as yet there were no roads leading from Upper Burma into any of the neighbouring countries. It was as if we were in a house with only one door and that door was locked. The only hope for the Army, if they were not to abandon all their transport, artillery and heavy equipment, was that the engineers would manage to make a motorable road out of the track leading from Ye-u to India. This track led, as I have said, to the Chindwin at Shwegyin, and there it ended. It was then necessary to travel six miles up the Chindwin by ferry to Kalewa. From Kalewa another track of about a hundred miles led through the malarial Kabaw Valley to Tamu, which lay just inside the frontier with India. From there the Army engineers from India were building an unmetalled road to Imphal, the capital of Manipur, from which a good road already existed to the Indian railway system. On the Burma side the road had in peacetime been little more than a cart-track, and it was necessary to widen it, to bridge streams and generally to make it fit for heavy transport. A further consideration was the imminence of the monsoon. We generally reckoned that it began about the 15th May, and once the rains broke the unmetalled roads would be a sea of thick mud, and heavy vehicles would be hopelessly bogged down.

We civilians were not of course aware of the decisions taken as to the line of retreat. But it appears from the histories which have subsequently been written that the original plan was for the 1st Burma Division to withdraw along the route which I have just described into India, while the 17th Indian Division should fall back along the railway line to Myitkyina, keeping in touch with the Chinese 5th Army, and enter China. The Governor accordingly decided that, when the time came for him to leave Maymyo, he would make Myitkyina his headquarters. Subsequently, on the 25th April, the Army's plan was changed, and it was decided that the whole of the British Corps should try to leave Burma intact along the Shwegyin-Kalewa-Tamu-Imphal route. The complete disintegration of the Chinese armies was a prime factor in prompting this decision. It appears, however, that the Army omitted to inform the Governor of this important change of plan. He moved to Myitkyina a day or two later in complete ignorance of the fact that the Army was now leaving by the other route.

The failure of the Army to keep civil officers informed of what was happening was one of our main causes of complaint. If we tried to obtain information by a direct question, we were never given a direct answer, and we felt sometimes that we were being treated like children asking their parents awkward questions. Obviously there must have been many matters about which the local military commanders were just as ignorant as ourselves; but there were many cases in which they had a pretty shrewd idea of what their next move would be. An officer who must have known very well that the next day he would be falling back would inform us blandly that there was no question of his withdrawing. In fact, we came to know from experience that, when we were told that a place would be held at all costs, we could prepare for its evacuation. It is, however, only fair to add that Field-Marshal Slim blames the lack of a clear, overall directive for obscuring immediate objectives.

Were we to risk all in a desperate attempt to destroy the Japanese Army and recover all that had been lost? Ought we to fight to the end on some line to retain at least part of Burma? Or was our task to withdraw slowly, keeping our forces intact, while the defence of India was prepared? Had we been given any one of these as our great overall object it would have had an effect, not only on the major tactics of the campaign, but on the morale of the troops. No such directive was ever received.

It now became obvious that we should not be staying much longer in Ye-u. Army stragglers, both British and Indian, were arriving and passing through on their way to India. Webster, who was now a Deputy Commissioner in Shwebo (one of three, I think), decided to move his headquarters to Ye-u, and I went and lived with him in a house occupied by the Administrative Commandant; Richards, a senior officer of the Indian Civil Service, joined us there. The evacuation staff were ordered to leave, and organised arrangements for refugees came to an end. The hospital had a number of civilian air raid casualties, but the Indian doctor in charge, who had lived long in the area and had, I think, a Burmese wife, intended to remain at his post even after the troops had left. This noble intention was, however, frustrated by the behaviour of two drunken British soldiers, who appeared one morning in the hospital with pistols in their hands and succeeded in frightening the doctor and his staff to such an extent that they hastened to leave the town.

Meanwhile I visited the headquarters of my two townships, both of which were easily accessible by road from Ye-u, and gave instructions to the Township Officers for the disposal of government cash, and permission to leave their stations if they so desired after they had paid their staff a month's salary in advance. I viewed the prospect of leaving Burma, for which I had so great an affection, with a heavy heart, and had thoughts of remaining behind, concealed in a Burmese village or in the hills. U Hla Pe and U Ba Win (one of the Township Officers) said that, if I decided to do so, they would help me as much as they could. But commonsense, I am glad to say, prevailed; I should have been able to do no good had I stayed in Burma, and it is most unlikely that the Japanese would not have learned very soon of my presence. In any case, Webster brought me written instructions from the Commissioner that I was to make my way to India and report myself at the office of the Special Officer for Burma in Calcutta. He had similar orders himself.

General Alexander established his headquarters at Shwebo,

twenty-five miles away, on the 26th April, and a day or two later an echelon of his headquarters arrived in Ye-u. I helped them to settle into their camp site by interpreting their requirements to the local people. That same evening, after we had had our dinner, I was reclining on an easy chair in our house, resting after the usual busy day, when two rather excited Army officers arrived, asking to be directed to Army headquarters; they said that they had heard a report that the Japanese were attacking Monywa. I was wearing a rather delectable pair of Chinese trousers, black silk patterned with silver pagodas, and, as I was the only one present who knew exactly where Army headquarters was and the matter was clearly urgent, I accompanied these officers, dressed as I was. It struck me at the time as being an incongruous garb for a European civilian to wear at the headquarters of a retreating army. I remember too my surprise when, on our arrival, it took some time before we could arouse anyone. I had assumed that in time of war, sentries were posted at night in British camps.

It was now arranged that Webster, Richards and I should leave Ye-u on the 1st May. On the previous day Webster went to Shwebo to close down the administration, while I did the same in Ye-u. I paid off all the staff and gave them permission to return to their homes, and I then had to destroy the currency notes in the Treasury. The troops guarding the Treasury vault were Indians and, knowing the general attitude of Indians to the destruction of good money, I prevailed upon some members of the police force, who of course were Burmese, to help me to burn the notes before they went home. I had just started to collect the money from the vault when Japanese aircraft appeared overhead. I locked the vault and we all took shelter in the trenches. The enemy's objective was the temporary bridge over the Mu, but they did not succeed in hitting it. When the raid was over, I looked for my police volunteers, but they were nowhere to be seen. I had therefore no choice but to call on the Indian troops to assist. I burned the notes in a slit trench and, whenever my back was turned, a sepoy would jump into the trench, grab a packet of notes and try to stuff it into his pocket. I don't think anyone got away with his loot, for I was constantly on the watch and, with a little assault and battery, managed to recover the notes. It was perhaps as well that I was not an army officer, or it would have been improper for me so to assault troops.

I paid off my servant Maung Nyunt and told him and his wife that they could go home. They had done very well by me in the short time that they had served me, and I gave Maung Nyunt, in addition to his wages, enough money to buy himself a bullock-cart, which was what he said he wanted. That evening I sorted out my remaining kit, leaving most of it behind to be distributed among the various servants in the house. What I kept went into one suitcase, for it was very probable that we should have to do a fair amount of walking before we reached Calcutta.

Some days previously a police officer had arrived in Ye-u driving an ambulance which he was using and had, I think, brought from the oilfields. As he was proceeding onwards on foot, he left it with me. Webster and I decided to use it when we withdrew from Ye-u. Some of our friends later suggested that we should not have taken an ambulance, which might have been used for transport of the wounded. But this was a civilian vehicle of pre-war type, with only two-wheel drive, and the road to the Chindwin was reported to be impassable by any vehicles without four-wheel drive. We were told that we had not a hope of getting through in the ambulance; we should probably get about half-way and should then have to walk; and indeed that was what we expected when we set out.

On the morning of the 1st May we left Ye-u, Webster and I in the ambulance, and Richards behind us in his own car; and so we ourselves became refugees. On the previous day, it is now known, the decision was taken that the British forces should begin their withdrawal to India, and that night the Ava bridge was blown. The movement of the Army began, as did ours, on the 1st May. The first twenty miles of the road were good. Then we got into dry, dusty forest, and in the next seventy miles passed, I think, through only one village. This was Pyingaing, which the British troops christened 'Pink Gin'. The track itself, though rough, was not very bad. The worst parts were the river crossings. There was little or no water in these rivers, but on either side were large areas of loose sand, and our wheels would simply revolve without moving the car. We had been warned of this, and had taken the precaution of carrying with us a spade and several pieces of timber to put under the wheels and give them something to grip. Richards soon had to abandon his car and came into our ambulance. At times we thought we were stuck for good, but Webster, who did all the driving, managed to get the vehicle out, all of us doing a fair amount of digging and pushing. We spent the night on the roadside, dossing down under some trees. We had brought with us the remains of our small store of liquid refreshment, and our uninteresting dinner was made more palatable that night by a few glasses of sherry and a bottle of French wine. The following morning we reached the Chindwin at Shwegyin.

The next stage, as I have already explained, was to go upstream for some six miles to Kalewa on the opposite bank. At Shwegyin we found considerable crowds of people, with transport both civilian and military, waiting for the ferry to come. (When, a few days later, the main body of the Army reached Shwegyin, it was to prove a dreadful bottleneck, with troops and vehicles offering a sitting target to enemy bombers.) At about midday the ferry arrived from Kalewa. Someone suggested to us that we should drive our ambulance on board, and Webster did so. A few other civilians did the same. When the Army officer who was in charge of the ferry found what had been done, he was most indignant, but he eventually decided that it would be quicker to make the trip to Kalewa with the boat loaded as it was and return, than to waste time in unloading our vehicles and loading Army transport in their place.

We soon reached Kalewa, and I spent much of the afternoon driving round in the ambulance in search of petrol, which I was able to obtain. The next part of the journey was through the Kabaw Valley to Tamu, a little over a hundred miles. We were told that the road was better than the one from Ye-u to the Chindwin, but that rain might well make it impassable; it had, we were told, rained a little a few days ago, but had recently been dry. Richards decided to leave us at Kalewa and to offer his help to the Deputy Commissioner there. Webster and I drove a mile or two out of the town and slept again on the roadside.

The following day we drove through the Kabaw Valley to Tamu, the journey taking the whole day. Apart from a few muddy passages, the road presented no difficulty. We passed crowds of Indians making their way on foot to Tamu; some 200,000 in all are said to have reached India by this route. In one place we overtook a European woman walking and picked her up; I think that she belonged to a mission. The Kabaw Valley acquired during the Burma campaign the name of the 'Valley of Death', not on account of the number of refugees who died there – for comparatively few died on this route – but because of the peculiar virulence of the malaria which could be contracted there. We reached Tamu after dark, and the first person whom we met was an officer of the Indian Medical Service who was in charge of medical arrangements. He drew our attention somewhat brusquely to the fact that we were travelling in a motor ambulance and requested us to hand it over to him. This we did as soon as we had reached the refugee camp.

The camp was administered by an officer of the Burma Forest Service, from whom Webster obtained passes for us to proceed onwards into India. There were some European officers of the Indian Police also on duty at the camp, one of whom was good enough to explain to us that, when we crossed the frontier into India, we should be regarded as refugees, not as government officials. We understood that from Tamu onwards we should have to walk for a few miles, as the road was not yet ready for motor transport.

On the next day a report went round the camp to the effect that no more European civilians would be allowed to leave for India; military personnel could, however, continue to go forward. The reason for this order was not at once apparent, and the officer in charge of the camp made no attempt to call the civilians together and explain exactly what was wanted of them. Eventually the story leaked through that the drivers of military transport which was being sent from India to help the retreating troops were so scared by the stories brought by refugees that some of them were purposely ditching their vehicles on the Tamu-Kalewa road or hiding them in the jungle; it was therefore proposed to send a European civilian beside the driver of each vehicle to ensure that he kept it on the road. I think that, had the position been properly put to us, many of us would willingly have volunteered, though we found it difficult to understand why only civilians should be required. We stayed in the camp for three whole days awaiting developments, and watching military officers marching out to India. As nothing happened, and as we were already in possession of passes to leave for India, Webster and I finally decided to wait no longer. I learned later that the proposal to attach civilians to Army drivers was dropped; military personnel were sent instead.

The enforced wait in Tamu was not without its compensations, so far as we personally were concerned, for the road into India was opened to motor traffic for the first time on the day that we left (7th May), and we passed through on an Army truck in the first military convoy to use the road. It was a winding and hilly road, and we passed gangs of Nagas, wearing nothing but loin-cloths, in some cases barely adequate for their purpose, who were engaged on road work. These primitive hill people gave sterling assistance to the British forces throughout the war. That day we travelled only about forty miles along the rough unmetalled road, and spent the night in a refugee camp at Palel in Manipur State, where refugees of all races slept on the ground. A good road ran from Palel to Imphal, the capital of Manipur, which we reached the next morning. Here too we were accommodated in a camp, but we had bamboo huts in which to sleep. I strolled out into the bazaar, where I found the peaceful atmosphere and the profusion of fruit and vegetables to which I had been accustomed in Burma before the invasion, but which now seemed so strange. In Imphal I met an old acquaintance from the Sahmaw Sugar Company, now on military service; he invited Webster and me to drinks in his mess, and arranged for a truck to take us the next day to Dimapur on the railway line, whence we should go direct to Calcutta.

We duly proceeded down to Dimapur, passing through Kohima, which achieved such fame two years later for its heroic defence against the Japanese. That evening we boarded the train for Calcutta, and on the following day, as we were crossing the Brahmaputra in the ferry, we met Sir Raibeart MacDougall (as he now was). He had gone with the Governor to Myitkyina in the last week of April and when the Governor, on instructions from London, left Myitkyina and flew to India on the 4th May, MacDougall had gone with him. He had had a few days' holiday in Shillong, the Assam capital and hill station, and was now, like us, on his way to Calcutta. He told us that we should report to Colonel Ewing of the Burma Commission, who was in charge of the Burma office which had been opened in Writers' Building, the Calcutta Secretariat. We reached Calcutta late that afternoon, and obtained accommodation in the Grand Hotel in Chowringhee, Calcutta's principal street.

CHAPTER NINE

Bewitched in the Naga Hills 1942

IT WAS NOW TIME to sit back and take stock of the situation. In the short space of five months the British had been driven out of one of their largest overseas possessions, and no one could deny that this was a humiliating experience. It was all very well for civilians to blame the Army and the Royal Air Force. They suffered from the lack of adequate preparations for the defence of Burma before Japan's entry into the war. As Slim has emphasised, no one had expected an invasion of Burma, and consequently arrangements for its defence had been regarded as being of comparatively minor importance. Once the invasion began, it was impossible for adequate reinforcements to be rushed in, owing to Britain's preoccupation with fighting nearer home. It was all very well for the Army to blame the Civil Government, to complain that many of the senior civil officials were too old and set in their ways, were lacking in energy and leadership to cope with the situation. They too had been caught unawares; they were handicapped by the disappearance of numbers of their subordinate Burmese staff, and on top of the normal work of administration they had on their hands the enormous problem of dealing with Indian refugees. It was some consolation to learn later that General Alexander had praised the civil organisation for evacuating refugees and had acknowledged that they had in no way hindered the Army in its withdrawal.

Uppermost in the minds of government officers was the feeling that we had let down the Burmese. The main justification for our presence in Burma had been that we maintained law and order and gave the people the protection of Britain. Now law and order had completely broken down, towns and communications had been subjected to heavy bombing, and finally we had run away and left the Burmese to the mercy of the enemy. What would be their attitude to us when we returned, as we hoped to do some day?

The general demeanour of the Army towards the Burmese was most distressing to us. They tended to look on every Burman as a potential enemy. It was true, as I have already mentioned, that units

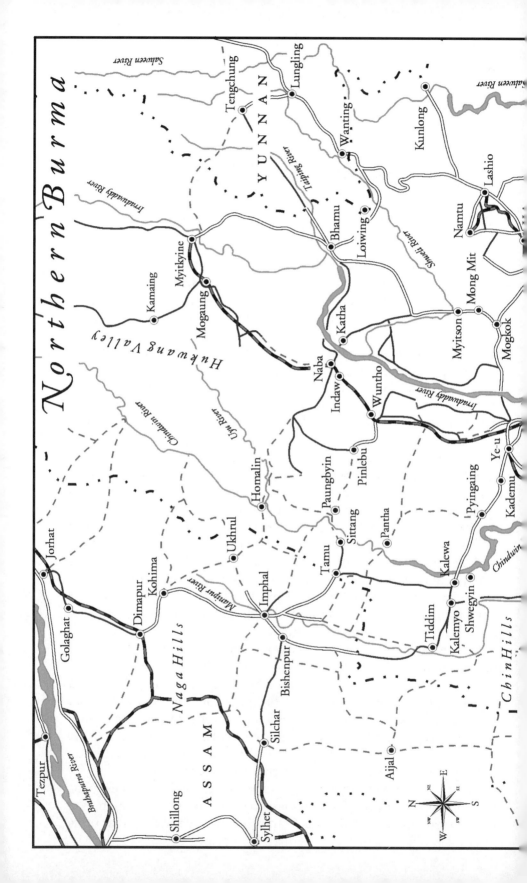

of the Burma Independence Army had been found fighting with the Japanese against our troops. It was true too that, in the general breakdown of law and order which followed the withdrawal of the administration, the criminal elements came to the fore. But, if the mass of the population had been actively hostile to the British, how many of our troops would have come safely out of Burma? It is significant that at no time was there any general rising of the people. On the contrary, innumerable stories are told of the kindness shown, and help given, by the Burmese to the retreating British, both civilian and military. I have said earlier that to the mass of the Burmese the war was a matter between the British and the Japanese and no direct concern of theirs. It has been said – and the estimate is probably not far wrong – that one-tenth of the Burmese were actively hostile to the British, one-tenth were actively pro-British, and the remainder were indifferent. It was a criticism levelled by the Army at the Civil Government that the majority were not pro-British, being the inhabitants of a British territory.

Webster and I reached Calcutta only nine days after leaving our last post in Burma, and had not had to walk at all. We were fortunate that our last postings had been to a station which lay on the only motorable route out of Burma. Those who at the end had been in northern or north-eastern Burma had a long and arduous march over mountain ranges before they reached the safety of India.

The weather was warming up when we arrived in Calcutta. In Burma the rains began about the middle of May, and brought the hot season to an end, but in Calcutta the temperature continued to rise till mid-June, when the first rains fell. Life in the city seemed to be following its normal course: the hotels and restaurants were in full swing, and in one hotel draught beer was still obtainable! There were, it is true, soldiers in uniform about the streets, but there was very little other indication that a victorious enemy was approaching the frontiers of India.

On the morning after our arrival we went to Writers' Building in Dalhousie Square to report to Colonel Ewing. We found a large crowd of Indians, evacuees from Burma, also hoping to see him. Ewing, who, despite his military title, was a civil official of the Burma Government, had been primarily responsible for the organisation of evacuation arrangements in Rangoon, and had left for Calcutta in the ship which took the 'last ditchers'. He had then been attached to the Bengal Government, with the title of 'Special Officer (Burma)', to advise and assist on matters relating to Burma. He was not directly concerned with the reception and accommodation of refugees; that was the responsibility of the Bengal Government. But employees of the Burma Government and of quasi-government bodies in Burma came to his office to apply for pay due to them, to ask for news of their families, and for a thousand and one other reasons. Ewing authorised the payment of their salaries to government employees, after first satisfying himself that the applicants were in fact government servants and that they had not left their posts without permission. As the flood of refugees – most of them Indians – grew, Ewing found it physically impossible to carry on without additional staff. At this time Mrs Donnison, whose husband later became Chief Secretary of Burma, was helping him to deal with the steadily growing pile of mail; apart from her, he had only a stenographer and an office assistant. When we reported to him, we found him in conclave with MacDougall, to whom he had explained his difficulties. MacDougall had evidently told him that Webster and I were now in Calcutta and had authorised him to employ us in his office, for, as soon as he saw us, Ewing informed us with a smile of relief that we were to start working with him the next morning.

And a hard and depressing job it was at first. Office accommodation was totally inadequate. All that the Bengal Government could spare us was one small room, which Ewing occupied, and another not much bigger for his clerical staff. The rest of us worked at a large table in the verandah-corridor outside Ewing's room, generally surrounded by an importunate throng of Indians from Burma. There were no fans there, and the heat of Calcutta and the crowds around us was not conducive to the preservation of an equable temper. But I hope that we dealt with our visitors courteously on the whole, though of necessity we could not waste much time.

My first task was to help Mrs Donnison to sort out the mails and to dispose of what I could myself. The volume of incoming mail was such that it used to take the two of us the whole day to open and classify it. As our office was at that time the only Burma office which had been opened in India, all refugees who had any claims or enquiries whatever would address them to us. Ewing used to be amused at the versions of his name which appeared on the envelopes; he was frequently addressed as 'Colonel Earrings' or 'Colonel Uring'. A good half of our mail was no concern of the government at all, and it had to be forwarded to the appropriate firm or other body as their official addresses in India gradually became known to us. A further difficulty which we encountered was that there was as yet no Burma Government established in India to which we might refer for instructions when required. The senior officials were enjoying a short holiday in India after the hectic last weeks in Burma, and in effect we in our miserable accommodation in Writers' Building represented the Government of Burma in India.

Things gradually improved. Fann, another of our Burma colleagues, joined us, though Mrs Donnison left to join her husband. Ewing was detached from the Bengal Government and became officially the 'Representative of the Government of Burma'. We left Writers' Building and rented our own office accommodation on the east side of Dalhousie Square, where we were able to work in some degree of comfort. The various quasi-government bodies and large Burma firms notified their India addresses in the press, and letters intended for them no longer came to us. Among my duties now was the meeting and accommodation of European government servants who were still coming out of Burma; the Bengal organisation dealt with the Indians. From all who arrived I obtained such information as they could give of other persons still missing whom they had met on their way out, and I compiled a dossier for use in answering enquiries. One of the most distressing things at this time was dealing with enquiries from wives and relations of men who had not yet arrived in India, as the answer was so often that there was no news of them.

I had myself suffered very little ill-effect from my evacuation from Burma. A few days after reaching Calcutta I went down with a bad attack of malaria and urticaria, doubtless contracted in the 'Valley of Death' and brought to the surface by the irregular meals and indifferent food of my last days in Burma; and Fann and I both spent a period in the Presidency General Hospital with dysentery. After a few weeks in the Grand Hotel, Fann, Webster and I had taken a flat; it had only one bedroom which the others shared, while I slept on a divan in the sitting-room.

A job which I took upon myself and particularly enjoyed, though it did not fall strictly within the scope of my duties, was that of dealing with the small group of Burmese refugees. Very few Burmese indeed left their country, and many of those who did were officers' batmen or personal servants who came with their masters. But a small number had found accommodation for themselves in a Burmese Rest House in Eden Hospital Road. Here lived two Burmese monks, who had spent some years in Calcutta, and who gave shelter to the refugees. There were about twenty young men in all. Financial assistance was given to them, as to other refugees, by the Bengal Government, but, as they spoke no language but Burmese, I was asked to interpret, and thereafter arranged with the Bengal officials that I would myself disburse their monthly doles. I kept a register of these young men, and tried to find them employment. I was glad to be among Burmans again and to speak their language, and I visited the Rest House once a week to see what newcomers there were and to discuss possible employment. There was no lack of Europeans from Burma who had always been used to Burmese servants and who looked with mixed feelings on the prospect of having to employ Indians to minister to their wants. None of my protégés in the Rest House had worked before as a personal servant, but quite a few were willing to try their hands, especially when the prospective employer was thought to be likely before long to cross the frontier back into Burma. In one way and another I managed, before I left Calcutta, to get all my Burmans into some sort of employment; though there were of course some failures, the majority made a success of their jobs. I became the good friend of U Tay-zeinda, the head monk, a pleasant and comparatively young man. He would not hesitate to call upon me in the office if the need arose, and he welcomed my visits to him. On one occasion he gave me a formal invitation to a Burmese supper in his Rest House; he sat at the table with me, but would not himself take any food, in compliance with the rule that no monk may eat after midday. He later left the Order and became a garage mechanic!

Meanwhile the exiled Government of Burma had established itself on the heights of Simla, and our work began to decrease. Fann was posted to Madras to open a Burma Government office there, while Webster asked for, and was granted, some leave. I remained as Ewing's only European assistant. I had no idea at this time what my future was to be and Ewing, a very kindly and charming man, was on the lookout for possible jobs for me. I was put in touch with a 'hush hush' organisation, which showed some interest in employing me. What exactly I should have had to do was not explained – it was much too secret! – but I understood that it would have involved my flying to China. I said that I should have to obtain permission from my government before I could accept the job, and I think that, had this been forthcoming, I should probably have been given it, for I had one or two telephone enquiries as to the result of my reference to the government, which in the end refused to release me.

When the Burma Government had had time to settle down and survey the position, it became aware that the Japanese, halted by the monsoon, had not occupied the whole of Burma. In the Chin Hills District, which lay on the frontier with India and to the south of Manipur, the British administration continued to function till the final Japanese offensive in 1944. And in other parts of the hill areas adjoining the Indian border there were pockets which the enemy had not penetrated. In peacetime these areas had enjoyed a very small measure of administration, but now the Government in Simla resolved to send out its young administrative officers to attend to the welfare of the hill peoples. This would not only give them profitable employment, but would enable the exiled government to justify its existence by having something to govern.

Towards the end of August I was warned that I was to be posted to the Arakan Hill Tracts, a remote hill district bordering on Bengal, but later my destination was changed to Shingbwiyang in the Hukawng Valley. I was to go there with Stanley Pollard of the Frontier Service, and we were to administer the Valley and supply its inhabitants with the necessaries of life.

The Hukawng Valley, which in the event I was never to see, lay to the north-west of my old charge of Mogaung. For years it had received no more than an annual visit during the cold weather from the Assistant Superintendent at Kamaing, within whose jurisdiction it lay. Shortly before the Japanese invasion, however, it had become a separate charge under its own Assistant Superintendent. It had a reputation for being swampy and very malarial during the rains. It had been one of the escape routes into India for refugees, and those who were unable to get through before the monsoon broke had a terrible time. They had to plough their way through deep mud, attacked by mosquitoes, sandflies and leeches, and many died on the way. But these were not the worst of their hardships. Groups of Indian military stragglers or deserters made their way out through the Hukawng, robbing, looting and murdering, and the troops of the Chinese 5th Army, who also went this way, behaved no better. A young officer of the Frontier Service, Neil North, who was passing through on his way to India, decided to stay at Shingbwiyang in the worst part of the Valley, to organise a camp for refugees. He remained there throughout the monsoon until every living refugee had been passed through; he did a very fine job, for which he was awarded the MBE. At this time he was still in the Valley, his camp being supplied with provisions dropped by air.

Pollard and I spent some days in Calcutta equipping ourselves. The Burma Government had now established there a Directorate of Supply under Mr Justice Sharpe of the Rangoon High Court, and this provided us with everything that was thought necessary in the way of foodstuffs and medical supplies. An Indian doctor, Menon, was to accompany us; the doctor first detailed for the job had unaccountably fallen ill when he learned our destination.

Our first objective was Margherita, a small station lying towards the Assam-Burma border and almost at the extreme end of the Indian railway system. The supplies which we were taking filled two goods trucks, the bulkiest single item being several dozen drums of chlorate of lime, to be used for disposing of the numerous unburied corpses with which the Valley was understood to be littered. The journey from Calcutta to Margherita by the direct route normally took two days, but passengers and goods had to be transhipped at the Brahma-putra ferry crossing. We wanted to avoid this transhipment, and had therefore to take a circuitous route which would enable us to cross the river by a bridge at another place and would not involve the unloading of our two trucks. Even so, we had to unload them once, in the middle of the first night after we left Calcutta (19th September), when we changed from broad gauge to metre gauge track. But this transhipment was merely from one train direct to another. Our journey to Margherita was a very tedious one: not only was our route devious, but we were not permitted to attach our trucks to any mail train. On most nights we dossed down on the floor of a railway station waiting-room alongside numbers of In-dians, and it was over a week before we reached our destination.

We had been instructed to break our journey at Jorhat, to report at the headquarters of 4th Indian Corps, which was now directly responsible for operations on the Burma front. Here we had an interview with the Intelligence Officer, my sole recollection of which is that he impressed upon us that, if we were captured by the Japanese, we should make every endeavour to pass the word to his headquarters before we were caught! It must have been very con-venient for the Army to have civilians going into the forward areas to do some of their work for them.

Towards the end of September we reached Margherita, which had until that time been a quiet little place with a few tea planters and a fine view of the distant snow-clad Himalayas. We had been told that the Political Officer would make arrangements for our onward journey, which would be on foot over jungle-covered mountains with native porters. The Political Officer was a young policeman, a little older than ourselves, called 'Johnny' Walker, very capable and extremely popular. He had arranged to accommodate us in his own house, and he warned us that it would be some days before he would be able to collect sufficient porters to take us on our way. Meanwhile we had our trucks unloaded and the contents placed in a store near the railway station.

Soon after our arrival, North reached Margherita from the Hu-kawng Valley with a young soldier named Katz who had stayed with him and assisted him. I had not met North before, and he struck me at the time as a rather dour young man – he was slightly junior to us both – who was firmly convinced that Pollard and I would make a mess of administering the Valley. Later, when I came to know him better, I had reason to revise my opinion of him, and can only suppose that his state of mind at our first meeting was conditioned by the experience which he had just undergone, marooned throughout the rains in Shingbwiyang with the heavy responsibility of keeping a miscellaneous crowd of refugees quiet and contented in the most uncomfortable circumstances.

We also met some of the Europeans of the Indian Tea Association, who had done such fine work in assisting refugees over the Indian frontier. They had gone to meet them through the almost trackless maze of forest and mountain, had organised camps for them, and had done all that was in their power to give them a hospitable reception on their arrival in India.

It was the best part of a fortnight before Walker was able to get us our porters, wiry little men belonging to the hill tribe of the Abors, who carried heavy loads on their backs in long baskets held in place by straps over the forehead and shoulders. He could not, however, find sufficient men to carry all our stores, for there were many demands for porters, chiefly from Army units. All our chlorate of lime, and much of our provisions, were left behind, and it was hoped that, after we had reached our destination, arrangements would be made for them to be dropped by air.

At last, in the middle of October, we set out. Besides Pollard, Menon, myself and our porters, the party consisted of a Kachin interpreter – who could speak Burmese, Hindustani and the languages of the hill peoples through whose country we should be passing – and our servants. I had two servants: Maung Tin, a Burmese refugee who had been working with me for about two months in Calcutta, and Moti, a little Bengali cook whom I had engaged only a few hours before I left Calcutta, another Bengali cook, whom I had taken on a few days previously, having disappeared after taking an advance from me to buy food for his family. Pollard had arrived in Margherita without servants, and had taken over from North a young Kachin, a rather timid little fellow, who somewhat irritated Pollard by his inability to understand his (Pollard's) Burmese. Pollard engaged a cook in Margherita who could speak Burmese of a sort but, when the time came for us to start, he was nowhere to be found. We also had an escort consisting of a platoon of Gurkhas belonging to the Assam Rifles, under the command of a little corporal.

We began with a short train journey to the end of a siding, where we said goodbye to Walker and set out to cross the mountain range. After about half an hour we were overtaken by Pollard's missing cook, who said that he was unable to come with us after all, but that he had brought a friend to take his place. Pollard was quite satisfied with this arrangement till he discovered, when we halted for the night, that the substitute knew nothing about cooking! He was, however, a willing worker, who carried out the less pleasant chores cheerfully.

Our journey over the mountains to the Hukawng Valley was, I think, to take us about ten days. The route had been surveyed by an officer of the Assam Government, and mat and thatch huts had been built at the night stops. These were in the vicinity of Naga villages, from which we were to get porters to carry us from stage to stage. We were told that American hard rations had been dropped at various points on the route and that the headmen of the nearest villages had taken charge of them.

The track was not an easy one, and we could cover only a short distance each day. The morning began with a long climb up a mountainside, during which we had frequently to haul ourselves up by grasping trees and bushes. Then came a descent, and at the bottom we generally found our camp at about 4 p.m. I do not suppose that we covered more than six to eight miles in a day. On arrival at our camp we had a welcome bathe in the cold water of a nearby stream, and then sought out the local headman, to ask for rations, if he had any, and to arrange for porters for the following morning. The villages were often so small that sufficient men could not be raised by the time that we wanted to start, and we had to kick our heels while more were fetched from elsewhere. The rations available were mainly American tinned foods of the stew variety and after a few days I came to loathe the sight of them; I am no lover of bully beef, but I would rather eat bully beef any day than meat-and-vegetable hash. It was virtually impossible to get any fresh food from the few villages through which we passed; even an egg was hardly to be had. I do, however, remember being treated to a very refreshing drink of rice beer (*zu*) in a village perched on the top of a hill, which we had reached sweating and panting with thirst.

On our first day out from Margherita we met a body of Chinese troops on their way from Shingbwiyang. We stopped, gave them cigarettes and sat down with them for a while, all smiling at each other and exchanging the only word which we had in common: '*Shingbwiyang*.'

On the third or fourth day we were walking along a forested path, when we saw in the distance one of the local civilians coming towards us. He disappeared behind a tree and then came out to greet us. Our little Gurkha corporal was suspicious, went behind the tree and found a shotgun lying against it. He asked the man if he had a licence to carry a firearm, to which he replied that he had none, but that he had merely borrowed it from a Chinese captain to do some shooting. I had no authority in this area, for we were still in India, but the corporal obviously expected me to do something, so I told the man that we should take his gun and hand it over to the police. There was a small police post at Tagap Ga, where we were to spend the night, and the Chinese officer was said to be there too. When we arrived at our camp, which lay near the police post on the banks of a stream of clear water crossed by a long bamboo suspension bridge, our civilian presumably went and told the Chinese captain what had happened to his gun. I do not know what a lone Chinese army officer was doing in this spot; perhaps simply having a shooting holiday! Anyhow, he came up to me and started to expostulate. I could not understand a word that he said, but managed to convey to him that I intended to hand over the gun to the officer in charge of the police post and leave it to him to do what he thought fit with it. My refusal to return the gun to the Chinese officer was alleged to have been the cause of my subsequent bewitchment.

On the following day – or it may have been two days later – we crossed the border into Burma. There was of course nothing on the ground to show that we had reached the frontier, but it appeared from our somewhat inadequate maps that we had done so. The next morning I awoke early with the most violent headache and itching all over with urticaria, and was promptly sick. I did another day's march but, as I was bringing up whatever I ate, Pollard decided that we had better rest for a day. This we did, but I still felt ill and weak. I suggested that he should go on and that I should follow the next day, hoping that two days on my bed would have done something to cure me. Pollard left Dr Menon behind with me.

I had fortunately managed to acquire a tin of glucose; whether I had brought it with me or had found it in one of the ration dumps I do not remember, but it proved my salvation, for I now lived almost entirely on glucose and water. I struggled on to the next camp, which I remember was at a place called Rukun; I doubt if it appears on any map. I cannot recall whether Pollard was waiting for me there or whether he had gone ahead, but there I met one Darlington, who in peace-time had been a missionary in the Hukawng, was now in the employ of the Burma Government and was also on his way into the Valley. I sat at Rukun for about two days, and then Darlington told me fairly bluntly that there was no point in my trying to go any further; I was clearly ill, and would only prove a hindrance to the others, and had therefore much better go back to Margherita.

So the next day I started on the return journey with my servants, Dr Menon, the Gurkha corporal and some of his men. The journey was one which I hope never to repeat. For most of the way I was being pulled by one of my servants and pushed by the other, and about every fifty yards I had to sit down and be fed with glucose and water. I was virtually carried into the camp and went straight to bed on the hard bamboo shelves which were provided for our rest. I spent the next day there, and poor Dr Menon did not know what to do with me. But in the evening a number of porters, who had been taking supplies into the Valley, arrived at the camp empty-handed on their way back to Margherita, and were persuaded to carry me with them.

The next morning I sent Menon to Pollard, and we set out for Margherita. First I was carried piggyback, but had not the strength to hang on. Various other methods of transporting me were tried, and eventually the most satisfactory was found to be to lay me in a groundsheet, which was slung from a bamboo pole carried on the shoulders of two men.

There is then a complete blank of a few days in my memory. I have a vague recollection of being at one time in a Naga house, and I was later told that we had in fact spent a night in one. I began to regain consciousness after we had left Tagap Ga – the scene of my encounter with the Chinese captain – and, when I was completely myself again, we were two marches from Margherita. I now felt clear in the head and much better, save for an acute pain on one side of my buttocks, which proved to be a large sore.

As we drew near to Margherita I began to feel that I could readily sit down to a meal. I was taken to the Political Officer's bungalow. Walker was away on tour in the hills, but he now had an assistant, a young Indian civilian named Murray. I must have looked like a down-and-out tramp: my bones were showing prominently, for I had been the best part of a fortnight without solid food, and I had nearly a fortnight's growth of beard. Murray was extremely kind. He called in an Army doctor who examined and treated me, and gave it as his opinion that I had had gastric malaria. I began at once to eat and soon felt well again, but Murray would not hear of my going to Calcutta till I had stayed with him a fortnight. I do not remember what I did in Margherita during that time, but I imagine that I spent much of it resting. Margherita seemed much busier than

A Burmese servant

it had been the previous month, with numbers of American troops about. They were working at Ledo – close to Margherita – on the building of the Ledo road into northern Burma, which was one of the main routes by which the Allied forces re-entered Burma.

Maung Tin, my Burmese servant, assured me that my illness was the result of my having been bewitched. He said that the Chinese captain, when I refused to return his shotgun, had said that he would cast a spell on me, and it was shortly after leaving Tagap Ga that I had fallen ill. Maung Tin also told me that, on the return journey, when he and the Gurkha corporal thought that I was not going to live, they had called in a Naga sorceress to treat me. I understand that her treatment consisted in pricking the soles of my feet with a needle, and doubtless in muttering some incantations as well. From that time, according to Maung Tin – and no doubt also after having repassed Tagap Ga – I began to mend. I had with me a bag of silver rupees for payment to the people of the Hukawng Valley, who preferred coins to currency notes. From this bag Maung Tin had taken two rupees and paid them to the sorceress as her fee. When finally I rendered my accounts to the Accountant-General in Simla, I entered this payment 'to Naga sorceress', pointing out that, under my terms of service, I was entitled to the best medical attention available, and that there was no other available at the time. No audit query or objection was ever raised!

To conclude this story, Pollard never reached Shingbwiyang: the Japanese got there before him. He established himself at a camp on the edge of the Hukawng Valley, where he was able to do little but send back wireless messages about his ration requirements. Eventually the Government of Burma recalled him to India.

I reached Calcutta at the beginning of December 1942. Before leaving Margherita I had applied for three months' leave; I had not decided how to spend it, but the first thing I must do was to see a doctor. I called on Ewing, who was much perturbed by my appearance, and who confirmed that my leave had been approved. I met an old Burma acquaintance in Calcutta, who had a flat in Chowringhee, which he invited me to share.

I spent the whole of December and the beginning of January in Calcutta. The appearance of the city had changed considerably. It was now full of troops – British, American and Chinese – and numbers of new Chinese restaurants had opened. The doctor found that I was suffering from malaria and two types of dysentery and for some weeks I had to take drugs. Japanese air raids on Calcutta now began, particularly in the dock area. Calcutta had much the same problem as Rangoon: the port labour, though Indian, was not Bengali, and the raids were followed by the familiar spectacle of crowds of people making their way north on foot or in carts. Around Christmas time the raids were at their height; though an occasional bomb fell in the city area, no great damage was done there.

In January I decided to go to Simla for a fortnight's holiday, mainly because some of my friends were working there at the headquarters of the Burma Government. In addition to its responsibilities for administering the frontier fringe, the government had established a Reconstruction Department, which was making plans for the restoration of Burma's economy after the war. Not only had the country suffered tremendous material damage through the destruction of its towns, its railway lines and its shipping, but intelligence reports showed that many of the people were short of food and clothing, suffering from disease, and unable to grow enough rice through lack of plough cattle, taken by the Japanese. It was at this time assumed that there must be a considerable period after the eviction of the Japanese during which the Governor would rule Burma directly without a Council of Ministers while the damage done by the war was repaired. When this task was completed, Burma would have the self-government which her political leaders had already demanded. The Reconstruction Department was not only planning to repair the material damage caused by the war; it was also reviewing the whole field of government administration, and all senior officers now in India were asked for their views and for their suggestions for improving the administration on our return to Burma. Unfortunately most of these reconstruction plans cost money, and the Governor was unable to get any firm promise of assistance from the British Treasury. Nor could he persuade the War Cabinet to agree to fix a date for the grant of self-government to Burma. At this time he himself thought that the period of reconstruction would last for five to seven years, but he felt with good reason that it was of the utmost importance politically that he should be able to make a firm pronouncement when he returned to Burma of the date when power would be transferred to the Burmese.

It was bitterly cold in Simla and there was snow on the ground. My servant Maung Tin had never seen snow before and was not at all happy in the cold, though I had bought him warm clothes. There was a certain attraction about Simla, but I found the constant walking up and down hills rather tiring. No cars were allowed in the main part of the town: one either walked or travelled in one's private rickshaw. The monkeys were a pest: they seemed to be everywhere, and would even come in through the hotel windows and steal anything which might be lying about. I was told that they were regarded as sacred by the local populace. I spent part of my time writing out a topographical description for the Army of that part of Bassein District which I knew; for the rest I had a complete holiday, reading or strolling in the town in the daytime and visiting my friends' houses in the evening. Since this subsequently proved to be the only opportunity I had for visiting this part of India, I have since wished that I had seen more than Simla. It is true that on my way there I had spent the inside of a day in Delhi, where I had seen the Red Fort and Humayun's tomb, and had driven to New Delhi, the imposing capital of the Indian Empire. I had also considered the possibility of stopping on my return journey at Agra to see the Taj Mahal; but this would have involved an arrival and a departure in the small hours of the morning, and I decided against it. I expected that I should have another opportunity.

CHAPTER TEN

In the Valley of Death
1943-44

I RETURNED TO Calcutta towards the end of January feeling very much better and was posted back to Ewing's office, where the work was now rather different. The emphasis was no longer on the troubles of those who had fled from Burma, but on sending supplies to the inhabitants of those parts of the country which we were still administering. Our only refugee problem was the Arakanese camp at Dinajpur in northern Bengal. North Arakan had been peopled by a mixture of Arakanese Buddhists and Muslims of Chittagonian origin. After the collapse of the administration in 1942, communal strife had broken out, with the result that the two communities had become segregated, the Chittagonians concentrating in the north and the Arakanese in the south. Between the two was a sort of no man's land. The area occupied by the Chittagonians now became so Indian that the Burmese and Arakanese languages were no longer understood; and all Buddhist pagodas and monasteries were destroyed. During the troubles large numbers of Arakanese Buddhists had fled into Bengal, and a camp had been established for them in Dinajpur. Our government had sent there as camp commandant a senior officer who was himself Arakanese, and it seemed that he did not always work in harmony with the Deputy Commissioner, who was an Indian. Moreover, the statistics of death and disease in the camp perturbed us. We had of course to deal very tactfully with the Bengal Government over these matters, and they gave us a considerable amount of anxiety.

In the matter of supplies for the people of the frontier areas we worked in very close conjunction with the Burma Government's Directorate of Supply, which was responsible for physically moving them. The main areas of Burma now administered by us were the Chin Hills, the northern part of the Kabaw Valley and the Arakan Hill Tracts, and in almost all cases new supply routes had to be opened up, for in peacetime there had been virtually no trade across these frontiers of India and Burma.

Off and on I spent the best part of a year in Calcutta, some four

169

months in 1942 and six in 1943. The friend whose flat I was sharing soon moved to an Army job in Delhi and I retained the flat. Calcutta seemed to grow more and more crowded. There was a large leave centre for British troops across the road from my flat, and the pavements of Chowringhee were thronged with troops, Indian, British and American.

Calcutta was a busy, but not a beautiful, city. The main streets were full of Bengalis in white shirts and *dhotis*, looking pretty prosperous. But as soon as you turned off these main streets, you were in dirty lanes of squalid shops and houses. Even the principal thoroughfares were beset by groups of beggars who stationed themselves on the pavements and exhibited their sores and deformities in the hope of exciting charitable feelings in the breasts of passers-by. Most of these were professional beggars, and it was said that the profession could be very lucrative. I have seen a small boy being instructed by an older beggar, no doubt his father, to cross his legs so as to make it appear that he was deformed. It was not until fairly late in the war that the authorities decided to clear these persons off the streets and to put them into some kind of home; they naturally met with opposition from those whose means of livelihood was thus abruptly terminated.

Another hazard of the Calcutta pavements was the bulls; one would not infrequently find one of these reclining on the wide Chowringhee pavement, sublimely unconscious of passing pedestrians. A disgusting spectacle was the refuse bins placed at many of the street corners. When these were full, scavengers would come and search through the rubbish for anything which might be of use. When they had finished, they invariably left the greater part of the contents on the pavement, and the stench of decaying vegetable matter heated by the tropical sun was frequently so foul as to force the pedestrian to cross the road in order to place as wide a berth as possible between himself and the garbage.

It was pleasant to walk in the late afternoon on the *maidan*, a long park running for about two miles between Chowringhee and the Hooghly River, and ending at the dome-capped Victoria Memorial, dazzling white in the sunshine. But war-time needs gradually encroached on the *maidan*; the Royal Air Force used its wide roads as runways, and little by little areas were fenced off and used for military purposes.

I have described how the frontier fringe of Burma, which was not occupied by the Japanese, was now being administered by civilian officials of the Burma Government; a Burma officer had been posted to Assam as Commissioner of the 'Frontier Division'. All these officers were responsible to the Government of Burma in Simla, though they naturally worked very closely with the military formations in their areas. The government had made proposals to the British Government which envisaged a continuance of the civil administration on pre-war lines; the control of civil policy would be in the hands of the government, but the civil administrative officers would work under the direction of the military authorities. As a result, however, of discussions between the War Office and the Burma Office, it was decided that the occupied parts of Burma should be governed by a military administration until such time as conditions permitted the return of the civil government. To give effect to this decision, the government seconded to the staff of the Commander-in-Chief (India) a senior officer, C.F.B. Pearce (later Sir Frederick Pearce), and other officers to work under him. They became members of a new service (or branch of the staff) known as the Civil Affairs Service (Burma), or CAS(B). There was considerable disagreement at high level on the question, which was not finally settled till months later, whether or not these officers should be commissioned. Meanwhile, however, they were given military designations – Pearce became a Major-General – and wore uniforms with the appropriate badges of rank. Pearce as Chief Civil Affairs Officer (CCAO) was directly responsible to the Commander-in-Chief. His duties were defined as follows:

> The CCAO is responsible for advising the C-in-C on all matters concerning the regulation of the civil population and the control and development of the economic life of re-occupied territories, having regard to the primary aim of facilitating military operations. The CCAO will advise the GOC-in-C on the co-ordination of immediate military needs with long term civil policy and plans.

In order that Pearce might keep the Burma Government informed of matters which might affect long term civil planning, he was appointed a Joint Secretary to the Government.

Officers of the Civil Affairs Service were to be attached, where possible, to military formations down to divisions. The main functions of these 'formation CAOs' were to enlist the co-operation and support of the local inhabitants, to ensure that they did not interfere with military operations, to arrange for the provision of civilian labour and supplies, and to assist as required in obtaining intelligence; the CAOs were also responsible for some measure of civil administration in the areas occupied by their formations. As the troops advanced into Burma, it would be necessary to take steps for the administration of the rearward areas, and this would be the function again of officers of the Civil Affairs Service. These 'territorial CAOs' would in fact perform the functions of a civil government, though the form of government and the basis of its authority would be military.

Officers of the Civil Affairs Service attached to the higher formations such as Army and Corps headquarters were called Deputy Chief Civil Affairs Officers (DCCAOs), and in the territorial phase they would become the equivalent of the peace-time Commissioners. Below them were Senior Civil Affairs Officers (SCAOs), the equivalent of Deputy Commissioners, and the humbler CAOs. At first the Civil Affairs Service had only administrative and police branches, staffed largely by officers of the Burma Civil Service and the Burma Police. Later came branches dealing with relief and labour, supply and industry, forests, prisons and the whole gamut of peace-time departments, all under high-ranking officers. The rapid burgeoning of Brigadiers and full Colonels was satirised in a scurrilous song composed in the frontier areas, set to the tune of 'The British Grenadiers', the refrain of which was:

> But of all this war's great heroes
> There's no one who compares
> With Major-General Freddy Pearce
> And all his Brigadiers.

The Civil Affairs Service (Burma) was formally created on the 15th February 1943. The intention was that a proclamation should be made in which a military administration would be formally established, but it was thought that the time was not yet ripe, partly because the area of Burma administered by the British was so small, and partly because it was thought politically undesirable that the Commander-in-Chief, India, should assume powers of government over Burma. The administration of the frontier fringe remained therefore for the present under the *de jure* control of the Governor of Burma, though *de facto* it was under the control of the Commander-in-Chief, India.

In April Ewing and I became members of the Civil Affairs Service, attached to Eastern Army headquarters, he as a DCCAO with the rank of Brigadier, and I as a CAO with the rank of Lieutenant. The headquarters of Eastern Army were at this time at Barrackpore, some fifteen miles out of Calcutta, in Government House, the country residence of former Viceroys. We did not, however, have to move out there: we remained in our Dalhousie Square offices, and Ewing used to go regularly to Barrackpore for discussions. Our work in the office proceeded on much the same lines as before, save that I now had a certain amount of routine work to do in procuring Army identity cards for our new officers, and in issuing a civilian form of pass to the subordinates (clerks and others) who were going to the frontier areas as civilians in military employ. An offensive had been mounted by our troops in Arakan at the end of 1942, with the limited objective of taking Akyab. This was unsuccessful, and during May 1943 members of the Civil Affairs staff who had been in Arakan arrived in Calcutta. Among them was George Merrells, now a Captain, who came and stayed with us for about three weeks before going off on holiday.

About the end of June I was warned that I was to be posted to the Upper Chindwin District; the only part of this which we were administering was the northern Kabaw Valley (the so-called 'Valley of Death') running alongside the Manipur border. I began again to make my preparations for departure. My servant Maung Tin had left me to take a job as a driver at Ramgarh, where some 30,000 Chinese troops were being trained by the Americans in readiness for the opening of the road to China through northern Burma; the Americans paid high salaries to their civilian employees. Since then I had had a succession of servants, all more or less Burmese, except for Moti, my little Bengali cook who stayed with me all the time. I decided not to take him to the Kabaw Valley, as I knew that there were several other CAOs there and that they were eating in a mess. My personal servant at this time was a young Indian, with probably a little Burmese blood, who had come from Burma and spoke Burmese. He was named Mohammed, but he called himself Maung Maung in Burmese.

I left Calcutta on the 15th July by train for Dimapur, together with another CAO from the Kabaw Valley, who had been on a few weeks' leave in India. The train was so full that even our suitcases had to be put in the luggage van. We left Calcutta in the middle of a very hot day, wearing shorts and with our shirt sleeves rolled up. When evening came, being unable to gain access to our luggage, we remained as we were. The Army treated malaria with great respect and had laid down very strict rules about malaria precautions: at sunset all ranks were to be in long trousers and long-sleeved shirts. In Calcutta I had not bothered myself much about Army rules and regulations, for I was to all intents and purposes doing a civilian job, though wearing a uniform. We both duly walked into the restaurant car for dinner. It was crowded, mainly with Army officers, some of whom were dressed as we were; there was also a fair sprinkling of civilian passengers. I had noticed at lunch-time a senior Army officer at the far end of the car, with a red band round his cap, and had assumed that he was some kind of General or Brigadier. I found him in the same position at dinner and, when everyone had taken his seat, he arose and said: 'Gentlemen, will all those of you who are wearing shorts or short-sleeved shirts kindly give your names to my ADC.' It appeared that this was General Sir George Gifford, who had recently taken over command of Eastern Army. The result was that some weeks later I received a letter from the DCCAO with 4th Corps, drawing my attention to my breach of Army rules and asking me to certify that I was aware of the regulations relating to malaria precautions. I am afraid that this provoked me into a correspondence as to what exactly were the regulations and how certain expressions were to be interpreted, and in the end the whole thing fizzled out without my giving any certificate.

In due course we reached Imphal, where 4th Corps had its headquarters. My companion pushed straight ahead for the Civil Affairs camp. I stayed to report to the DCCAO, and then joined John McTurk, who had left Calcutta a few days after me and was also bound for the Kabaw Valley. As we moved eastwards towards Burma, we found the Army withdrawing westwards to Imphal. The rains were now in full spate and, the campaigning season being over, the troops were falling back to less uncomfortable and less malarial stations. A few units were left behind in the forward areas, but they were relieved at regular intervals. The road was the same by which I had left Burma in the previous year, but very considerably improved, though there was still much work to be done.

The Civil Affairs organisation had at this time two camps in the area, neither of which was actually in Burma. The main camp was at Moreh in the Kabaw Valley, some two miles inside the Manipur border and about three miles from Tamu. The subsidiary camp was at Sibong, which lay up on the hills about six miles away; it was a much healthier place, and was being used as a sort of rest-camp to which our staff could retire during the rains after a spell of duty in Moreh. We had been ordered to report to Sibong, where we found Thomas, the Deputy Commissioner, just off on leave in India. He had been in the area before the Civil Affairs Service came into being, still regarded himself as a civilian and dressed as such; for the same reason he retained the old civil designation of Deputy Commissioner instead of its Civil Affairs equivalent of SCAO. His place was taken by his second-in-command Keely, whom also we met at Sibong; he had come to see Thomas off and returned at once to Moreh.

At our Sibong camp we had only a clerk and a platoon of Kumaonis from the Burma Regiment company stationed at Moreh, and there was no administrative work for us to do, as we were so far from the Burma frontier. We made work for ourselves by putting into order and cataloguing all the stores in the canteen. No attempt had been made to do anything about this, and they were accountable stores, having been sent by the Burma Supply Organisation. While we were at Sibong, Toby Fforde, the Civil Affairs police officer from Moreh, passed through on his way to India for a short spell of leave. His job, he told us, was mainly the collection of intelligence. We learned that there were in the camp at Moreh about a dozen Burmans, who were known as 'armed peons'; they were mainly employed in the camp, but from time to time were sent out to the villages, to collect what information they could. In addition to these we had groups of men in the more distant villages, principally on the banks of the Chindwin, called 'kin scouts' (*kin* is a Burmese word meaning a guard or sentry-post), who were also responsible for the collection and transmission to us of any news of enemy movements.

The dispositions of the Civil Affairs staff during the rains had not yet been finally settled. Thomas had told us that he thought they should all withdraw to Sibong, and take it in turns to go into Imphal for a break. But one of the main purposes of our remaining so far forward during the rains, when practically all the troops had gone back, was to show the people of the Kabaw Valley that the British administration was still with them and still cared for their welfare. Keely decided – rightly, I think – that we could not achieve this if we sat on the top of the hills in Sibong, which was some eight miles from the Burma frontier and could be reached only by a steep and muddy road. He arranged therefore that we should maintain our forward camp at Moreh, and go back periodically for rest and recuperation to Sibong.

After repeated requests for a jeep to be sent to convey us and our kit to Moreh, Keely at last sent it when we had been the best part of three weeks kicking our heels at Sibong. Moreh was quite a busy camp. Besides our Civil Affairs staff, there was the main body of our Burma Regiment escort, and the Elephant Corps, whom Thomas had permitted to settle there. This latter consisted of two former European employees of the Bombay Burmah Trading Corporation and a number of Karens and Burmans employed by them. The elephants had been recovered during the last open season from the northern part of the Upper Chindwin District, most of them being the property of the Bombay Burmah, and they were employed mainly on hauling logs to make corduroy roads and bridges. Within a day or two of our arrival in Moreh we went over the border to have a look at Tamu. The villagers had abandoned the old village because of the cholera which had broken out among the refugees who had passed through in 1942, and had built themselves temporary huts a mile or so away. It was a great pleasure to me to be back in Burma, to see real Burmans and to hear the Burmese language spoken again.

This seems a convenient point at which to pause and see what had been happening inside Burma since the British retreat. The arrival of the Japanese had been heralded by the promise that they would give Burma independence within the Greater East Asia Co-Prosperity Sphere, in which of course Japan would be the dominant member. I have told how the thirty young men, members of the extreme nationalist Thakin party, had come into Burma with the Japanese, and had raised a Burma Independence Army. Units of this force had fought with the Japanese against the Allied troops and, though their presence had no effect on the ultimate result of the campaign, they were responsible for creating among our troops considerable fear of fifth column activities. But the brutality displayed by the Burma Independence Army, particularly to the Karens and to loyal servants of the former administration, caused the Japanese to disband it almost at once. In its place they formed the Burma Defence Army, which they placed under the command of the leader of the Burma Independence Army, Thakin Aung San, who was now given the rank of Major-General. At the same time Thakin Tun Oke, another of the Thirty, was put in charge of the administration of Burma. He was, however, soon replaced by Dr Ba Maw, who on the 1st August 1942 became Chief Executive. Dr Ba Maw, it will be recalled, had been the first Premier of Burma, and had been imprisoned for sedition by U Saw's Government. He was not a member of the Thakin party, but his administration contained a number of Thakins. When appointing him, the Japanese commander proclaimed that it was the intention to give the Burmese freedom, provided that they co-operated with Japan. Exactly a year later (1st August 1943) the Japanese declared Burma to be an independent state, and Dr Ba Maw became its Head; its first act was to declare war on Britain and the United States.

It was not until a good deal later that we in the frontier areas obtained a full account of what had been happening in Burma, and of the budding resistance movement we knew next to nothing. But it is now known that the extreme left wing of the Thakin party, whose leaders were Thakins Soe, Than Tun, Tin Shwe and Thein Pe, and whose opinions on the rights and wrongs of the war had changed radically with Russia's entry into it in 1941, had, even before the last British officials and troops had left Burma, started a resistance movement against the Japanese. In July 1942, Thein Pe and Tin Shwe made their way overland to India to ask for British assistance. Once the British were satisfied of their bona fides, they put them in touch with Force 136, a secret service organisation of which I shall have more to say later. Thein Pe published a booklet in India called *What Happened in Burma*, in which he attacked the Japanese for their behaviour, and also criticised the British administration. Tin Shwe was sent back into Burma in the dry season of 1942–43, and on his return to India he brought with him an Arakanese called Nyo Tun, whom I was later to meet. In due course information reached India that some of the leaders of the resistance now held important posts in the nominally independent government. Dr Ba Maw had appointed General Aung San to be Minister for Defence, and Thakins Than Tun, Nu and Mya to hold other ministerial posts; and a few months later news was received in India that Aung San was secretly planning to turn the Burma Defence Army against the Japanese when opportunity offered. I repeat, however, that we – and, I think, most of the Civil Affairs staff – knew nothing of these things; had we been kept informed, or at the very least been given a full account later when secrecy was no longer necessary, our whole attitude to the left-wing organisations in Burma might have changed.

But to return to the Kabaw Valley. The northern part of the Valley, which was the area directly administered by us, consisted only of some sixteen village tracts, and measured about fifty miles from north to south; its breadth, from the Manipur Hills to the Chindwin, was about twenty miles on an average, but in practice our administration barely reached the Chindwin. During the rest of the rains we were virtually confined to Moreh, for we had only one motor vehicle (a jeep), and in any case the roads in the Valley were impassable to motor traffic.

I was given the job of Supply Officer, and my duties were to arrange for the procurement and distribution of their essential needs to the local people, to obtain from them the Army's requirements of materials and labour, and to ensure that our own camp was supplied with rations and the other necessaries of life. At first my work was light. The Army had left behind sufficient hard rations to last till they returned after the rains; local villagers brought in rice and vegetables, and we supplied one Burman with a shotgun and cartridges on condition that he brought in fairly regularly a leg of deer or some other meat. The Army at this time had no demands on us for supplies, for there were no troops in the neighbourhood except a company of Gurkhas stationed in Tamu, which was relieved every month. My supply work was therefore at this period confined to issues to the local villagers. During the rains our Civil Affairs trucks could not come down from Imphal with supplies, but stocks of salt and sugar had been built up before the rains, and from time to time I would make an allocation to the villages and send out notices to the headmen through our armed peons, telling them how much had been allocated and how much cash they must bring. The weighing of the bags took a long time and caused a considerable amount of trouble for, owing to damp or evaporation, some weighed more or less than others, and I used to get complaints from the headmen that, on their return home, they had weighed their pur-chases and found the weight to be less than they had paid for.

Not far from our camp we had a village in which a number of Burmese refugees, who had fled before the Japanese advance in the previous campaigning season, had been settled. The Army had agreed to supply them with rations, which they obtained through us. Other refugees who arrived from time to time were also housed there.

I spent some three weeks in Moreh, dealing with supplies, talking to the villagers from the Kabaw Valley – who were always coming in, partly for advice and, I have no doubt, partly to assure themselves that we were still there – and from time to time accompanying the doctor on his visits to the villages to deal with cases of malaria, yaws, and so forth. Now and then pieces of information about enemy movements would be brought to us, which we would pass on to Army intelligence.

Towards the end of August we heard that there was to be a change in the high command. Hitherto the British forces in Burma had been units of Eastern Army, whose Commander was responsible to the Commander-in-Chief, India. Now a new South-East Asia Command was to be formed, entirely separate from the India Command, with Admiral Lord Louis Mountbatten as Supreme Commander; the American General Stilwell ('Vinegar Joe') was to be his Deputy. We did not know much about Mountbatten, but his appointment was generally welcomed, if only on the score of his age; he was forty-three. The new Command did not come into existence until October. General Giffard became Commander-in-Chief, 11th Army Group, which controlled all the British troops in Burma (but not the Ameri-cans or Chinese), and General Slim was appointed to the command of the new 14th Army, which was directly responsible for British operations on the Burma front.

At the beginning of September I went up to Sibong for a short rest. We had two Indian doctors on our staff who in turn went on leave to India during the rains; as we had small hospitals for the personnel of our Burma Regiment escort at both Moreh and Sibong, one had consequently to be left without a doctor. The junior doctor, Balwant Singh, was a most useful fellow who was willing to turn his hand to any job. He had been working in Tamu before the Japanese invasion and was known and liked by the local people. He was in Moreh when I went up to Sibong, and I arranged with him to look after the Sibong hospital, and to get any advice which I might need from him by telephone. Having nothing else to do, I decided to apply myself seriously to hospital work! I had charts posted at the foot of each bed, and did a regular morning inspection, taking temperatures, giving medicines, massages, etc. The subadar in charge of the platoon used to accompany me on my rounds, and was highly amused at my carrying a Hindustani phrase book, from which I read out such apposite sentences as 'Are you feeling better to-day?' or 'I shall have to give you an aperient.'

From time to time the Army raised objections to our being so far forward during the rains. It seems that we were not supposed to do any more than occasionally send a Civil Affairs Officer with an escort of six men to visit Moreh. One Brigade Commander, when he found that we had a permanent camp there, gave instructions that no one was in future to go to Moreh without permission. I do not remember how we circumvented his orders, but we stayed. Meanwhile Keely made proposals, which were accepted by the Army, that, when the rains were over and the troops had come back, we should move our camp to the old deserted village of Tamu.

Early in October we received information that a small party of Japanese had come to the most southerly village in our area of administration and taken away some of our kin scouts. The following morning before dawn we were awakened by a report that a Burma Regiment picket, which we kept on the bridge across the river between Moreh and Tamu, had seen two figures approaching from the Burma side and had also seen a couple of Very lights. The picket had fired on the men and had then withdrawn. We stood to till dawn and alerted the nearest units. Inspection by daylight showed nothing but buffalo prints, but it was difficult to explain the Very lights. For a couple of nights we officers kept telephone watch, ringing up the Gurkha camp at Sibong at half-hourly intervals, but nothing ever came of the incident. So far as could be discovered, no enemy had been near the place, and we came to the conclusion that the picket commander had heard a bullock or buffalo, had panicked and had imagined the Very lights.

With October and the end of the rains, the road from Imphal again became motorable by heavy vehicles, and we could expect the Army to start moving forward. We had been asked to lay in stocks of bamboos in readiness for the building of camps. It was my job to arrange with headmen for loads of bamboos to be brought to Moreh, to check the amounts and to pay for them. Roofing materials were not generally required, for the Army had plenty of tarpaulins. In advance of the main bodies of troops came various officers who had been working on their own in intelligence jobs and had withdrawn to India for the rains. They generally spent a night or two in our camp before moving forward into Burma. Williams of the Elephant Corps, popularly known in military circles as 'Elephant Bill', arrived and took up his quarters at Moreh. Relations between ourselves and the officers of the Elephant Corps were not very friendly. I think that this was mainly due to the fact that Williams had worked in this area before the war as a forest manager for the Bombay Burmah Company. He knew it therefore much better than we did, but he also thought that his local knowledge made him better qualified than ourselves to advise the Army on the handling of the civil population. This was of course our function, but some of the commanders of subordinate formations did not always realise this. In the evenings arguments frequently developed in the mess between ourselves and the Elephant Corps officers, and this encouraged us to hasten our departure to Tamu.

Many of the houses in the old village were of solid construction, with good timber floors and joists. We decided to dismantle two or three of the largest and to use the materials to build houses on our new camp site in the vicinity of the old Government Rest House, which was still standing. The headman and elders helped us to fix a fair price to pay to the owners. Orders had recently come from Civil Affairs Service headquarters that in future officers in the field were to be charged rent for their accommodation, even if in fact no accommodation was provided. We took the view that, if we had to pay rent, we should have something better than the ordinary bamboo *basha* (hut) to live in. The houses which we built had stout timber floors, walls of matted bamboo and thatched roofs. Thomas returned in the middle of October, and was by no means enamoured of the proposed move to Tamu. He thought we should open an office there, but he considered that Tamu would be an obvious target for enemy aircraft when units of troops had taken up their positions all round it, and that we ought therefore to retain our possession of Moreh. But he remained for only three weeks, during which he was continually ill with malaria and later developed a pain in the stomach which proved to be appendicitis.

Meanwhile the first units of the returning Army began to arrive.

It amused us, who had spent the rains in Moreh without any special security precautions, to find road blocks springing up near our camp with Indian sentries on duty at night, challenging anyone who approached. The end of the rains also made it possible for Civil Affairs supply trucks to come down again with goods from Imphal. The Rest House at Tamu was to be our new office, and we had the bottom of it walled – for it was built on posts – for use as a supply store.

Thomas asked me to go to Mintha, our most northerly village, to help to investigate a charge of rape brought by a Burmese woman against an Indian soldier. It was not yet possible to drive to Mintha, so I obtained an elephant from the Elephant Corps to carry my bedding and went on foot, accompanied by Chit Maung, one of our armed peons, who was a brother of the Tamu headman. I also took a few sepoys from the Burma Regiment on the first stage of the journey, to give them some exercise and to let them learn something of the country. It was only about fifteen miles to Mintha, but I took the journey easily, stopping for the first night at a village on the way. Here I was called upon to deal with a case in which a woman had run away to her father's house because her husband had beaten her, and refused to return. The husband accused his father-in-law before the headman of restraining his wife from returning to him, and the headman, not knowing what to do, passed the case to me. As the wife herself told me that she never wanted to see her husband's face again, there was little that I could do beyond calling all the parties together and asking the father-in-law and the elders of the village to try to patch up the quarrel.

Next day I went on to Mintha, where I met an officer from the accused's regiment who was to hear the rape case with me. As the witnesses were not all present, we had to postpone the hearing till the following day. The accused, a strapping great Pathan, was stripped of his arms in front of the headman and elders and placed under arrest, and the inquiry then took place. We both thought the case a true one, but all that we were doing was to record a summary of the evidence with a view to a court-martial being convened at a later date. On my way back to Moreh I spent a night at the same village, where the case of the runaway wife was again brought up. I was asked to issue an order to her to return to her husband; this I refused to do, but I called up the husband and the woman's father separately and tried to persuade them to settle the matter quickly.

Towards the middle of November we moved our camp, and were at last on our own and actually living on Burmese soil. Soon afterwards we moved the refugee village too to Tamu. John McTurk had some time previously been recalled to Imphal and, since Thomas never came back except for a flying visit at Christmas, there were now four administrative Civil Affairs Officers and Toby Fforde, the police officer. By this time we had a couple of jeeps – one of which was usually out of order – and two 15 cwt trucks, and most parts of our charge could be visited on a day trip from Tamu.

Apart from my visit to Mintha, I never slept away from my headquarters, but I was of course the Supply Officer and was not doing a normal administrative job. The view was once expressed by a formation commander that Civil Affairs were not doing their job properly, as their officers hardly ever slept away from Tamu; but we were continually visiting our villages and keeping in touch with the people, and there was no particular virtue in sleeping out when there was no necessity to do so. We regarded ourselves as being territorial rather than formation Civil Affairs Officers; for the Army, once it arrived in the Kabaw Valley, settled down and did little but patrol. There was only one division (20th Indian Division) in the area, whose headquarters was only a couple of miles from our camp, and normally a formation lower than a division had no Civil Affairs Officer. I think the Divisional Commander, General Gracey, was perfectly satisfied with our activities. We found him very friendly; he came once to our mess for a Burmese curry lunch, some of our staff took him out to shoot jungle-fowl, and once we put on a Burmese *pwè* for his benefit. Some of the subordinate commanders were difficult, but on the whole our relations with the troops in the area were good. Many officers, however, had but an imperfect understanding of the functions and status of the Civil Affairs Service. It was something new to them and, even though we wore uniform and badges of rank, they could never quite make up their minds whether we were soldiers or civilians; sometimes our ambiguous position was an advantage.

One of the most important tasks of Civil Affairs Officers in the early days was to create in the minds of our troops a right attitude towards the Burmese. Many members of the forces which retreated from Burma in 1942 were firmly convinced that the great majority of the Burmese were hostile to them, and that this hostility had contributed in large measure to the British defeat. It was very necessary that these ideas should be corrected before Burma was reoccupied. The British Government, through the Secretary of State for India, had announced that, when the British returned, it would be 'in no spirit of vengeance against those civilians who have been forced by events beyond their control to conceal for a time their loyalty to the cause of the United Nations provided they have not deliberately assisted the enemy's war effort or taken part in injuring or persecuting British or Allied prisoners or interned civilians or minority communities or British or Allied nationals'.

Under pressure from the Government of Burma and from the Chief Civil Affairs Officer, India Command had issued a directive in March 1943, over the signature of Field-Marshal Wavell, on the treatment of the inhabitants of Burma. This stated that 'Burma is a British and not an enemy country. Its people have the rights, and are subject to the duties of British subjects; they should therefore be treated as such.' And it went on to say that a policy of leniency would serve the ends of the Allied troops better than one of harshness, always provided that there was no relaxation of security. Before I came to the Kabaw Valley our staff had had considerable difficulties with the Army in this matter, and there had been one scandalous incident in which an officer in charge of a patrol had shot a number of village elders without trial or justification. I do not remember personally having any disagreement with the troops about their attitude towards the Burmese. I was, however, somewhat amused by the fact that, whenever military reports had occasion to mention the presence of units of the Burma National Army (as the Burma Defence Army had been renamed after the Japanese had granted Burma independence), they referred to them as the 'BTA' – Burma Traitor Army.

On the 1st January 1944, Admiral Mountbatten issued a proclamation in which he assumed full responsibility for the administration of Burma. A British Military Administration now existed in name as well as in fact. The terms of the proclamation were as follows:

1. I, Admiral the Lord Louis Mountbatten, GCVO, CB, DSO, ADC, Supreme Allied Commander, South-East Asia Command, do hereby declare that until further notice I assume for myself and successors full judicial, legislative, executive and administrative responsibilities in regard to all the territories of Burma now or at any future time occupied by the Forces under my command and exclusive jurisdiction over all persons and properties therein.

2. I delegate to the military officer for the time being holding the appointment of the Chief Civil Affairs Officer, Burma, full authority to conduct on my behalf the military administration of the civil population in the said territories, subject always to any orders and directions which I may issue from time to time. And for this purpose the said Chief Civil Affairs Officer is authorised to delegate sufficient powers to any officers under his command.

On the same day the Supreme Allied Commander issued a directive to the Chief Civil Affairs Officer outlining his duties, and the latter issued a proclamation on the 'Maintenance of Order'. This stated that all laws in force in Burma should continue in force unless suspended or amended by subsequent proclamations or regulations; it also dealt with the jurisdiction of courts, with confirmation of death sentences, and with the review of judicial proceedings.

Mountbatten himself paid a visit to the Kabaw Valley early in February. None of the Civil Affairs staff was invited to meet him, though even the head Burman of the Elephant Corps' employees did so. In an address to the troops Mountbatten is reported to have said that, so far as he was concerned, there was no monsoon; in other words, the rains would not henceforth be regarded as putting an end to military operations.

Among other visitors was the Political Agent from the neighbouring state of Manipur. He came on foot across the hills to the north of Tamu, and I went up by jeep to meet him and bring him to our camp, where he spent the night. Some weeks earlier we had had a visit from three members of the Manipur State Durbar (or Council); there had been a rumour in Manipur that the British had evacuated Tamu, and the Army had arranged a conducted tour for them, so that they could see that we were still there.

Soon after we had moved to Tamu we were told by General Gracey that he wanted the southernmost villages under our administration to be evacuated and the inhabitants distributed among the villages in the north; the Army would feed them. A few days later the Army Commander, General Slim, came down; Keely went to see him and came back with orders to go ahead with the evacuation. We began to make our plans, but on the following day were told that nothing was to be done till the villagers had reaped their crops. This meant a delay of at least a month. But in fact it was not for nearly two months that anything happened.

About the middle of February information came through that enemy forces on the east bank of the Chindwin were increasing, and it seemed likely that they were preparing to cross. We made plans to move our refugee village and some of the less essential members of our own staff back to Manipur, to a camp not far from Imphal, but General Gracey told us not to do so, as we should be given ample warning of any enemy infiltration. The question of evacuating the southern villages did, however, come up again a few days later, and it was decided that the operation should be carried out. There were three villages involved, and one Civil Affairs Officer was allocated to each.

We drove down to the headquarters of the battalion which was to be in charge of the exercise, and in the late afternoon set out in three parties, each with an escort of troops under their own officer. My party slept on the roadside; I remember that it was a beautiful clear night, and Orion was shining brightly overhead. At 2 a.m. we moved on again, and reached my village an hour later. We reconnoitred the village, a long straggling one consisting of three separate groups of houses, and all seemed quiet. I had in my water bottle cold coffee heavily laced with rum, a most refreshing substitute for early morning tea on a cold morning. At dawn we moved into the village, and I went round to each house telling the occupants to collect what they could carry of their possessions and be prepared to leave. It was very hard on these poor people, who were not really concerned in a quarrel between Britain and Japan. But they took it very well, and by 8 a.m. were ready to walk to some Army trucks which had arrived and were waiting not far off, and which took them to Tamu. After a couple of nights there, they were moved back to camps in Manipur, where I suppose they remained until the Japanese had been driven out of the Kabaw Valley.

My supplies work was now becoming very heavy. I was responsible for indenting on our Civil Affairs organisation in Imphal for the essential requirements of the civil population, taking delivery of all supplies sent, allocating them to the villages, arranging distribution and collecting payment. The principal items which I handled were salt, sugar, cooking oil, cloth and cotton yarn. We also tried to meet the requirements of individuals, when they were likely to be of benefit to the community. For instance, we got the Tamu carpenter a new set of tools; we tried to get the local sawyers a special sort of file for use with their saws, but those which were supplied proved to be the wrong kind. We occasionally purchased supplies ourselves locally for distribution, as when we bought from a shopkeeper from a village on the Chindwin (an Indian who was going back to India) his entire remaining stocks of cloth and clothing. The items enumerated above were the principal needs of the people which could no longer be satisfied locally. Rice, their staple diet, was fortunately available. Most of the villages grew enough for their own consumption, but towards the end of my time in Tamu I was engaged in a calculation of the amount of rice which each village had available, how much they required themselves and how much could be bought from them for sale to deficit areas. The average Burman's estimate of his own needs was always much higher than I thought was justified, but, as one Burman on our staff told me, Burmans always reckoned to cook much more rice than they required for a meal, and to throw out what was left to feed the dogs and poultry.

The Army's requirements from the local people were not great and, apart from labour, were in the main limited to bamboos, cane baskets for carrying earth (used by civilian labour working on the roads), and *pwènyet*, a sort of beeswax obtained from trees, which the boatmen used for caulking their boats. The Army was now operating a civilian boating company on the Yu River which flowed through the Kabaw Valley, and my old acquaintance of Monywa days, Stanley White, was put in charge of it.

Once a week I had to go with our trucks to the Field Supply Depot to collect the rations for our camp and for the refugee village. As this was a malarial area, rum was issued as a regular item in the rations. In my weekly indent I always asked for a rum issue for our camp alone, but was invariably given an issue based on the total ration strength of both camp and refugees. We naturally did not distribute rum to the refugees, and so we built up a comfortable surplus for ourselves, to which we were able to treat our numerous visitors. I was also responsible for collecting our canteen require- ments. These included the monthly issue, on payment, of alcohol, amounting to one bottle of whisky, one of gin and six of beer for each officer; and the various items which our Burmese staff required, such as cigarettes, soap, toothpaste, hair cream and so forth.

All this time the Army had remained more or less stationary; at all events, the Divisional and Brigade headquarters stayed in the same place, though roads were being pushed forward. At the be- ginning of March there seemed to be a general impression that we should soon be advancing, even if only as far as the Chindwin, and there was talk of our having to evacuate villages on the west bank of the river to facilitate operations. But a few days later a Japanese push was being talked about, and it was being hinted that our camp might have to be moved back to Moreh. About this time there was a great deal of aerial activity at night, which we assumed to be the second Wingate expedition moving into Burma. In the previous year Wingate had led his 'Chindits' several hundred miles into Burma behind the enemy lines, blowing bridges and cutting communica- tions. The raid had been a very daring feat, but a third of the force failed to return and the damage done to Japanese communications was soon repaired. From our point of view it was a most unfortunate operation, for the force was welcomed by some of the pro-British Burmese, who suffered cruelly after it had withdrawn. This year the Chindits were to combine with Stilwell's Chinese and American troops in an attack on Myitkyina, towards which Stilwell's men had been advancing down the Ledo road from northern Assam since the end of the rains.

In the second week of March the Japanese started their great offensive, which was to carry them right up to Imphal and Kohima and, they hoped, ultimately to Delhi. General Mutaguchi said in his Order of the Day on the opening of this campaign: 'This operation will engage the attention of the whole world and is eagerly awaited by a hundred million of our countrymen. Its success will have a profound effect on the course of the war, and may even lead to its conclusion. We must therefore expend every ounce of energy and talent to achieve our purpose.' Though we knew nothing of this at the time, it appears that our high command had been aware since January that a Japanese offensive was being planned, and had predicted fairly accurately when it was likely to begin. It was carried out by three Japanese divisions coming from across the Chindwin. The central thrust, made by the 15th Division, was aimed at the Kabaw Valley. On the 11th March we heard that the Japanese were in the area from which we had so recently cleared the inhabitants and that our troops were withdrawing. Keely sent me up to Imphal to discuss the situation with the DCCAO at the headquarters of 4th Corps. It now appears, from histories which have been written of the Burma campaign, that General Slim decided at the start of the Japanese offensive to withdraw the British forces to the Imphal plain and meet the enemy there. We Civil Affairs officers were not informed of this. We continued to do what we could, though it was little enough, but clearly, if there was no intention of trying to hold the Kabaw Valley, there was little point in our staying.

On my return from Imphal I began making arrangements to move our stores back to Moreh. We also gave our armed peons and such kin scouts as were in our camp practice in manning the perimeter. It seemed likely that the enemy would cut the road behind Moreh, and an attack on Tamu was expected soon. On the night of the 18th/19th March a great 'battle' took place in Tamu. Firing began at 10.30 p.m., and we all stood to and went to our allotted positions. The firing continued all night, and we remained in our positions till dawn. Next morning we found two casualties in the camp: one was a prisoner in the lock-up, who was so scared that he tried to break out through the barbed wire and was promptly shot by the sentry; the other was a buffalo which had strayed too near to the perimeter. So far as we could discover, there were no enemy in Tamu at the time, and the firing all came from units of our own forces.

The Army was now on the move backwards, and the next day Keely went to General Gracey to find out what we were to do. He was apparently surprised to learn that we were still in Tamu, and said that we should move to Imphal the next day. Our Burma Regiment company was to remain behind and to be placed under the command of the local formation.

I hastily did some packing, leaving behind a quantity of my possessions in this, my last evacuation, and next day (20th March) we set off about 6 a.m. in a jeep and six trucks containing the officers, clerks, armed peons and kin scouts. Our Burmese staff were given the option of coming with us, and most elected to do so, for they would be marked men when the Japanese arrived. My servant Maung Maung had been sent back to Calcutta many months before; he was too much of an Indian to fit well into a predominantly Burmese camp. In his place I took on a young Burman, Maung Tun Che, who had been sent to us from the Chindwin area on, I think, a charge of buffalo theft. As no evidence was ever brought against him, we made him a mess servant, and subsequently he became my personal servant. He stayed with me until I left Burma nearly four years later.

On arrival in Imphal we reported to the DCCAO, who was surprised to see us. I asked if I could be given a job in Imphal, as I had no particular desire to return to Calcutta, but he told me that it was expected that the Japanese would cut the road between Imphal and Dimapur at Kohima, and that Imphal would soon be under siege; the Corps Commander therefore wanted no more mouths to feed that were absolutely necessary. We were instructed to place our Burmese staff in a refugee camp at Dimapur and then to take twenty-eight days' war leave. We spent the night in a camp at Khangampat, some nine miles from Imphal, and the following day proceeded to Dimapur. Fforde and I stayed there a couple of days to see our Burmans settled into their camp. We also visited another camp to which the villagers from the southern Kabaw Valley were just being moved, and found them reasonably pleased with life. We then took the train to Calcutta.

Certain changes had taken place in our Calcutta staff in the eight months that I had been away. Ewing had died, and Lindop, his successor as DCCAO, was with 14th Army headquarters at Comilla, which lay east of Calcutta. The Burma Government supplies organisation had been taken over by the supplies branch of the Civil Affairs Service, and to its office reported all Civil Affairs staff who passed through Calcutta for railway warrants and instructions. There was now a small rest house for officers, to which I went. Fforde's wife was in a flat in Calcutta, and of course he joined her.

Fforde and I had already decided to seek permission to return to

Dimapur for our leave, to give our Burmese staff some training in police work and to show them that we had not forgotten them as soon as we reached India. Marsh, the head of the supplies organisation, was sympathetic, but said that I should have to refer to Lindop, to whom accordingly I wrote. A few days later we had news that the Japanese advance might make it necessary to evacuate Dimapur, and this seemed to make it even more urgent that we should go there, to ensure that none of our people were left behind. But I now received a rather curt reply from Lindop, who wrote that, while he appreciated our desire to look after those who had served us well, we must recognise that our Burmese staff had now passed out of our charge and had become the responsibility of the welfare branch of the Civil Affairs Service, and that he could not have either Fforde or me butting in on the administration of the refugee camp. He added that Dimapur was not a recognised leave station, and that we should not be permitted to proceed there even on leave.

That seemed to close the matter so far as I was concerned. But Fforde, who had put forward the same request through police channels, now received instructions to proceed to the camp. We also heard that the inmates of the Dimapur camp were being moved to a small place called Palasbari, which was close to Gauhati and the ferry over the Brahmaputra. Having obtained information from Marsh that, so far as he was aware, there was no reason why I should not spend my leave in the Gauhati area, I arranged to accompany Fforde. Neville Hill, one of our Burma police officers whom I had known in my Mogaung days, was already at Palasbari in charge of an interrogation centre, and we sent him a telegram to say that we were coming.

We left Calcutta on the 9th April, and reached Palasbari the next day. It was fifteen miles from Gauhati and the camp was pleasantly situated on the banks of the Brahmaputra. Here I spent an enjoyable two and a half weeks in Neville's hut. Our Burmans were delighted to see us; we were told that, when our telegram had been read out to them, they had all applauded. We did what we could to make life more interesting for them: we gave them some instruction in police work, we organised games of football, and we occasionally took them into Gauhati to do some shopping or to have a Chinese meal. Meanwhile Neville was obtaining a great deal of information which was of interest to us from the persons brought to him for interrogation; a number of these were members of the 'Indian National Army', a force raised by the Japanese from Indian civilians and prisoners-of-war. The news from the front was not good: the Japanese had cut the main road between Kohima and Dimapur and were closing in on Imphal, but there was a general feeling that their offensive would soon receive a terrific setback.

I had left my address with Marsh, and in due course received a signal that I was to report to the DCCAO with 15th Corps; this meant that my destination was Bawli Bazaar in North Arakan. The one area which I had hoped to avoid was North Arakan, since the part under our control was populated entirely by Chittagonians, and there were no Burmese or Arakanese there. Tun Che, who had been with the rest of our Burmese staff since we had reached India, said he would go with me, though I warned him that he would probably find himself the only Burmese. On the 28th April we left Palasbari.

At this moment I decided to promote myself to Captain. I have said that there was considerable argument whether or not officers of the Civil Affairs Service should be commissioned, and consequently the question of ranks had not been settled. I found that most of my contemporaries were now Captains, and had been told unofficially some months before that it had been decided that members of the Burma Civil Service with four years' seniority were to be Captains; I had now had more than five years'. I do not remember ever being formally promoted, but henceforth I signed myself as Captain and was so addressed. We found that a formation Civil Affairs Officer could carry no weight unless he was at least a Captain.

CHAPTER ELEVEN

North Arakan and the Refounding of the Old Town 1944-45

WE TRAVELLED BY ROAD from Palasbari over the Khasi Hills, through the Assam capital of Shillong, and down again into the heat of the plains to Sylhet, where we boarded the train for Chittagong. We arrived the next day and spent the night in an Army rest camp. There was an office of the Civil Affairs supplies branch in Chittagong, which provided a truck to take us on to Bawli Bazaar, the headquarters of the Military Administration in North Arakan and some one hundred miles distant. We arrived in the late afternoon of the 30th April.

The area which was at that time under British administration was a small portion of the extreme north of the Akyab District, consisting of little more than the two narrow and parallel valleys of the Pruma and Kalapanzin Rivers. The Civil Affairs organisation in North Arakan provided both territorial and formation CAOs; there were no fewer than four divisions operating in the area, each with a CAO attached to it. Bawli Bazaar was a small village on the Pruma, which in peacetime had been of absolutely no consequence. The Senior CAO was Apedaile, and there was a territorial CAO, Peter Murray, stationed over the hills to the east at Goppe Bazaar in the Kalapanzin Valley. Peter had done his Burmese course with me at Oxford; after the outbreak of war he had joined the Burma Navy, and he continued to wear his naval badges of rank in the Civil Affairs Service, causing some confusion to military personnel. As a result of the communal disturbances which occurred in 1942 after the British evacuation from Arakan and to which I have referred before, the entire population of this area was now Muslim. They were Chittagonian by race and spoke a type of Bengali. Only a very few could speak Arakanese, a dialect form of Burmese, and we relied almost entirely on interpreters for communication with them.

Our camp at Bawli was on the river bank and consisted of a

miserable collection of bamboo huts. The one allotted to me looked as though it might once have been a cattle shed. Another camp was, however, being built a little further up the river, and it was not long before we moved to it. The size of the Civil Affairs staff in our headquarters astonished me after what I had been used to in Tamu. In the early days the Service had consisted almost entirely of Burma civilians or Burma police officers. But now new branches were being formed: Supplies, Relief and Labour (also known as Welfare) and so forth; and all sorts of people who had come out of Burma were drafted into them as officers or civilian subordinates. Indeed it was not long before about three separate branches were employed on the type of work which I had been doing single-handed in Tamu.

I was told by Apedaile that he proposed to use me to relieve the formation CAOs as one by one they went to India for some leave. I was first posted to 36th British Division; as it was just leaving Arakan, I did not go to live in its camp, but paid an occasional visit during the week or so before it went. I was then sent over to Goppe to relieve Peter Murray, so that he could go to Bawli for a short rest. The Kalapanzin Valley seemed a very peaceful spot at this time. Peter had built himself a bamboo bungalow on a slight eminence, from which he looked down over the sunny valley. We used to hear the birds singing, especially the Indian cuckoo with its tuneful song of four notes. The people went about their business in the normal way, and once a week there was a market day in the little bazaars of the valley. There was a refugee camp at Goppe, under the charge of one of our welfare officers. We also had fairly large stocks of paddy, which had been requisitioned after the previous harvest; this was used to feed the refugee camp, and from time to time we sent supplies of it over to Bawli for use in the Pruma Valley. When Peter came back after about a week, I returned to Bawli, a depressing place by comparison with Goppe, with evidence of the Army everywhere.

My next job was to relieve John McTurk, who was now in Arakan attached to the 26th Indian Division. The divisional headquarters was withdrawing for the rains some miles inside the Indian frontier, but some of its units were to remain in Burma, and there was a brigade headquarters in Bawli. We suggested that there was little point in the CAO living outside Burma with the divisional headquarters, and were told that Corps insisted that he should move there. But when we went to see what accommodation was available, the Army quickly changed its mind. There was a great shortage of building materials and accommodation was already very cramped, and within a few hours 26th Division persuaded Corps that the CAO would be far more useful in Bawli. It was agreed that I should continue to live in our own camp and should go about twice a week to brigade headquarters to liaise with the Intelligence Officer and see if there was anything for me to do. And so I used to plough across the waterlogged fields every three or four days, have a cup of tea with the Intelligence Officer and trudge back again.

On my arrival in Calcutta from the Kabaw Valley I had written to ask if I could go on home leave. I had not been in England for five and a half years, and it seemed unlikely that there would be much work for me during the coming rains; there was clearly going to be no offensive on the Arakan front. But several months later I was told that I could not yet be spared. Meanwhile my services had been in such great demand at Bawli that I was able to do a good deal of reading, and even started to teach myself shorthand. My work with the troops – apart from my regular social visits to brigade headquarters – included such matters as agreeing in what areas civilians could carry on their cultivation without endangering the security of any units, dealing with complaints that they were cultivating too near to military camps, warning the local villagers when a unit wanted to do some firing practice, investigating complaints when their cattle were hit in such practices, and arranging for the maintenance of the airstrip at Bawli. None of this took up very much of my time. On the purely civil side, I had occasionally a few petty cases to try. Most of these arose out of an order issued by Apedaile that all civilians were to declare what stocks of paddy they held, for a number were prosecuted for making false declarations. We were now well into the rains, and the Arakan coast had an annual rainfall of about 200 inches. There was therefore little question of our doing any touring save by boat, and we had only open boats driven by outboard engines. Among our civilian staff were a number of Township Officers appointed by the Military Administration. They were local men who spoke English. Some had been government servants before the war, but they were schoolmasters or clerks, not administrative officers. With few exceptions they did most valuable work, and they were particularly useful to us in an area where we could not converse directly with the people.

I took over the commissariat side of our camp, as I had done in Tamu, and was the officer in charge of the mess. Some weeks later we were fortunate in acquiring five Burmans to work as mess servants. They had been picked up by the Navy while fishing off the Bassein coast and had been brought back for interrogation. The Army then handed them over to us, and I found that they were about to be sent to the Arakanese refugee camp at Dinajpur in

Bengal. I suggested keeping them and training them as mess servants and, since we were the only people in the area who could speak to them in their own language, they accepted the proposal with alacrity and served us cheerfully and well.

One grew rather tired of seeing only Chittagonian civilians, wearing their little white Mohammedan caps, and with their shirts invariably hanging outside their longyis. They were not a people who could inspire much affection, but they had their good qualities, and I was told of Chittagonians who went unconcernedly about their work in the fields while fighting raged around them. Across the Indian border there were some settlements of Arakanese Buddhists, whose forbears had fled into British territory during the Burmese invasions of Arakan at the end of the eighteenth century. They spoke their own dialect of Burmese and dressed in the Burmese fashion, and it was something of a paradox that we in North Arakan should have to cross into India to see Burmese villagers and to hear Burmese spoken.

Though on the Arakan front nothing of military interest was happening, things were going very well for the Allied forces on the other two Burma fronts. In northern Burma the area round Myitkyina and Mogaung was recaptured by the combined action of Stilwell's Chinese-American forces and the Chindits, while the Chinese had mounted an offensive from Yunnan to the east. Mogaung was taken before the end of June; Myitkyina was besieged for two and a half months, and fell at the beginning of August. On the Assam front the great Japanese offensive was halted by the middle of May, and on the 23rd June the road from Imphal to Kohima was cleared. Then began the pursuit of the Japanese by the troops of the 14th Army, which continued till the end of the war; Tamu was re-entered at the beginning of August. Sitting in what seemed to me a foreign country, I hoped – but with little optimism – that someone might realise that I knew the Mogaung area well and that I might be posted there; or at least that I might be sent back to the Kabaw Valley. But I spent the rest of the war in Arakan.

When John McTurk arrived back from leave towards the end of July, I went south to relieve George Merrells, who was CAO with 25th Indian Division. The divisional headquarters was at Maungdaw, some twenty miles south of Bawli, which in peace-time had been a township headquarters, but Merrells was living with an Engineer unit on Kappagaung, an island north of Maungdaw and joined to it by a bridge. We were here virtually on the shore of the Bay of Bengal, for Kappagaung and Maungdaw lay on the wide estuary of the Naf River, the boundary between India and Burma. Here I had a much busier and more interesting time, for my job included elements of the duties of both a formation and a territorial CAO. The central part of my area, which included Kappagaung and Maungdaw, had been cleared of civilians, and consisted only of military units. To the north there were some villages, and a large refugee camp at Balukhali, where the people evacuated from the Maungdaw area had been settled. To the south again there were a number of villages. Merrells had evolved a routine whereby he visited Balukhali and the southern area – called Fadaungza – on a fixed day each week, allotting the whole day to the visit. The rest of the week was occupied with office work, trying cases and going into Maungdaw to keep in touch with divisional headquarters, and in particular with the Field Security Section, whose work was very much connected with ours.

Balukhali was run by an officer of the Civil Affairs welfare branch, with his staff, and medical arrangements were in the capable hands of the inimitable Arakanese doctor, Captain Kyaw Zan. One of our township officers also had his headquarters in the camp. My work with the Army was mainly of a security nature, issuing passes to Army contractors to enter protected areas, restraining civilians from cultivating too near to military camps, and so forth. Security was a matter of some importance for the Japanese were only twenty miles to the east of Maungdaw at the end of a motor road. My dealings with the staff of 25th Division were very amicable. The commander, General Davies, who did not arrive back from leave till I had been in the area a month, at once invited me to tea, and showed a considerable interest in my work and the greatest willingness to give me any assistance possible. For the first time I felt that I was part of the Army and working in co-operation with the other branches, and I should have liked to remain with this division. But I was told that my destination was 26th Division, which was said to have asked for me.

I enjoyed my short time in the Maungdaw area. There was plenty to do and the work was interesting. The main drawback was the weather: on a rainy day the flat expanse of Kappagaung, with the Naf estuary on one side of it and the wind whistling over it, could be most depressing. But north of the island on a fine sunny day the scene was a very pleasant one, with the dark-green mass of the Mayu range standing out in the distance against the blue sky, and in the foreground the light-green carpet of young paddy plants and green trees with white paddy birds perched on their topmost branches.

Merrells went into hospital in Calcutta with suspected sprue and his leave was extended. One of our police officers was therefore sent down towards the middle of September to relieve me. I had been informed that the period which I had spent in India in March and April after leaving the Kabaw Valley would not be regarded as leave, and I was therefore now entitled to take the regulation twenty-eight days. I spent three nights in Bawli, where Leo Edgerley of the Burma Forest Service had now succeeded Apedaile as SCAO. Here I met an American civilian engaged on what he called 'black' radio propaganda; I understood this to mean propaganda purporting to emanate from enemy stations (such as Rangoon or Saigon), as opposed to 'white' propaganda, which is straightforward propaganda. He had come to learn something of the Burmese, presumably from us as he would not have found any Burmans at Bawli apart from our mess staff.

I left for Calcutta with Tun Che on the 11th September. The journey involved travelling by road to Chittagong, where we spent the night, by rail the next morning to Chandpur, by river steamer all the rest of the day and all night up the Brahmaputra and Meghna to Goalundo, and finally another five or six hours in a train before we reached Calcutta, where I again stayed in the Civil Affairs rest house.

I had made no arrangements in advance for my leave, not having been certain till nearly the last moment when I should be able to take it. I should have liked to go to Darjeeling, but that was a very popular leave resort for Army officers and I should have had little chance of obtaining accommodation there at such short notice. I heard, however, that Merrells was at the Himalayan Hotel in Kalimpong, so wired and asked him to arrange accommodation for me. I went up with no firm booking a week after arriving in Calcutta, and found that Merrells was just leaving and had arranged for me to take over his room – or rather, half room, which he had been sharing with an American captain.

Kalimpong lay nearly 4,000 feet above sea level in the Himalayas, not far from Darjeeling. We travelled by train all night from Calcutta, and the next morning reached Siliguri, where we changed to the comic Darjeeling-Himalayan railway. This took us to a station twelve miles from Kalimpong, whence we were given a lift in a military truck. Kalimpong was a quiet little place, lying on the saddle between two ridges (Deolo and Rinkingpong), and the hotel looked out over a green valley towards the protected state of Sikkim. One of the overland trade routes to Tibet started here. The Tibetans came in with mules laden with wool, and went back with tea. They were rather dirty-looking people, wearing long gowns with high collars and long sleeves, which were tied tightly round the waist and looked like dressing-gowns. Other races to be seen in Kalimpong were Gurkhas from Nepal, Lepchas from Sikkim and Bhutanese from Bhutan. The Lepchas had peculiar marital customs, being both poly-androus and polygamous: a man might cohabit with his wife's younger sisters, and the eldest brother's wife was common to all his brothers. It was a change to find a town in Bengal that was not full of Bengalis.

Kalimpong seemed a healthy place, and I did a fair amount of walking as well as riding. Ponies could be hired in the town for one rupee an hour and Tun Che and I rode most days on Deolo or Ringkingpong. Unfortunately there was a good deal of mist during our stay, but occasionally, when it cleared, we had a fine view of the snow-capped peak of Kanchenjunga (28,000 feet) some forty-seven miles away; it was a magnificent sight, this huge mountain which seemed almost to reach to the sky. The Church of Scotland had established in Kalimpong the St Andrew's Colonial Homes for the education and training of poor European and Eurasian children, the latter being, I believe, mainly the children of tea-planters. They were polite little boys who used to wish us good morning as we rode past.

The proprietress of the Himalayan Hotel was of mixed European and Gurkha parentage with, I think, a dash of Tibetan. Her father had been the British Trade Agent in an area of Tibet and was living in the hotel; his family seemed to know everyone round here. His daughter, the proprietress, was a friendly soul and, if she met one of her guests in the town, she would take him or her for a cup of coffee in one of the shops. At one of these coffee sessions I met Raja Dorje, the Bhutanese Minister, a picturesque figure in a long purple cloak with white cuffs. I understood that he was in effect the Prime Minister of Bhutan, though he spent a good deal of his time in Kalimpong, acting as intermediary between the Maharaja and the Indian Government. He spoke excellent English and had just re-turned from the Darjeeling races, a sport in which he apparently took a considerable interest.

I decided to motor down to Siliguri, a journey of forty miles, which took nearly three hours. I spent a little over a week in Calcutta, met a number of my friends passing through the rest house, and had some nights out with Hanson who was still there. I enquired into the possibility of returning to Chittagong by sea, but found that I could do so only if I would take charge of a leave party, collecting them in Calcutta, looking after them on the ship and disposing of them in Chittagong. I chose the uncomfortable rail and river route.

At Chittagong I obtained Civil Affairs transport, which I shared with a Chinese sanitary officer. I stopped on the way at the head-quarters of 15th Corps, where I learned that there had recently been a Japanese infiltration into Goppe, which was my ultimate destination. 26th Division, to which I was to be attached, now had its headquarters in Bawli, and I called on General Lomax. It was agreed that I should not live with the division, but should go over to Goppe, where a brigade had its headquarters. I was told that 26th Division would soon be relieved by 82nd West African Division, and that I should remain with the new division. Edgerley, who was still SCAO, told me that I was to be entirely under the orders of the division, though I should liaise with him in such matters as obtaining staff to deal with refugees, supplies for the civil population, and so forth. When this additional work became so heavy that I could no longer manage it as well as my formation work, a full-time territorial CAO would be sent to the area.

I went to Goppe on the 18th October, with Captain Kyaw Zan, the Arakanese medical officer whom I have already mentioned, an active and cheerful little fellow who was very popular in the mess. The Japanese in their raid some twelve days previously had overrun the Civil Affairs camp, and my predecessor and his staff had had to make their way as fast as possible into the 'stronghold', where brigade headquarters and the other military units were concentrated, and where they were now living. The Japanese had carried off some civilians from the Goppe villages, and in due course I recorded statements from those who had been released or had managed to escape and return home. Meanwhile it was hardly prudent to go back to the old Civil Affairs camp outside the 'stronghold', and we continued to live under tarpaulins with brigade headquarters; very hot it became under these tarpaulins in the middle of the day. As it was difficult for civilians who wanted to see me to get into this military area, I obtained permission to build two small bamboo huts just outside the perimeter, one as an office and the other as a dispensary; as a result, our out-patient attendance rose from seven to forty a day. My staff consisted of a clerk named Abdul Rahman – an invaluable fellow – and some half a dozen policemen, while Kyaw Zan had a hospital assistant.

Here I spent the best part of two months. My work for the Army consisted of the usual issuing of passes to civilians; arranging contracts for the supply of timber, posts to support tarpaulins, hay and paddy straw for mule fodder; helping mess sergeants to buy eggs, fruit and vegetables in the local bazaar; providing guides when required, and labour to carry rations or water roads (to keep down the dust). It was my job to advise the Army on the prices which should be paid for labour and supplies, and to assess the compensation payable for damage done to crops when roads had to be driven through them.

The West Africans took over the area from 26th Division at the beginning of November. I remained attached to the brigade operating in the Goppe area. The new Brigade Commander was most anxious that his men should get on well with the locals. He told me that all villages had been put out of bounds to troops, except for patrols and military police, and that he would like my headmen to report to me if this order was disobeyed. He thought his troops would give no trouble with the local women, but advised the villagers to keep their women at home as far as possible and, above all, not to sell any liquor to the Africans. There was little danger of this, for most Chittagonians were pretty strict Muslims and did not drink.

But it was not long before civilians began to come to me with complaints against the troops, at first mainly of a minor nature; for example, they had taken goods from a bazaar-seller without paying for them. The first African troops to arrive were from the Gold Coast. They were generally small and often cheerful fellows and they seemed to get on quite well with my civilians. But after a while they were replaced by Nigerians, tall, dour-looking men with scars on their faces, who rather frightened the locals, and shocked them by their habit of bathing naked in the river.

The worst incident in which the troops were involved during this period was at a village some miles south of Goppe. Some African soldiers had gone into the village looking for women. The villagers resisted them, with the result that the Africans killed three and set fire to many houses. I sent my police to investigate, but we were just about to start our advance, and I had to leave the settlement of the case to those who came after me. No doubt by the time the investigation was completed the culprits had moved well ahead with their unit, and the case probably fizzled out.

The most unsatisfactory feature about dealing with offences committed by military personnel was the complicated legal procedure which had to be followed and the great length of time which consequently elapsed before the case came to trial. The following is an example. I was sitting one morning in my little bamboo office when a young civilian came and complained that two Sikh sepoys belonging to a mule company, who were cutting fodder about half a mile away, had robbed him of his money as he was on his way to the bazaar. I went at once to the place with some of my police. When they saw me, the Sikhs began rummaging in a pile of freshly cut grass, in which I found the stolen money. I arrested them and took them to their commanding officer. Two days later a very inexperienced Sikh lieutenant took a 'summary of evidence', with some assistance from me. This went to the Judge Advocate General's branch, which in due course sent it back with certain criticisms of the manner in which the evidence had been recorded. Meanwhile the advance began and the two sepoys, who had first been put under close arrest and then under open arrest, were allowed to go about their normal duties. Whether in the end anything happened to them, I did not hear, and this was a case in which the accused had been caught red-handed.

Complaints against civilians by the military were dealt with by me, and I tried cases by virtue of the magisterial powers with which I had been invested. There were very few cases, and they were generally of a petty nature, such as pilfering of Army rations. The sentence was usually a fine or a few strokes of the cane, which disposed of a case much more satisfactorily than one of imprisonment, which would have meant sending the offender back to our Civil Affairs headquarters at Bawli to serve his sentence.

I had of course a fair amount of administrative work of a non-military nature. Apart from dealing with the large number of civilians who used to attend my office every day on their own private affairs, I had the question of food supplies to consider. I arranged with Edgerley – with whom I had telephone conversations almost every day – for salt to be sent down to me for distribution to the villagers. The hill tribes of the area, Mrungs and Kumis, who practised shifting cultivation, came and said that their paddy crop had suffered severely from the depredations of birds and monkeys, and I had to issue rice to them. Once Edgerley sent me some seed potatoes for distribution among the headmen, the idea being that we should buy back part of the crop. And traders would frequently come to ask for permits to go to Chittagong District to buy goods for sale locally.

Unfortunately my movements were restricted, as my only transport was a 15 cwt truck, and at this time most of the tracks in the valley were passable only by jeeps. Unless therefore I could occasionally borrow a jeep, I was unable to go further from Goppe than I could manage in a day's walk. This meant that the main bazaar centres to the north and south of Goppe rarely saw me, and to some extent the local V Force commanders did such administrative work as was required.

V Force was primarily an intelligence organisation, which operated in several sectors of the Burma front. It had started after the British retreat from Burma, when a number of British officers were sent into the forward areas. They gathered round them a group of local civilians and built up a network of agents operating behind the Japanese lines. No doubt V Force did much excellent work, but there was occasionally friction between it and the Civil Affairs Service. Though some of its officers had local knowledge, many had no previous experience of dealing with Eastern peoples and were inclined to put overmuch trust in the truth of what their civilian subordinates told them about the attitude of the local people. The persons employed by V Force were not the most reputable, and indeed many of their agents worked for both sides. But these people now found themselves suddenly quite important personages in their villages, as the 'staff' of the local V Force officer, and they were not averse from getting their own back on other civilians against whom they had a grudge by reporting them to V Force as being anti-British or at the least obstructive. The more sensible officers would consult us before taking any action on these reports, for in any case V Force was not concerned with civil administration. But some of the younger and more impulsive might take it upon themselves to arrest the persons reported against.

In the Kalapanzin Valley there were two V Force commanders. The one to the south of me was extremely co-operative and would consult me on the telephone about matters affecting the administration; we had a working arrangement that, until such time as I was able to pay regular visits to his area, he should have a free hand in day-to-day administrative matters, save those affecting policy. The other officer, to the north, was continually issuing orders to my headmen, threatening to arrest them, and generally acting outside his proper sphere. I tried several times to arrange a meeting with him, so that we might reach an understanding as to our respective functions, but the meeting never took place, and I was much relieved when the V Force post in that area was withdrawn.

On the Chindwin front the British advance continued. Our troops were pushing down the Kabaw Valley and through the Chin Hills, and early in December they entered Kalewa. The time had now come for the forces in Arakan to start moving too. Brigade headquarters went south from Goppe to Taung Bazaar, and towards the middle of December I joined it with my staff, consisting of my clerk Abdul Rahman, my servant Tun Che and some police. I was at last provided with my own jeep as well as a 15 cwt truck, and another CAO was sent to take over the territorial administration of the area which the Army was leaving behind. I had an interview with the Brigade Commander, Brigadier Ricketts, who showed me on a map the plan of operations for the first few days of our offensive, so that I should know where I stood. This was the first time that any Army officer had taken the trouble to give me a clear picture of the Army's plans – perhaps a sign that it was at last realised that the Civil Affairs Service was a branch of the Army.

The 14th December was 'D-Day', and on the 15th our headquarters began to move. Soon we were passing through villages which a few days earlier had been occupied by the Japanese. Just before Christmas I moved from brigade to divisional headquarters, where I remained so long as I continued to advance. My main tasks now were to obtain labour for the troops and to listen to the complaints of villagers. Unfortunately the latter were becoming numerous, and we were moving so fast that I had little time to investigate them. I arranged, however, with the division that a fresh order should be issued putting villages out of bounds to troops, and took the first opportunity of raising the matter with the Divisional Commander, General Bruce. I told him that we were about to enter the Arakanese area, where the local people were unlikely to be so submissive as the Chittagonians had been, and that there might be serious conse-quences if the troops continued to misbehave. About this time the Army decided that it would be useful if the division had two CAOs, one apparently to sit in headquarters and the other to work slightly forward in liaison with the Field Security Section and the Burma Intelligence Corps. Another officer was accordingly sent, but the arrangement was not satisfactory.

The advance continued and early in January we were among Arakanese villagers, and I was at last able to speak Burmese again. But as soon as I entered a village and the people found that I could speak their language, they would come to me with complaints about the African troops. On one occasion I found two Africans making a nuisance of themselves in a village; I arrested them and handed them over to the military police. This sort of behaviour naturally had its effect on the supply of labour for military purposes, as fear of attack by the troops on their womenfolk made the men reluctant to turn out for work.

The West Africans had no animal transport of their own. The division had been provided with some mules with their Sikh attend-ants, but for the rest it relied on its corps of porters, known as the Auxiliary Group, to carry its baggage when motor transport was not available. These porters were military personnel and, in addition to carrying their own packs, bore up to some forty pounds' weight of baggage on their heads. When we reached the stage at which we had to send back our vehicles, I was allocated a few porters for myself and my staff; they were from the Gold Coast and were cheerful little men. On the whole, I far preferred the Gold Coast to the Nigerian Regiments.

Hitherto the Auxiliary Group had prepared the camp sites for the next move, but, as we were now entering a more populated area, it was decided that sites for divisional headquarters should in future be made ready by civilian labour. This meant that the CAO would go ahead of the main headquarters at every move with the reconnaissance party in order to collect, instruct and pay the labour force. It was later agreed that the Field Security Section should also move with us. This arrangement suited me well, as it meant that we could move in our own time, and that I could be well settled and in touch with the local villagers before divisional headquarters arrived. Fortunately my relations with Captain Leslie of the Field Security Section and his staff of three sergeants were very cordial; one of them was a Burmese speaker.

On the 5th January we learned that Akyab, the district headquarters, had been captured a few days earlier by 25th Indian Division, and that our division was to cross over into the valley of the Kaladan River to the east, to relieve 81st West African Division, which had been advancing southwards down the valley. A range of hills separated us from the Kaladan. It was possible to cross them by jeep, but orders were issued that only a limited number of jeeps would be permitted to go over; all other motor transport was to be sent back, and mine went with it. My little unit now consisted of Abdul Rahman, Tun Che, three policemen, the staff's cook and our Auxiliary Group porters.

General Bruce, who was suffering from a poisoned foot, had meanwhile been relieved by General Stockwell (later Sir Hugh Stockwell), who sent for me two days after assuming command to discuss the behaviour of the troops in the villages. He said that he wished me to report to him any incidents which came to my notice, and that he would have no hesitation in removing any Battalion Commander whose men were frequently involved.

Our move to the Kaladan Valley was delayed for a few hours by the visit of the Supreme Allied Commander, Admiral Lord Louis Mountbatten, who arrived by air and spent an hour with the division. He met all the officers, and had a brief chat with me about the Mogaung area, having discovered that I had served there in peacetime. He then gave a short address. Rumour had it that he enjoyed standing on soap boxes to make his speeches, and the Deputy Adjutant was hovering about with a box held behind his back which, however, he was not called upon to produce.

In the Kaladan Valley we generally found the villages deserted as a result of Allied bombing, though my inquiries almost invariably elicited the information that the Japanese had withdrawn two or three days before the air raid. The people were living in huts in the fields, but they were not far away, and they soon came back when they heard that a Burmese-speaking officer had arrived. Wherever I stopped, I made copious notes about the political and economic situation and the principal needs of the people, and sent them back to our local Civil Affairs headquarters for the use of whichever officer should be sent to administer the area. As we advanced further, former government employees – members of the police, the sanitary services, revenue surveyors and occasionally administrative officers – came and reported to me. I had authority to pay them a certain amount of salary, provided that there was no reason to believe that their conduct during the Japanese occupation had been improper. They began to help me to collect labour for the Army.

The Japanese had made large issues of their own paper currency in Burma and the other occupied territories of South-East Asia. After careful consideration of the advantages and disadvantages of recognising the Japanese currency, it had been decided not to do so, and our payments were made in Indian currency notes overprinted 'British Military Administration, Burma'. At this stage, when Japanese currency was valueless and our notes had yet to find their value, the people preferred payment in kind for their labour, and what they particularly wanted was cloth. A considerable amount of this was available in the form of parachutes which had come down with supply drops, and I used to fix the price of work or local supplies in terms of pieces of parachute cloth.

81st West African Division coming down the Kaladan Valley from the north, and our own division advancing from the west, were now converging on Myohaung, the old capital of the Arakanese kings. It was decided that 81st Division should occupy the town on the 24th January, after which it would be withdrawn from Arakan. On the previous day I arrived at a place some five miles west of Myohaung with the Field Security Section and the reconnaissance party consisting of one platoon of troops, to select a camp site for the next move of divisional headquarters. I settled into a fairly substantial house in the village, made the usual arrangements for labour, and the following morning was busy on the camp site ensuring that the labourers understood what they had to do.

As I was returning to my house, I saw from a distance a crowd of civilians in front of it, surrounding a man who was tied with a rope. I assumed that this was some miscreant brought to me for trial; I was hot and tired and certainly in no mood to settle down to try a case. As I approached, I saw that the prisoner was dressed in a white shirt and had a short towel round his waist; he was somewhat battered about the head, looked unusually fair-skinned and had a few days' growth of beard. Before I reached the crowd, someone shouted to me that a Japanese had been caught, and this was indeed the case. I had never before seen a Japanese prisoner. Until the collapse of the Japanese Army began, prisoners were very rarely taken; the Japanese soldier preferred death to capture. I went to the officer in command of the reconnaissance party and asked him if he could look after a Japanese prisoner for me; he laughed and said he was always ready to do that. When I produced my prisoner, he had the surprise of his life. The Divisional Commander had promised fifty rupees for every prisoner, and I paid this out at once to the men who had captured this Japanese. I later heard that they were somewhat aggrieved at my having appeared and taken the man off their hands, as they were hoping to hand him over to V Force, which paid higher prices for prisoners.

When I entered Myohaung two days after its capture, the town was completely deserted. Japanese ammunition and clothes were lying everywhere, evidence of the enemy's very hurried exit. Later I found quantities of bombs and grenades scattered about the town. For the next few days I was busy with civilian visitors, especially with government servants coming in to report. I met the CAO with 81st Division, who had engaged a number of local people, mainly police, to start an administration; these he handed over to me before he left the area. On the day after my arrival I was informed that some troops had found a quantity of files and other documents in a field. Myohaung had been the district headquarters during the Japanese occupation, and these papers proved to be the records of the district office. I later found a good deal of interest in them; it was amusing to see that the Burmese civil officials and the Japanese Army had to correspond with each other in English, the only language which they had in common.

I now received orders that I was to report to the headquarters of the Senior Civil Affairs Officer, now in Akyab, to await posting, probably as SCAO myself in some other district. I represented, however, that it was essential that a CAO should be stationed in Myohaung, and my instructions were altered: I was to detach myself from 82nd Division and to stay in Myohaung as territorial CAO. I got a lift to Akyab in a small American L–5 aircraft, which carried only a single passenger behind the pilot, and spent a few days there. I was told that I could use my discretion about engaging staff for the administration, and I made arrangements for rations to be sent for them. When I returned to Myohaung on the 5th February, I found the last of the Army moving out.

Myohaung had a long history. Its name is Burmese and means simply the 'old town'; the old Arakanese name was Mrauku. Early archaeological remains have been found there which show pronounced Indian features. In the middle of the fifteenth century King Narameikla of Arakan came to the conclusion that the site of his existing capital was ill-omened; his astrologers told him that Myohaung was an auspicious site for a new capital, but that, if he moved, he would die within the year. Expressing the view that his own life was of little importance in comparison with the good of his people, he founded Myohaung in 1433 and died the following year. Myohaung remained the capital of Arakan till the country was conquered by the Burmese in 1785.

It has been described in its heyday as 'an eastern Venice, like modern Bangkok, a city of lagoons and canals, connected with the sea by tidal rivers. Its outer walls had a circumference of about twelve miles' (D.G.E. Hall, *Burma*). King Minbin (1531–53) fortified it with strong walls and a deep moat to withstand siege by the Burmese. Myohaung was at the height of its prosperity in the seventeenth century. European travellers painted glowing pictures of its wealth, and one of them described it as the richest city in that part of Asia. In those days Arakan was far more advanced than Burma through its contacts with people of other races. Merchants from many foreign countries traded in Myohaung and the Dutch for many years had a factory (trading settlement) there. As in so many eastern capitals, there was a palace-city within the walls, which was built on an eminence and dominated the town. Myohaung was taken by the British in 1825 and, by the Treaty of Yandabo (1826) which ended the First Burmese War, Arakan was ceded to Britain.

The old palace buildings had long vanished, and the government offices had taken their place, for Myohaung became the headquarters of a subdivision in the Akyab District. When I entered Myohaung, there was not a single building left on the Nanragon (the palace hill) except the small strongroom in which the government treasury had formerly been housed. There was also a tall wooden post covered with Japanese characters, which was said to commemorate the heroic deeds of the Imperial Japanese Army. On several occasions I was asked by the townspeople why I did not have it pulled down; I felt, however, that it served to mark an incident in the history of Myohaung, and it was still standing when I left. In the rest of the town many private houses had been destroyed, though there had been less damage on the outskirts.

Myohaung was by nature admirably adapted to defence against attack by land or water. Around it to the north and east was a series of hills, the narrow gaps between which were easily filled with stone; to the west were numbers of tidal creeks; and to the south were two fair-sized lakes. Three or four pagodas of historic interest had been scheduled as archaeological monuments and had been maintained at government expense. The chief of these was the great Shitthaung Pagoda; the name means 'eighty thousand', perhaps because at one time it had contained that number of statues of the Buddha. It was an unusual type of pagoda: around the central shrine was a double row of cloisters, and it has been described as 'more a fortress than a pagoda, ... undoubtedly used as a place to which members of the Order could retire, were the city attacked' (Collis, *The Land of the Great Image*). It was certainly used by the Japanese in these circumstances, for, when I visited it two days after my arrival in Myohaung, there was abundant evidence of their recent presence in the outer cloister. Food was scattered about, and I even found the enamel container from a commode.

My first task was to re-establish an administration in the area, and it was a most interesting and satisfying experience to watch it start virtually from nothing and gradually consolidate itself. Most of the staff handed over to me in Myohaung had been over-hastily re-cruited, had never been government employees and had to be discharged almost at once. But all government servants living in the vicinity came and reported to me and, as soon as there was work for them to do, I re-engaged them, provided that there was no adverse report of their behaviour during the Japanese occupation. Police were sent from Akyab, under an elderly Inspector of pre-war days, and in due course I received township officers for my two headquarters of Myohaung and Kyauktaw, and a young Assistant Township Officer. We took over a number of houses in the western quarter of Myohaung for government use. They were still in good condition, and I supplemented them by building a few bamboo huts. We soon had a fair-sized bamboo building ready for our hospital, which was under the charge of an Arakanese doctor. On the ground floor of the house used as a police station we prepared a lock-up.

Within a few days I was able to send a Township Officer and his staff to Kyauktaw on a steamer which had come to us with rations. Soon afterwards two platoons of Tripura Rifles arrived on attachment to us; they were commanded by a young Lieutenant Burman (or Varman), a relation of the Maharajah of Tripura. A Signals detachment also came to us, to maintain our wireless communications with Akyab and the other administrative centres of the district. We constructed an airstrip for use in the dry season, which involved merely cutting down the bunds over a wide area of paddy field and levelling the uneven portions. The strip was ready on the 1st March and the next day our first aircraft landed with mails; a thrice-weekly service was thereafter operated. Before long the relief (or welfare) branch of the Civil Affairs Service sent us a Sikh Lieutenant to open a supply shop in Myohaung, at which the people could purchase their requirements of cloth goods and other essential commodities.

Now that I was no longer attached to an Army formation on the frontier, but was administering an area well inside Burma, I inevitably became involved in some degree in internal Burmese politics. I have described in Chapter Ten how a resistance movement had started among the extreme left wing Thakins even before the British had left Burma in 1942. The Communist sympathies of this left wing made it naturally hostile to the Fascist powers. I have told how Thein Pe and Tin Shwe came to India to ask for British assistance, and how they were put in touch with Force 136. I must now trace briefly the history of this association, first emphasising that much of what I am about to relate did not come to my knowledge till long afterwards, and that even the high command was kept considerably in the dark in the early days.

Force 136 was a branch of the Special Operations Executive (SOE), originally formed for clandestine warfare in Europe. This organisation was responsible directly through the Minister of Economic Warfare to the War Cabinet. It did not come under the Army nor was Force 136 ever under the control of the Supreme Allied Commander, South-East Asia Command. Its responsibilities towards the military and political authorities were not clearly defined, and consequently a considerable part of its activities took place without the knowledge of either. In the early stages these activities were directed to the obtaining of intelligence from inside Burma and the establishment of contacts which might be useful later. The result of the association of Force 136 with Thein Pe and Tin Shwe was inevitably that these contacts were largely with extreme left wing elements. I have mentioned that Tin Shwe was sent back into Burma in the dry season of 1942–43, and that he brought back an Arakanese called Nyo Tun. In the next open season Nyo Tun was sent back into Arakan overland, and, when he eventually emerged about the middle of 1944, he brought back information that Arakan had its own underground movement under a notorious monk called U Pyinnyathiha.

On the 1st August 1944, the first anniversary of the establishment by the Japanese of the puppet independent Government of Burma under Dr Ba Maw, the leaders of the resistance held a conference at which the Anti-Fascist Organisation (AFO) was formed. This was a group of parties, dominated by the Thakins, who now formed the national front of the resistance; they ranged from moderate to extreme left wing. It was not, however, till considerably later that anything of this was known to our intelligence organisations. General Aung San, the Commander-in-Chief of the Burma National Army, was the leading spirit in the formation of this united front, and he declared that he and his army would lead the nation in revolt against the Japanese as soon as the time was ripe. Shortly after this some soldiers of the Burma National Army were captured by our troops on the Chindwin front, and they said that they had been told by their officers that they must be prepared, when the time came, to rise against the Japanese. The Burma National Army was some 10,000 strong; it had Burmese officers, and Japanese sergeant instructors.

About the same time, Thein Pe – now working with Force 136 – prepared a document in which he asked for trust in the Thakins, for the arming of civilian guerrillas and for the post-war Burma Army to be built up on a foundation of these guerrillas. The commander of Force 136, apparently without consulting anyone, informed Thein Pe that he recognised him and his associates as the 'Anti-Axis Association of Burma', that he would give them full military support, but that the question of the absorption of the guerrillas into the Burma Army was one for the Government of Burma to decide. He added, however, that, if the guerrillas showed their worth, the government would be unable to ignore their demands. Neither the Supreme Allied Commander nor the Chief Civil Affairs Officer had any knowledge of these negotiations. It appears that the Government of Burma was aware of them. But the government, acting on the advice of the two Burmese Ministers (including the late Premier Sir Paw Tun) who had come out to India, took the line that the Thakins and their associates were by no means representative of the Burmese people, who indeed hated them for the atrocities committed by the Burma Independence Army, and that after the war they would be of no account; meanwhile there could be no harm in making use of them. This was the cardinal error: it was not realised now, nor till long afterwards, that the Anti-Fascist Organisation had become a Burmese national front, whose aim was independence for Burma.

Now that the Allied offensive was well under way, the role of Force 136 changed from the collection of intelligence to the more active one of harassing the Japanese, and it was about this time that its activities came to the notice of General Pearce, the Chief Civil Affairs Officer. The 81st West African Division, advancing down the Kaladan Valley, captured a number of civilians who were wanted for murder and collaboration with the Japanese. These persons claimed to belong to guerrillas raised by Force 136, and General Pearce had little option but to grant them an amnesty. And this sort of thing continued as our advance proceeded. But now at length protests from 14th Army at their ignorance of the activities of Force 136 led to the establishment of closer liaison and control.

In February, Force 136, making plans for the extensive arming of members of the AFO Civil Affairs, protested on the ground that the organisation was an extremist group with communist affinities, and that to encourage it now by asking for its assistance would lead to political difficulties after the war was over; an armed left wing would imperil the security of the country. General Leese, Commander-in-Chief of the Allied Land Forces, South-East Asia (ALFSEA) – the successor to 11th Army Group – upheld the Civil Affairs objection and ordered that no further arms should be supplied to the underground movement. But Force 136 appealed to Admiral Mountbatten, who reversed the ruling. His view was not only that no offer of assistance against the Japanese should be rejected, but that, with Kachin, Karen and other tribes already armed as guerrillas, a refusal to accept similar help from the Burmese might ultimately lead to his having to divert his troops to suppress the Burma National Army. He ordered, however, that arms were to be issued only to specified individuals for specific operations; they were not to be issued to the AFO as an organisation. This ruling, however, proved impossible to enforce.

As soon as I started to work in Myohaung, I met members of these Force 136 guerrillas. Before the reoccupation of the district a dossier had been compiled of known criminals and collaborators. By this time we knew that many of these people would turn up as our gallant allies of the resistance, and we had been instructed that no action should be taken against any of them save for specific offences against other persons. Force 136 had undertaken to supply Civil Affairs with a list of the local members of the 'Patriotic Front', as they were called, so that he could ensure that the amnesty was not extended to those who were not entitled to it. But it seemed that Force 136 had no authoritative list of their own; they apparently had to rely on the local leaders to produce lists of their men, and there was of course nothing to prevent these leaders from including certain wanted men who had never taken part in the activities of the 'Patriotic Front'.

We were perturbed by the amount of arms and explosives left in the area. Besides those issued by Force 136, there were those which had been abandoned by the Japanese in their retreat. Our troops too, when they moved on, had left a house in Myohaung full of ammunition; I had to place a police guard on it for about a month till the Army made arrangements for some of the ammunition to be removed and the rest destroyed. Japanese bombs had been left lying about the town, and there were also some Allied bombs which had failed to explode when dropped. I asked for a bomb disposal squad, who spent about ten days in Myohaung and exploded all the bombs that they could find. From time to time a villager would be brought to our hospital who had picked up something which proved to be a grenade and had had part of his hand blown off.

The Inspector and I toured our charge as much as we could. Our only permanent transport was a sampan, rowed by a man employed by the police, and our tours were naturally restricted in range, for we could not be away too long from our headquarters. Occasionally, however, we had the use of a tug sent from Akyab for our longer tours. Our main objects as we went round the villages were to assure the people that the Japanese had gone for good and the British administration was back, to call on all persons in possession of firearms to bring them in for licensing, and to ask for the villagers' co-operation with the police in reporting the presence and movements of dacoit gangs. For there were frequent reports of the presence of armed gangs from various parts of our jurisdiction; some were former members of the 'Patriotic Front' or persons who had been closely connected with them; others no doubt were criminals pure and simple, taking advantage of the unsettled condition of the countryside and their possession of firearms. Meanwhile it was necessary to re-establish the village administration on a formal basis. Where the pre-war headman was still available and willing to carry on, he was reappointed. In other cases the headman appointed under the Ba Maw administration was confirmed, provided that nothing serious was known against him. As was but natural the personal enemies of this latter group of headmen would come and say how they had collaborated with the Japanese and oppressed the villagers, but, unless some specific crime was alleged – and I do not remember that it ever was – I normally refused to investigate the matter. I had no doubt that the majority of the headmen had done their best in difficult circumstances and had sometimes had no choice but to assist the Japanese; and I could not see that any useful purpose would be served by my dismissing all those who had been appointed by the puppet Burmese administration.

One of my early tours took me to two villages somewhat removed from the main waterways to which many of the Arakanese gentry had withdrawn at the time of the Japanese invasion. They had remained in these secluded villages throughout the occupation and were, I think, genuinely glad to see us back. The educated Arakanese had always mixed socially with the European much more easily than the Burman did, and these men were government officials, serving or retired, and prominent business men. These little communities made such arrangements as they could to welcome me and to celebrate the arrival of the first British official since our evacuation. I was invited to meals in their houses, and one evening a Burmese *pwè* was organised. The people were really out to enjoy themselves, and one of the items in the *pwè* was a song composed in my honour.

Life in Myohaung returned gradually to normal. The townsfolk were eager to come back and rebuild their houses. I would not permit them to do so till I had obtained adequate information as to land rights, for I did not want to let a man build his house on a plot of land, only to find that someone else claimed the land. I was able to re-engage the former Myohaung revenue surveyor, and he produced a plan of the pre-war layout showing the owners of each plot. Building was further delayed by the difficulty experienced in obtaining materials, but little by little houses began to rise – of semi-permanent construction with timber floors and walls of bamboo matting – and Myohaung again wore the appearance of an inhabited town.

I inspected all the historic pagodas to find out what repairs, if any, were needed. One of the smaller ones had collapsed on one side, but most of them required only to be cleared of grass and scrub. No maintenance had been carried out since the Japanese invasion, and I thought that, for both archaeological and political reasons, it would be a good move to pay for the pagodas to be cleared. I obtained permission to do this, and the local people turned up willingly to work; they even agreed to give one day's labour free. When we had finished the pagodas, we started clearing the site of the old palace-city and the walls. Before the war a collection of old stone inscriptions had been housed in a small building near the government offices. These I found lying scattered, some with pieces broken off. I was fortunately able to find the former caretaker who, to my surprise, produced from memory a diagram showing where each stone had stood, and could tell me exactly how many were missing. In fact very few were lost, and I had the stones collected and set up in a temporary shed until such time as an archaeological expert could come and examine them.

It was now March. The 14th Army advancing southwards had crossed the Irrawaddy and taken Meiktila and was now preparing for the assault on Mandalay, whose capture would complete the reconquest of Upper Burma. Meanwhile contacts with the under-ground movement had been intensified, prominent among the members of the latter being Thakin Than Tun, a minister in the Ba Maw administration. Early in March news was received that on the 16th the Burma National Army would leave Rangoon for the Ir-rawaddy front, ostensibly to fight with the Japanese against the Allied troops, but that in fact the Burmese troops would come over to the Allied side. The rising took place on the 27th March.

Admiral Mountbatten had had to consider what attitude he should adopt towards the Burma National Army. Should he accept their co-operation and give them full recognition and support, or should he decline their assistance on the ground that they were disreputable and extremist elements, lacking the support of the majority of their own people, and moreover many of them guilty of criminal acts and of treason towards the legitimate government? His military com-manders considered that the rising of the Burma National Army should be supported on operational grounds; on political grounds the Chief Civil Affairs Officer pointed out the dangers of such a course and the offence which it would give to the more respectable elements of the population. Mountbatten put both views before the Chiefs of Staff, recommending that the rising should be supported, and the Chiefs of Staff referred the problem to the India Committee of the War Cabinet. On the 20th March this Committee approved Mountbatten's recommendation, but emphasised that no undue pub-licity must be given to the part played by the Burma National Army; that its leaders must not be allowed to consider their contribution of great importance; that they must be warned that they had much to do to atone for their past collaboration with the Japanese; and that no grounds should be given to them for thinking that they would have any claim to political control or concessions after the return of the Civil Government.

The help of the Burma National Army was accordingly accepted, and overnight the term 'BTA' (Burma Traitor Army) in military communiqués was changed to 'PBF' (Patriotic Burmese Forces)! I think it is important to stress that the views taken by most of us officers in the field were coloured by two fundamental misconcep-tions. In the first place, many of us were not aware that the rising of the Burma National Army against the Japanese had been planned long ago; we assumed that it was the certainty that the Japanese were now defeated that had caused the Burmese forces to desert them for the winning side. And secondly neither we nor, for that matter, anyone else either in the Civil Affairs Service or in the emigré Government of Burma realised how large a measure of popular support was commanded by the supposedly left-wing and unrepresentative elements which had combined to form the Anti-Fascist Organisation – or Anti-Fascist People's Freedom League (AFPFL), as it now began to call itself.

In Myohaung the maintenance of law and order was still a matter giving us considerable concern. The air was full of rumours of armed gangs, some merely criminals, others (as I have said) members of the guerrilla groups which had been employed by Force 136. The monk U Pyinnyathiha, who has already been mentioned, had been the head of the underground movement which called itself the 'Arakan Defence Force'. After the reoccupation of Akyab District Force 136 arranged for him and his principal lieutenant Kra Hla Aung to be taken to India for a holiday and as a reward for their services. The headquarters of U Pyinnyathiha's secret organisation had been a little village in my area called Pyade, which I always found a most unfriendly place, in marked contrast to the other villages. Though most of the headmen had hastened to report themselves when the administration was re-established in Myohaung, neither the pre-war headman of Pyade nor the headmen appointed by the Ba Maw Government had done so. On my first visit to the village, I asked to see them but, though I waited for two hours, neither appeared. There was an air of aloofness – almost of hostility – about the whole village and hardly anyone came to speak to me.

In the latter half of March arrangements were made by our headquarters in Akyab for a wing of the Royal Air Force Regiment to tour the more disturbed areas of the district with the object of rounding up wanted persons and searching villages for hidden firearms. It consisted entirely of British troops, who spent a little over three weeks with me. For most of that time I accompanied them, explaining to the villagers that we had not come to give them any trouble, but to search for arms so that criminally-minded persons might not get hold of them. We visited a very large number of villages and searched many houses. The material results of this operation were but meagre: a few arms and explosives and some other military stores were recovered, but, so far as I can recall, no wanted men. But I think that the moral effect of British troops marching through the countryside was very beneficial. Though none of them spoke the local language, they succeeded in the British soldier's inimitable manner in cultivating friendly relations with the people. In one place the villagers arranged a *pwè* for them, and they were delighted with a young Arakanese boy who got up and sang an English song, 'Pistol-packing Momma'. Sometimes, if the patrol party was not too large, the people would arrange a curry meal for us when we arrived for a halt in a village. But the highlight of the operation was when we were returning by tug from our last trip and landed to have our lunch in a village. It was the time of the Burmese New Year, when it is customary for people to throw water at each other. The festival had, I understood, been little observed during the Japanese occupation when – as they used to tell me – they felt in no mood to be gay, and now the villagers were determined to have a real New Year again. Our troops joined in the fun and caused much hilarity. They ended by distributing a good deal of their surplus rations in the village and, as our tug moved off, the whole of the usually undemonstrative Arakanese population lined the banks and cheered.

While the RAF Regiment was in the area, poor Burman, who was in command of the Tripura Rifles, died. So far as we could make out, his death was due to hydrophobia. He passed on his last requests to me, and I conveyed them in a letter to the Maharaja. Shortly afterwards the Tripuras were replaced by a company of Gurkhas of the Burma Regiment; company headquarters and one platoon were stationed in Myohaung.

It was now two months or more since U Pyinnyathiha and Kra Hla Aung had been taken to Calcutta, and the rumour was gaining currency among their followers that they had in fact been detained there and would not be allowed to come back. Reports came in that Kra Ni Aung, the brother of Kra Hla Aung, was planning a revolt; arms, it was said, were being collected by former members of the 'Arakan Defence Force' with a view to a rising at Pyade before the end of April. On the day after my return to Myohaung after my tour with the RAF Regiment I received a message from the officer in charge of a small police outpost to the effect that there were armed men in uniform in the neighbourhood and that he feared an attack. Fortunately a motor launch had arrived that afternoon from Akyab bringing a new doctor, so I took a section of Gurkhas to the outpost and left them there. In the event nothing happened. A few days later I heard that another group of armed and uniformed men under Kra Ni Aung was at a village a few miles north of Myohaung. I sent some troops, but they reported that the villagers were unwilling to speak. So I went myself and entered the village at dawn. One or two of the villagers, who were said to have taken a leading part in entertaining the gang, were not to be found, but I called the others together and warned them that their village would be burned if the gang continued in the area and information was not at once given to me. I left a Gurkha section to stay there for about a week in the hope that they might capture some of the gang.

On the 1st May I went down to Pyade, the reported centre of the rebellion. I found it just as unfriendly as ever and was about to leave when, by an extraordinary coincidence, U Pyinnyathiha and Kra Hla Aung arrived, having just returned from Calcutta. Seeing a British officer, the monk came towards me with his hands outstretched and muttered a welcome in broken English. When he learned who I was and that I could speak his language, we sat down and had a long talk. I told him that his followers were reported to be organising a rising because they thought that he was being kept in Calcutta; that I wanted him to send messages to them at once to say that he was back and that their preparations must be stopped; and that I then looked to him for assistance in bringing in all the arms that were in their possession. He gave the appearance of being friendly and ready to co-operate, and I think he was genuinely surprised to learn what Kra Ni Aung and his men had been doing.

A few days later Nyo Tun and Kra Hla Aung came to my office. I have mentioned Nyo Tun previously as an early member of the resistance movement who had twice during the Japanese occupation of Burma made his way into India with information. He was an educated man, unlike U Pyinnyathiha and Kra Hla Aung, quite young and spoke good English, and I liked what little I saw of him. He and Kra Hla Aung said they were trying to gather in all the arms and to hand over to me the wanted men in the gangs; meanwhile they asked that we should not yet start making arrests. It was difficult to know how far they were to be trusted, but the question proved to be of merely academic interest to me, for a few days later I was no longer in Myohaung.

During April I had been promoted to be a Deputy SCAO with the rank of Major, and John McTurk, who was now SCAO, had told me that he would like me to come to Akyab to assist him. Towards the end of April my successor arrived. Having introduced him to the routine work of the office and taken him on two short tours, I prepared to depart. Before I left two important events happened in the war. The troops of 14th Army had been advancing at speed into Lower Burma in order to reach Rangoon before the rains broke. They were forestalled by 15th Corps, which mounted a seaborne attack from Arakan. It was my old division (26th Indian Division) which landed in the Rangoon River on the 2nd May, and entered the city on the following day, to find that the Japanese had already withdrawn. And three days before I was due to leave Myohaung

news came of the surrender of Germany, followed the next day by
the announcement of the end of the war in Europe. On my last night
I gave a dinner party, to which were invited the officers of the station
and a number of prominent unofficial Arakanese guests to whom
hurried invitations had been sent. This party served the dual purpose
of celebrating the defeat of Germany and my departure from the
old capital, which I had seen built for the second time, and of which
I felt that I might with some justification claim to have been the
second founder. I left for Akyab the next day, and returned to
Myohaung only once a few weeks later to complete the trial of some
criminal cases which I had left unfinished.

The town of Akyab had suffered severely from Allied air raids.
There were no civilians living in it now, and the few habitable
buildings were occupied by military units. The Civil Affairs headquarters was some six miles away at a place called Narigan, where
a large camp had been built. Most of the buildings were bamboo
huts, but it was by no means uncomfortable.

After the recapture of Rangoon, General Pearce, the CCAO, had
urged upon Admiral Mountbatten the desirability of declaring the
AFPFL and its army illegal, and of arresting Aung San and bringing
him to trial for treason. This attitude was fundamentally opposed
to Mountbatten's own, and on the 10th May he replaced Pearce by
General Rance, a military officer with no knowledge as yet of Burma
and the Burmese, but who was later to become – as Sir Hubert Rance
– the last Governor of Burma. Pearce took Rance round the Civil
Affairs stations, and they came to us a few days after my arrival in
Narigan, accompanied by Air Marshal Sir Philip Joubert de la Ferté,
who was the Deputy Chief of Staff for Information and Civil Affairs
at Mountbatten's headquarters. They had dinner in our mess and
just after we started a great gecko or house lizard – in Burma called
a tuctoo – dropped from the roof and landed with a resounding
smack in front of Rance's soup. These creatures were often a foot
long or more, and I think Rance had only recently arrived in the
East and had never seen one before. His reaction may well be
imagined.

Three days later (17th May) the British Government published a
White Paper in which it declared its future policy towards Burma.
Ever since he had left the country the Governor had been urging on
the British Government the importance of making a clear pronouncement on Burma's future after the war. Both he and the British
Government accepted the fact that there would have to be a period
of direct rule by the Governor, without either a Council of Ministers
or a Legislature, while the plans for reconstruction were put into

operation. Dorman-Smith suggested that this period might last for five to seven years; at the end of this time a free parliament would be elected and Burma would be handed over to the Burmese a prosperous country again. But the Cabinet, engrossed in the war, refused to consider the matter and to fix a time limit to the period of the Governor's direct rule. In December 1944, a group of young Conservative Members of Parliament published a 'Blue Print for Burma', in which they proposed that the Governor should exercise direct rule for six years, during which period he should not only restore the country to its former condition, but should also draw up a new constitution for an independent Burma with Dominion status. The Blue Print was debated in the Commons, but the Government would not yet declare its policy. Now, however, it was announced that the period of direct rule by the Governor would last for three years; elections would then be had, and the Burmese would put forward their own proposals for a form of constitution which would give them full self-government within the Commonwealth. This meant a considerable reduction in the period of direct rule previously envisaged, but it was unfortunate that the British Government gave no indication of the length of the second stage and of the target date for the achievement of full self-government, and it soon became evident that the terms of the White Paper were unlikely to commend themselves to the AFPFL.

For on the previous day (16th May) General Aung San had arrived by invitation at General Slim's headquarters. This young man of thirty began by informing the commander of the victorious 14th Army that he came as the representative of the Provisional Government of Burma, which had been established by the people of Burma through the AFPFL. He said that, as commander of that government's national army, he was prepared to co-operate with the British, provided that he was recognised as, and accorded the status of, an Allied commander. Slim replied that, so far as he was concerned, there was only one Government of Burma, which was His Majesty's Government, now acting through the Supreme Allied Commander, South-East Asia; he could defeat the Japanese without the assistance of Aung San's forces; and, if he accepted their offer of help, it was on the clear understanding that this implied no recognition of any provisional government, and that Aung San would be regarded merely as a subordinate commander who would obey the orders of Slim or of any other British commander under whom they were placed. He also took the opportunity to point out to Aung San that he was liable to be brought to trial for his past actions. At a subsequent interview, when Slim told him that after the war the old regular Burma Army would be revived, Aung San asked that his forces should be incorporated as units in the new army; Slim gave him no reason to hope that this might be agreed, though he said that suitable individuals might well be accepted for enlistment. How would the leaders of the provisional government of what they claimed to be a sovereign and independent Burma view the British Government's proposal that a British Governor should rule their country for three years without a parliament, after which an unspecified period would elapse before Burma would govern herself? It should also be noted that the proposals outlined in the White Paper were not to apply to the hill areas inhabited by the Chins, Kachins, Shans and Karens unless these people specifically expressed a desire to become merged with Burma proper.

My first task in Narigan was to dispose of the arrears of routine office work which had accumulated as a result of the preoccupation of the senior officers with establishing law and order. For example, all criminal cases tried by a subordinate magistrate had to be reviewed by the SCAO or his deputy. This was very necessary, for some of the persons appointed to be magistrates in the Military Administration had never exercised magisterial powers before. I found that of some three hundred cases tried since the beginning of the year only about fifty had been duly reviewed, and I set to work to dispose of the rest. I then turned to financial matters. All civilian employees of the Civil Affairs Service were issued with what was known as a pay/pension book. These books were also to be issued to Burma Government servants and pensioners who had not been re-employed when they applied for arrears of pay or pension; thereafter they would come in monthly for payment. But before any arrears could be paid – they were limited to three months in the first instance – and books issued, a board of inquiry appointed locally had to record a finding that the conduct of the applicants during the period of the enemy occupation had been fit and proper. This work was also in arrears. Other routine office work consisted in arranging for the regular despatch of rations and stores to our outstations, periodically checking the cash balance in the Treasury, and occasionally trying criminal cases.

The rains began soon after I left Myohaung. Our main centres could in any case be reached only by water, and we continued to pay them frequent visits. John McTurk and I generally took it in turns to go on tour. Once I went back to my old stamping-ground of 1944 – Bawli and Kappagaung – and found it greatly changed. In place of military camps and dusty roads there were now thriving villages and green paddy fields. The area was still completely

Chittagonian, but the people had a pretty good idea that it could not be long before the Arakanese refugees were allowed back. One of the Muslim Township Officers assured me, in the course of this tour, that a promise had been given in 1943 by one of our earliest Civil Affairs Officers that North Arakan would remain exclusively Muslim for ever. Since, as I have explained, large parts had been predominantly Arakanese Buddhist before the war, it was inconceivable to me that any such promise could have been given. The claim smacked a little too much of Mr Mohammed Ali Jinnah, whose map of the future state of Pakistan was said to have included north Arakan. Before I left Arakan we were making preliminary plans for resettling the Arakanese in the north.

On my last tour I tried my first and last murder case. I had been invested with the powers of a Special Judge, which meant that I could try almost any case. A young Arakanese was accused of murdering his wife. He admitted doing so, and said that he had killed her because she had committed adultery with a Japanese soldier. He gave his evidence in a perfectly straightforward manner and I accepted it as true. I could do no other, as the law stood, than find him guilty of murder, for which there were but two penalties, death or transportation for life (which in practice meant imprisonment for twenty years). I sentenced him to the latter, but would gladly have given him a lesser sentence, had I been able to do so.

Meanwhile negotiations had been going on between our military leaders and Aung San about the future of the Burma National Army, now officially known as the Patriotic Burmese Forces. After much discussion and a good deal of misunderstanding, it was agreed that its personnel should proceed to centres where they would hand in their arms and be paid off and disbanded. Those who wished could register for enlistment into the regular Burma Army and would be accepted if they were found medically fit. Disbandment and registration began at the end of June, and continued for the rest of the year, by which time 8,324 members of the Patriotic Burmese Forces had passed through the centres, of whom 4,763 had applied for enrolment in the Burma Army. Of the 3,500 who did not apply many appeared before long as members of the People's Volunteer Organisation (PVO), which I shall have occasion to mention in subsequent chapters. Some 14,000 weapons of all kinds were handed in, but I think no one was under any delusion but that a very large number had not been surrendered.

The views of Mountbatten on the one hand, and of the Government of Burma and the senior officers of the Civil Affairs Service on the other, on the attitude which should be adopted towards Aung

San and his colleagues were entirely different. Immediately after Aung San's meeting with Slim, Mountbatten asked the Governor if Aung San might be told that, on the restoration of Civil Government, the Governor would consider including representatives of the AFPFL in his advisory council. Dorman-Smith did not wish to commit himself at this stage and refused to associate himself with any such undertaking. Mountbatten took the view that with proper handling Aung San might prove to be another Smuts or Botha; his policy was to treat him with respect and to offer him full co-operation. The Burma Government and Mountbatten's Civil Affairs advisers adhered to the argument that the AFPFL leaders were extremists who did not represent the Burmese people, and that to cultivate them now would have unfortunate repercussions after the return of the Civil Government. In July Mountbatten called to Rangoon the senior officers of the Civil Affairs Service, told them that it was his policy to work with Aung San and the AFPFL leaders, and directed them to conform to his policy. Aung San was offered an appointment as a Deputy Inspector-General in the Burma Army, but declined it on the ground that his colleagues in the AFPFL wished him to give up his military career and enter politics.

At the end of the first week in August the Americans dropped their atom bombs on Hiroshima and Nagasaki, and the Japanese made their offer of surrender. On the 15th August they accepted the Allied terms and the war in Asia was at an end. It took some days, however, before the local Japanese command received its instructions and acted on them. We celebrated the end of the war with parties and sports, and decided that henceforth Sunday should be an office holiday; up to this time we had all worked a seven-day week.

A few days later John McTurk departed for India on a month's leave, and I took over the district in his absence. A week later instructions came that I was to report to Rangoon for posting as a SCAO. The Deputy CCAO in Arakan – who was now virtually the equivalent of the peace-time Commissioner – said that he could not release me till McTurk's return. The issue was postponed for another ten days, when orders came that I was required immediately for posting to a new area. I found that there were now no regular air services operated by the RAF between Akyab and Rangoon, though there was occasionally an aircraft making the journey. I spent another week in trying to find some means of reaching Rangoon direct either by air or by sea, till it finally became clear that I should have to fly to Calcutta and make my way thence. These delays enabled me to postpone my departure till the day after McTurk's return, and on the 16th September 1945, I boarded a RAF transport plane with my servant Tun Che and such kit as I was permitted to take, and said farewell to North Arakan.

CHAPTER TWELVE

Return to the Delta

1945-46

THE GRAND HOTEL, Calcutta, to which I went, had now been taken over by the Army, and I found numbers of officers who had been waiting there for weeks in the hope of obtaining transport to Rangoon. The only people who could get passages almost at once were those who had volunteered for service with the organisation known as RAPWI (Relief of Allied Prisoners of War and Internees), who were urgently required. Enquiries through normal Army channels elicited the information that an air passage to Rangoon was out of the question without a very high priority, and that a ship was expected to sail about the end of September, for which some five hundred officers had already registered their names. I then approached our Civil Affairs supplies organisation, and was told that a ship would be leaving in about ten days for Rangoon from Vizagapatam with Civil Affairs personnel, and that I could travel in this. I accordingly went south to Vizagapatam in Madras Province and spent nine hot and uncomfortable days living under canvas in a Civil Affairs transit camp, which was affectionately known as 'Belsen'. There was a fair number of British officers in the camp, but the bulk of the inmates were Indian civilians; there were about a thousand of them, of whom about eight hundred were going as dock labourers to work in the Port of Rangoon and nearly 150 were subordinates of the Prisons Department. I was detailed to take charge of the party, as I held the highest rank; I was now, as a SCAO designate, disguised as a Lieutenant-Colonel. The ship did not sail till the 1st October, and three days later we berthed in Rangoon.

The Syriam refinery installations had been knocked flat by air raids, but outwardly the city looked little changed; many of the buildings had, however, been completely stripped inside. I was accommodated in a Civil Affairs mess, where I heard the arrangements which had been made for the resumption of the administration of Burma by the Governor.

Here I must go back a few months. In June the Governor had, with the approval of the British Government, gone to Rangoon to meet Burmese leaders and explain the British intentions as set out in the White Paper. As it would not have been appropriate for a civil Governor to set foot in a country which was still under military government, the meeting took place on a British warship HMS *Cumberland* in the Rangoon River. Among those invited were not only the AFPFL leaders Aung San and Than Tun, but also representatives of the older political parties, including some who had been ministers before the war; and the former Premier Sir Paw Tun came with the Governor. Dorman-Smith made a speech in which he asked for co-operation, goodwill and trust. But in a private conversation with him Aung San and Than Tun made it clear that in their view, as soon as the Military Administration had come to an end, a National Provisional Government should be established.

In the same month the CCAO set up an advisory council of twenty-six members, which met fortnightly and served both to convey to him the general views of the Burmese and to channel their grievances and criticism. It was representative of all shades of opinion and of all communities, and the intention was that its establishment should lead towards the creation of an Executive Council, which was envisaged by the White Paper.

In July planning began for the gradual handing over of the administration of Burma to the Civil Government. But the work of the planners was overtaken by the unexpected surrender of the Japanese in August. It was decided that the whole of Burma except the Tenasserim Division should be transferred as soon as possible after the 1st October; Tenasserim was to follow at the end of the year. Certain departments were handed over at later dates, the last being the Civil Affairs Supplies Department, which remained under military control until the end of March 1946.

I was told in Rangoon that the Governor was expected to arrive on the 16th October to resume the administration. I reported at the Civil Affairs headquarters and was informed that my destination had been Mergui; owing to my delay in reaching Rangoon, however, someone else had been sent there, and it was now proposed to post me to the charge of Bassein District in place of George Cockburn. I had suspected that I might be intended for Mergui; though in many ways it might have been more interesting than Bassein, I should not much have relished returning to the district from which I had made such an ignominious escape in 1942. Bassein I knew pretty well, and was pleased to be going back.

I spent a few days in Rangoon awaiting transport, and lost no time in visiting my old friend Ohn Maung, whom I had not seen since the Far Eastern war began. He had remained in Burma, but had withdrawn with his family to a village and had not accepted employment under the Ba Maw Administration. A few months earlier I had managed to get in touch with him by letter, after the reoccupation of the area in which he was then living. I was glad to find him looking well. His wife Ma Thein Kywe had just given birth to a third and last son and, as he did not at present wish to move his family from Rangoon, he had not asked for employment under the Military Administration.

I have referred earlier to the fact that, before any former government servant or pensioner could be placed on the payroll, a finding had to be recorded to the effect that his conduct during the Japanese occupation had been loyal and proper. In the case of lower-ranking staff, an informal board was convened locally and, if nothing was known against them, they could be employed or at all events paid. In the case of officers of the superior services, however, a formal inquiry was necessary. This procedure did our cause no good. The reason for it was obvious: both the loyal members of the services and the public in general would have resented the employment by the Military Administration of public servants who had been collaborators. But what were the feelings of the senior Burmese officers, who had stayed to administer their country when their British colleagues had fled and who had discharged their duties to the best of their ability, when they were told by the returning British that they could not be offered employment until inquiries had been made to ascertain that their behaviour had been loyal and proper? And meanwhile the nationalist leaders of the AFPFL, who had certainly been guilty of collaboration with the Japanese, were treated with honour and respect.

George Cockburn had left Bassein before I arrived, and I met him in Rangoon and had a long talk about conditions in the district. In due course I left on an old steam-tug which was towing a number of flats. The journey took three days, as against some fourteen hours in peacetime, and we reached Bassein after dark on the 11th October. I was given a great welcome from the Burmese officers and some of the townsfolk whom I had known before, and most of my first day in the office was occupied in receiving visitors. Among the first was the monk U Narada of the Anti-Crime Association.

It was a pleasant change after North Arakan to find all the government buildings, both offices and houses, intact. One section of the town had suffered from air raids and two of the big schools had been destroyed, but apart from this Bassein looked much as it had done before the war. The Civil Affairs officers were occupying rooms in two houses, one of which – the old Commissioner's bungalow –

was also used as a mess. The government houses at Kanthonsint near the golf course and the lakes were being used by the troops, a battalion of the Karen Rifles under Burmese-speaking British officers.

I had barely settled into my new job when the Civil Government resumed the administration, and on the 16th October I reverted to the civil designation of Deputy Commissioner, and ceased to be a military officer. On that day the Governor, with the two Burmese Ministers who had accompanied him to India and senior officers of the Civil Service, landed in Rangoon, and on the following day he was given a civic reception at the City Hall. He read a message from the King, in which Burma was promised self-government within the Commonwealth as soon as this could be arranged after elections had been held. In his own speech he explained the policy laid down in the White Paper, and emphasised that the British were not coming back to Burma with the same old ideas; they had learned from the experiences of the war.

This is perhaps a convenient place at which to pause and examine the economic condition of Burma at the time of the restoration of the Civil Government. Before the war Burma had exported a small number of raw and semi-finished products, principally rice, timber, petroleum and other minerals. Her imports included a great variety of manufactured goods and machinery, but to the ordinary Burman the most important of these were cloth goods. Most of the external trade was in the hands of Europeans and Indians, and four-fifths of it passed through Rangoon. So far as internal trade was concerned, Upper Burma, which did not grow sufficient rice for its own consumption, was dependent on Lower Burma for this staple element in its diet. Conversely, Lower Burma relied on Upper Burma for its cooking oil in the form of sessamum, groundnut or coconut oil. Before the war an excellent inland water transport system had been developed, as well as railways and roads.

But the Japanese occupation completely wrecked the country's economic system. Great damage was done to most of the towns by air raids. British denial measures and Allied bombing destroyed oil refineries and pipe-lines, mining equipment and river transport, and kept the railways virtually out of action. Internal transport stopped save for the movement of Japanese troops. The traditional external markets (Britain and India) were lost, and the majority of the big non-Burmese traders had left the country. Though the Japanese exported small quantities of minerals – lead, zinc, tin and tungsten – the export of rice virtually ceased, through their failure to take the surplus crop. They are said to have exported a mere 300,000 tons annually as against the pre-war figure of some 3½ million tons. The natural result was that the Lower Burma farmers grew little more rice than was required for local consumption, and the breakdown of the internal transport system meant that the dry zone of Upper Burma suffered a serious shortage. It is estimated that the paddy crop amounted to about 3 million tons a year against the pre-war figure of 6 to 7 million tons. At the same time, transport difficulties prevented Lower Burma from obtaining its requirements of cooking oil from the dry zone. Not only did the Japanese fail to export the country's main products, but they did not import the most wanted consumer goods; they were unable to bring into Burma anything but the essential supplies for their forces.

'Both in internal transport and external trade, Burma was thrown back a century without warning or previous preparation' (Andrus, *Burmese Economic Life*). At the time of the British reoccupation there was a shortage of rice in Upper Burma, while Lower Burma had only about one-third of its normal surplus. This does not mean, however, that the average Burman was starving. Most people had sufficient food of a simple kind, but it lacked variety and many suffered from an unbalanced diet. Housing presented no difficulty, for bamboos were easily obtainable. But the most serious lack was clothing, and other imported commodities were practically unobtainable.

Bassein had always been a rice-exporting district. Now the bulk of the surplus paddy available was what remained from the 1941–42 harvest, the last before the Japanese occupation. The Burman turned up his nose at this old and rather smelly paddy, but the health experts pronounced it fit for human consumption, and much of it was exported direct from Bassein to feed the population of Malaya. There were also stocks of fresher paddy, which had been bought from the producers either by the Japanese or by the Ba Maw administration. These stocks of what we called 'booty paddy' were naturally taken over by us, but I found that our action in taking them caused considerable resentment. The producers complained that they had been virtually forced to sell at very much less than the true price, and that we should have handed the paddy back. Legally of course we were perfectly within our rights; politically it might have been wise to return it and repurchase it, but the need for rice to feed the starving peoples of South-East Asia and our other heavy financial commitments arising out of a war which was none of our making would have made such a course unjustified.

Cultivators' loans had already been issued by the Military Administration, and we had to do all that we could to persuade cultivators to plant more paddy. Government announced that it would grant a subsidy of so much per acre for every additional acre brought under the plough. But one of the main obstacles to increased cultivation was the shortage of plough cattle. Large numbers had been killed to feed both the Japanese troops and the civil population, and we had to place very severe restrictions on the slaughter of cattle for meat. Only if they were over a certain age or otherwise unfit for use in the fields might they be killed. I once spent two days bargaining with the Muslim community of Bassein about the minimum number of cattle which they would require to kill for their religious festival of Bakr-Id.

The distribution of essential commodities was a matter of great importance to the people. There was a unit of the Civil Affairs supplies organisation in the district, but I had to lay down the policy and to keep a close control over its activities, for applications or complaints were constantly coming in. Moreover, some of the staff employed had to be watched carefully, as the distribution offered a fruitful field for corruption, and at least two officers were removed at my instance. But for most of the time I had as my principal supplies officer Captain Ruttonsha, an Indian who had been born in Burma and who had run his own business in Rangoon before the war. He spoke excellent English, was not afraid of expressing his own opinions, and did his job most efficiently.

Distribution points were opened in the main centres. The aim was ultimately to replace them by authorised dealers, but the fact that goods were still rationed as between one village tract and another delayed the change. The principal commodities handled were sugar, milk, *longyis* and cloth, and of these the cloth goods were much the most sought after. During the Japanese occupation many men had been reduced to wearing pieces of sacking in place of *longyis*, and women had made themselves skirts of palm leaves sewn with fibre stripped from the leaves of banana trees.

In order to facilitate the transport of essential supplies to the northern part of the district, I persuaded the villagers living on the route to make a road which could be used by our trucks during the dry weather. This ran for most of its length across paddy fields, and construction work consisted mainly of cutting down small sections of the bunds dividing one field from another. In this way a road of some thirty miles was made, and it cost nothing. The villagers were prepared to give their labour free in the knowledge that supplies would come to them more regularly, and in fact the headmen were instructed to give priority in distribution of cloth to persons who had worked on the road. On the Bassein sector, where I went myself and made arrangements with the headmen, no complaint was raised, but an article appeared in the Burmese press which referred to work at the other end of the road and compared it with the forced labour exacted by the Japanese. It may well have been that my Burmese officers in the area were over-zealous and used something more than gentle persuasion.

In the course of my touring I generally carried some *longyis* for free issue to destitutes. These had been supplied by the Red Cross, and I asked the headmen in each village to send for the people who were really too poor to pay for them; they were generally the aged and infirm. I authorised my township officers to use their discretion in making free issues up to a maximum of five per cent of the inhabitants of a village. But in fact comparatively few real destitutes were to be found.

Immediately after his return the Governor prepared to appoint an Executive Council in accordance with the terms of the White Paper. He first decided that it should consist of fifteen members, but later reduced the number to eleven. His intention was that Sir Paw Tun should be the Home Member, that Sir Htoon Aung Gyaw (the other Minister who had gone with him to India) should deal with Finance as he had done before, and that two British Members should be responsible for Defence and the Frontier Areas. Since most of the other pre-war parties were now merged in the AFPFL, the Governor made it known that he was prepared to consider nominations from the League for the remaining seats on the Council. But the League demanded that all its nominees should be accepted or none; that it should decide which portfolios they were to hold, and that the Home portfolio must be one of these; and that all its members should report the Council's proceedings to the Supreme Council of the AFPFL and take orders from it. The Governor could not accept these terms – and he was supported by the British Government – and was consequently unable to invite any member of the AFPFL to serve on the Council. The attitude of the AFPFL was of course quite consistent with its claim to be the Provisional Government of Burma. The Governor appreciated by now that Aung San was the most important man in Burma, and that the AFPFL was far and away the most powerful political organisation. What he could not know without an election was the extent to which the old parties and the old leaders had become discredited; and there was of course a natural disinclination on the part both of the Governor and of the British Government to discard men like Sir Paw Tun, who had stood by them loyally for so long. Sir Paw Tun had, however, been out of touch with Burmese affairs during the crisis of Burma's history.

U Saw, who had been away even longer from the country, was allowed back early in 1946, but under instructions from the British Government was not offered a seat on the Council. Towards the end of 1945 the AFPFL announced its intention of sending a deputation to England for discussions; but the British Government made it clear that it would not receive such a deputation, since it would represent not the Burmese people but merely a single political group.

In Bassein District the AFPFL was the only political organisation with any following. As I have explained, the League was composed of a number of left-wing groups; these ranged from moderate socialist to extreme communist, and for the present they all remained within the League. The local Bassein President, Mya Sein, who represented the more moderate section of the AFPFL, was a graduate of Rangoon University, a young man with whom I was always on excellent terms and who was, I think, genuinely eager to help the people of the district and to co-operate with the Government officials; but towards the end of my time I heard that he was beginning to tire of politics. The League's communist element, however, seemed to be the most prominent, and its local secretary was Cho Hla Aung, son of one of my Subdivisional Officers U Aung Pe – a source of some embarrassment to his father. He was a sincere and intelligent youth with a great love of books, but he was a leper, and his ailment after a time made it advisable for him to take a rest from political life. His prospective successor was an overgrown schoolboy of limited intelligence. Another of this type – but of the socialist wing – came to the district and went round organising cultivators' meetings, at which he was reported to have advised his audience to pay no land revenue to Government or rents to their landlords. I warned him against doing this, but of course he denied that he had said anything of the sort.

There were widespread rumours that the 27th March 1946, the first anniversary of the rising of the Burma National Army against the Japanese, had been fixed for a rebellion against the Government. But the day passed with nothing more than an orderly procession in the town. From the time that the Civil Government was restored till independence was in sight, such reports were periodically passed to the districts by police intelligence in Rangoon.

It was while I was in Bassein that I first heard of the PVO (People's Volunteer Organisation). I mentioned it briefly in the last chapter as having had its origin in those members of the Burma National Army who did not enlist in the regular Burma Army. Its numbers had, however, been greatly increased by fresh recruits. The PVO was one of the principal constituents now of the AFPFL, and was in effect the League's private army, the successor of the Burma National Army. Many of its members had strong communist leanings, and the PVO and the Burma Socialist Party (BSP) tended to be uneasy bedfellows beneath the AFPFL blanket. The PVO generally dressed in a uniform of a sort, and had access to hidden stocks of arms; and, as will appear later, they pressed with a considerable degree of success for the Government to issue them with arms. Since some of their members had been prominent in the resistance movement, they were able to trade for a long time on their reputation for heroism. There were no doubt many perfectly sincere young men in the PVO, but many were thorough scoundrels who made use of their uniforms and arms to rob villages and waylay travellers. Later I was to find the PVO a real thorn in my flesh, but in Bassein I heard no more than casual references to their existence. In retrospect, I am inclined to regard Bassein as an oasis of comparative peace in my life between the disturbances of Akyab District and the general lawlessness of Pyapon, to which I was next posted.

For the administration of the district I had professional civil servants, with the exception of a few Assistant Township Officers, who had been engaged by the Military Administration and were retained temporarily by us. My two Subdivisional Officers were U Aung Pe in Bassein, an experienced and capable man whom I had known before the war, and U Mo Myit in Kyonpyaw. Mo Myit was a member of my own Service, who had done his training in Australia and arrived back in Burma just as the British were retreating. He remained in the country during the Japanese occupation and was employed by the British Military Administration. He was an active young fellow, who spoke excellent English and had a very Western outlook. His wife too spoke English – an unusual thing for a Burmese official's wife – and I used to stay with them when in Kyonpyaw; they had no children. I had one outstanding township officer, U Sein Maung, an unassuming young man who was one of the most level-headed and reliable officers who ever worked under me. I did all I could to get him promoted, but encountered the usual red-tape obstruction: he was a comparatively junior officer and could not be promoted over the heads of his seniors unless it could be demonstrated that they were not fit for promotion! U Sein Maung grew dispirited; he had been five or six years in charge of the same township and saw no prospect of advancement. He went on leave soon after I did and, when I last saw him, he was seriously considering leaving the government service.

My Commissioner was U Ka Si, whom I had last met in Tharrawaddy in 1942, when he was taking his census records to Upper

Burma. He was a good Commissioner to work under, clear-headed and hard-working, and could be relied upon for sound advice when it was needed. He later became the last Chief Secretary under the British Government and, as I have related earlier, the independent Government of Burma appointed him to be their Ambassador in London.

A post-war innovation in district administration was the establishment of an advisory committee composed of unofficials. In pre-war days Deputy Commissioners and their subordinate administrative officers had gone ahead and done what they thought was right and good for the people without giving much thought to the people's own views. Now it was accepted government policy that Deputy Commissioners should appoint advisory committees consisting of representative members of the public and should consult them at frequent intervals. They could be of considerable assistance, provided that the members accepted the fact that they were advisory only, and in Bassein I think they worked well. My committee represented all races and most shades of political opinion; we met once a fortnight, and there was a two-way exchange: the committee would express their views on any matter on which I sought their advice, and I would listen to their complaints, criticism and suggestions. I arranged for the establishment of similar committees in those of my subordinate headquarters where communications were fairly easy.

The government now ran a Public Relations Department, whose local representative had an information room in the town, where newspapers and photographs were displayed and a wireless set had been installed. This information room was very popular. Unfortunately the Department's allocation of funds was meagre in the extreme, and everything was done with an eye to economy: material was sent from Rangoon by private sampan or chance railway passenger to save postage or freight, and it sometimes arrived and sometimes did not. Our local man, who had been a schoolmaster, was very keen, but he was working entirely on his own, with little support or encouragement from his superiors in Rangoon.

As I have said, there was a large number of Karens in Bassein. The total population of the district at the time of the Japanese invasion was some 665,000; it was the third most heavily populated district in the country. Karens constituted about one-fifth of the residents, Burmese and allied groups rather over three-fifths. Communal disturbances had broken out in parts of the Delta between Burmans and Karens after the British withdrawal in 1942 and the Karens, being the weaker party, had generally come off worse, some frightful atrocities being committed. Bassein was almost untouched by this communal strife, though in one small area there had been trouble and one Burmese and several Karen villages had been burnt.

The veteran Karen leader Sir San C. Po was still alive, but he was growing too old to take any active part in the affairs of his community, and a Karen army officer, who was, I think, a relation of his, was setting himself up as the new leader. He had been employed in supplies work when I arrived in Bassein, and I had been largely instrumental in securing his recall to Rangoon. But a month or two later he was back with a new job, that of Custodian of Enemy Property for the area. He left all the work to his assistant, while he spent his time on tour, ostensibly searching for enemy property, but in fact doing propaganda work among the Karen villagers. He travelled on one occasion with a Karen missionary, who is alleged to have made insulting remarks about the Buddha and Buddhism. I duly reprimanded him for associating in missionary work of this nature and, when the Custodian's Department was transferred to the Civil Government, I hoped that he would be withdrawn. When I found that he was to stay, I reported to government that in my view it was a waste of public funds to employ this officer in other than a military capacity, and that I was willing to supervise the Custodian's Department myself. When I returned from leave at the end of the year, I found that he had been appointed a Minister of the Government! He later led a Karen rebellion against the independent Government of Burma.

The crime rate in Bassein was high, though I believe that the figures compared favourably with those in many other districts. During the open season detachments of armed police were posted in various areas, and they undoubtedly helped to prevent crime. Even so, dacoities numbered between thirty and forty a month. Hold-ups on the smaller creeks by armed gangs were frequent, and the villagers would persist in travelling in their sampans by night and taking short cuts, which was asking for trouble. Down in the south, certain Karen villages were suspected to be harbouring dacoits, and the inhabitants were presented with the usual warning that their houses would be burned if they continued to do so. No doubt they were more frightened of the dacoits than of the police. Village defence guns were issued from police stocks in an endeavour to protect law-abiding citizens from attack by gangsters.

U Narada reorganised his Anti-Crime Association, which now had its headquarters in Rangoon. Hall (the Superintendent of Police) and I had numerous discussions with him and, at his suggestion, one monk in the jurisdiction of each police station was nominated as the Association's representative and was given an appointment order signed by Hall and me. U Narada spent much of his time travelling and I cannot say that the results produced by his Association were at all remarkable. At first its activities seemed to be confined to complaints against headmen, but these were firmly discouraged.

Opium smoking had in the past been a source of minor crime. I have described how before the war the government ran shops at which opium was issued in rationed amounts to registered addicts. The theory was that an addict could not exist without opium, but that the supply must be rigidly controlled, and that an increase in the number of smokers must be prevented. The Military Administration had made no attempt to re-establish the opium shops, and it was with some astonishment that I received from the Civil Government orders to open them again. I argued that, as they had been closed for nearly four years, the addicts had either died or learned to do without the drug, and that it would be a most retrograde step to encourage its sale now. In this attitude I had the support of my advisory committee, and I wrote to government and protested. Ultimately the order was countermanded.

During November a brigade of 82nd West African Division moved into the district. After my experience as Civil Affairs Officer with the division, I looked forward to their coming with some apprehension, but fortunately they were mainly Gold Coast troops and they gave very little trouble. Rumours did indeed come to my ears to the effect that as soon as they arrived they went round the town looking for drink and women, but no formal complaint was ever lodged against them. On the contrary, the local prostitutes did a thriving business, and I was asked by the military authorities to try to prevent these women from appearing in the vicinity of their camps. There was a squatter village not far from the Deputy Commissioner's house, to which I had now moved; before the war, as Subdivisional Officer, I had started an inquiry into its origin with a view to getting it moved, but had not completed this before I was myself transferred. It lay alongside the golf course and was not far from some of the African camps. I found that prostitutes were in the habit of coming in the evenings from the town to this village to wait for African customers. I therefore told the titular headman to do what he could to discourage the use of his village by these women and to report to me if they continued to come. On my next visit there I found a large notice posted in Burmese: 'By order of the Deputy Commissioner no prostitute may enter this village'!

I was gratified to learn in the course of my tours that the troops were getting on very well with the local people. This friendliness went once to such an extreme that an African soldier and a Burmese girl presented themselves before me and requested permission to get married. I explained that this was not within my competence and that the soldier should approach his commanding officer. I did, however, do my utmost to dissuade them from marrying. The African could speak no Burmese and the girl had no English or African tongue, and how they managed to communicate their affection to each other was a mystery. The Burmese are the most insular of people, and I tried to make the girl realise what life would be like in the Gold Coast with probably not another Burmese speaker in the country. I believe that the result was that the man was quickly transferred.

I toured as much as possible, and so did Hall, the Superintendent of Police, both to find out what was happening and to show ourselves to the people and make it clear that the old administration had been restored. Most of the touring was by launch, though there were roads in the Kyonpyaw Subdivision, the northern part of the district. The quickest way to reach Kyonpyaw was by rail, but a bridge about half way had been demolished by bombing, and passengers had to trans-ship and walk along a footbridge. The section between Bassein and the bridge was covered by an ancient engine drawing a few goods waggons, in which we sat on chairs provided by the station master. On the other side of the bridge there was a better engine and a few passenger carriages. I used occasionally to carry sweets with me and hand them out to the children at halts along the line.

I travelled across the Arakan Yoma to the west coast, a tour which I had been unable to do before the war. This took about a week; I went with one of my assistant township officers, and took a quantity of Red Cross clothing for distribution. When we reached the coast, I was suffering so much from blisters on both feet that I had to travel from one village to the next in a cart drawn by two buffaloes; the track was extremely rough and the journey was most uncomfortable. We spent two nights at a delightful little place called Sinma. The village was built in a little cove, and the water's edge was fringed with coconut palms. Here my diet was somewhat varied by the gift of an octopus, which was cooked with my curry; its only taste was that of salt. For our return journey over the hills we rode on a couple of elephants sent for us by a wealthy Karen timber trader called U Shwe Hlaw, our kit being carried by porters. We travelled along forest paths, the gradient being sometimes so steep that I wondered whether the animals would maintain their foothold. But we arrived on the Bassein side without mishap and spent the night in U Shwe Hlaw's house, where some Karen singing was arranged.

My last tours were undertaken almost exclusively for the purpose of selling fishery leases. It was the practice for the Deputy Commissioner personally to auction these and even in normal times he had sometimes to exercise a restraining influence if he thought the bidding was going to a figure higher than the fishery was worth. Now, with the sudden fillip given to trade by the end of the war, the price of fish had soared, though it seemed likely that it would start to drop before very long. Moreover, the value of the new British currency was still finding its proper level. As a result, in nearly every case where there was competition the prices bid rose – or would have risen – far beyond what my advisers considered to be the economic value of the fishery. In most cases I stopped the bidding and leased the fishery to the previous year's lessee, provided that he had paid his rents in full. This could not have given much satisfaction to the unsuccessful bidders, but the alternative was probable ruin for the highest bidder and endless trouble to government officers in trying to extract the instalments of rent.

About a month before I left Bassein I attended an interesting ceremony in the town's principal pagoda, the Shwemoktaw. Shortly before the war a valuable jewel had been stolen from it, which had later been recovered in, I think, Madras. In addition, the *hti* (or umbrella) at the pagoda's top had collapsed either just before or during the Japanese occupation. The *hti*, which was in fact shaped something like an umbrella, was made of wrought iron and surmounted every pagoda; on it hung a mass of gold and silver bells and jewels which tinkled with every breeze. The trustees had now collected sufficient money for a new *hti* to be placed on the pagoda, and this was to be a great occasion. All the Burmese officers were to be present, and I too was invited, the invitation being conveyed with characteristic Burmese delicacy. It was the practice for Burmans to remove their footwear when going up to a pagoda. In the early days British officials had entered pagodas wearing shoes and no objection had been raised. In the 1920s, however, this became a political issue. The Burmese insisted that anyone visiting their pagodas should conform to the usual custom – on the face of it, a not unreasonable demand – and most Europeans thereafter kept away. (I once asked my friend Ohn Maung to take me up to the platform of the great Shwe Dagon Pagoda in Rangoon, but he said it would be so filthy – with dogs' droppings and so forth – that he was not particularly keen to go himself.) Now the pagoda trustees in Bassein sent a verbal message through U Aung Pe, the Subdivisional Officer, to the effect that they would like to invite me to the *hti*-raising ceremony; they did not, however, know my views on the shoe-wearing question and, if I was not prepared to remove my shoes in the pagoda precincts, I might find it embarrassing to have to refuse the invitation. They wished therefore to enquire whether I should like to be invited. I replied that I should be delighted to witness the ceremony and was formally invited.

The proceedings lasted for two days. On the first day I went up to the pagoda platform with two other European officials – the Commissioner's assistant and the Supplies Officer. U Tsoe Maung, the chairman of the trustees, showed us the golden *hti* and the weather-cock which would surmount it; they were to be hoisted into position the following day. We then moved on to visit the clerks' association, which was engaged in presenting gifts to the monks, an essential part of any religious occasion in Burma. I had received an invitation from the clerks too, but they probably did not really expect me to come, and they seemed delighted to see us. My office boys rushed forward with outstretched arms and wanted to seat me among the monks. I declined this honour, however, and sat among the Burmese Government officers, who were all there from the Commissioner downwards. In the evening we went up again to the pagoda platform and were entertained by the bazaar-sellers' association. There was a *pwè* in progress, the first of any size to be held in Bassein since the Japanese invasion, and we watched this for a time, and then strolled round the food stalls which were always erected on these occasions.

The next day was the big day, and I went along early to the pagoda platform. Again most of the Burmese officials were there. A wooden carriage had been built, which was to be hoisted to the summit of the pagoda on ropes in the manner of a cable railway. The *hti* was in three parts, one of iron, one of silver and one of gold; the lower portions (the iron and the silver) were already in position, and it remained to hoist the golden *hti*, the weather-cock and the *seinbu* (the spherical ornament surmounting the weather-cock). The principal officials were asked each to hold the golden *hti* for a few seconds, to give it what the Burmese call *tago*, which may be translated as 'power' or 'influence'. The Commissioner held it first, then it was passed to me, and so on down the line. The man who was to place it on the top of the pagoda then mounted the carriage, said a prayer and received the *hti* into his hands. We officers were asked to assist in the first few hauls on the ropes – again to give *tago* – and we then left the job to tougher men than we were. The carriage gradually rose into the air and started its slow journey to the top of the pagoda. It seemed to be a very long time before the *hti* was properly placed. Then the carriage was lowered and preparations were made to place the accessories above the *hti*. These were less important and we did not stay to watch them. A group photograph had been arranged for the Government officials, the pagoda trustees and the leading citizens; the Supplies Officer and I were the only Europeans in it, wearing our khaki bush shirts, while the Burmese officers were in Burmese costume. I still have the photograph.

I felt that this ceremony was the highlight of my time in Bassein, when I was really able to feel at one with the people and to share their religious observances and their enjoyment. And I think that many of them were genuinely pleased to see a British Government official associating himself with them in this way. A month later was the New Year festival, with the usual water-throwing. This was celebrated with greater gusto than I had ever yet encountered. When I went out into the town driving my jeep, I had to wear a waterproof. When they saw me coming, the people on the roadsides got ready their bowls and pails of water and hurled them. They thoroughly enjoyed themselves and so did I. In Rangoon this practice of throwing water at the drivers of cars during the festival frequently led to fatal accidents, but we had none in Bassein.

Though Bassein District was comparatively quiet, there was an undercurrent of unrest running through much of Lower Burma. Aung San and the AFPFL persisted in their refusal to join the Governor's Executive Council save on their own terms, and by numbers of incidents they sedulously fostered the fear that a rebellion was likely to break out at any moment. The senior officers of the Civil Service advised the Governor to arrest Aung San on the ground that his speeches at mass meetings were seditious; this, they thought, would have a sedative effect upon the unruly elements in the country. But it might well have the opposite effect and set off a national uprising. The British Government, busy demobilising its armed forces, would have been in no mood to send troops to Burma to suppress such a rising, and the Governor had been advised that public opinion in India would have been strongly opposed to the use of Indian troops for this purpose. The terms of the White Paper forbade him to accede to Aung San's demands, and the British Government's view was that elections must be held in order to make clear which party, if any, had a mandate to speak for the people of Burma.

The Governor appointed a Legislative Council, consisting of thirty-five non-officials nominated by him, and in the course of its first session, which began at the end of February, Thakin Tun Oke (who, it will be recalled, had been one of the Thirty, and had been placed by the Japanese in charge of the administration of Burma immediately after the British retreat) accused Aung San of murder during the Japanese invasion. The government could not ignore this public accusation, and the facts were transmitted to London. The Labour Government ordered Aung San's arrest, but countermanded the order before it had been executed. The Governor represented the impossibility of carrying on the administration in this state of suspense and unrest, and urged a review of the policy laid down in the White Paper.

I had now been in the tropics for seven and a half years and had renewed my application for home leave. It was approved in April. I was beginning to feel in need of leave. The last three years had been very strenuous, and a Deputy Commissioner's job was now far more arduous and exhausting than it had been before the war. He had responsibility for departments which had not existed before, such as the distribution of supplies. Added to this was the very considerable increase in lawlessness which had followed the Japanese occupation and the periodical rumours of rebellion which kept one always on the alert. Towards the end of April my successor's name was announced; he was a Burman. I was told that, if he had not arrived by the end of the month, I should hand over the district to my most senior officer and proceed to Rangoon. On the last night a farewell dinner party was held on the verandah of the District Office, at which some (myself included) sang Burmese songs.

A District Commissioner's house

I travelled with Ruttonsha, the former Supplies Officer, along our new supply route as far as Kyonpyaw, U Aung Pe accompanying us for part of the way. After that we were on a tarmac road and we spent the night at Henzada, the headquarters of the neighbouring district, which lay on the Irrawaddy. The following morning we were ferried over the river in an Army amphibious 'duck', had a short train journey to Letpadan, where the Japanese had nearly bombed me in 1942, and then obtained government transport to take us into Rangoon.

Ohn Maung had invited me to stay with him. I did not know how long I should have to wait in Rangoon. I was to sail in the *Reina del Pacifico*, then running as a troop ship, but her exact sailing date was as yet undetermined. In the event, I had over two weeks in Rangoon. I saw a fair amount of Ohn Maung's two elder boys, nice little youngsters who were just going to school. It was a mission school which insisted that all children should be given a Christian name. Ohn Maung's elder boy was called Tin Maung Thein, and the mission decreed that his surname was Maung, as this was his father's last name. Ohn Maung and I compiled a short list of Christian names, from which Tin Maung Thein was instructed to select one; he accordingly became transformed into Winston Maung.

I saw something of my Oxford friend Maung Wun, the poet, who, it will be recalled, was a lecturer at Rangoon University. He took me round the university and introduced me to Luce, the Professor of Oriental Languages and an expert on Burmese epigraphy, who was interested to learn the fate of the Myohaung inscriptions.

I had left in Calcutta a trunk containing such civilian clothing as I had acquired since my evacuation from Burma, and had written and asked for it to be sent to Rangoon. Alas, it reached the docks and was never seen again. Cloth was in such short supply that there was no possibility of my getting clothes made in Rangoon, and I boarded the *Reina del Pacifico* on the 19th May with practically nothing but khaki bush shirts and shorts and the minimum of essential underwear. The passengers were almost all members of the Services, and there was a mere handful of civilians, among them Freddy Wemyss, John McTurk and Hall, late Superintendent of Police in Bassein. The trip was not a particularly comfortable one: we were six in a cabin, the ship was 'dry', and we were not allowed to go ashore at Colombo. But in due course we landed at Liverpool on the 11th June 1946, and I was back in England after an absence of close on eight years.

CHAPTER THIRTEEN

Tribulations in Pyapon
1946-47

ON MY ARRIVAL IN England I called at the Burma Office, which was housed in the same building as the India Office. The Burma section was quite small, and a friendly reception awaited members of the Burma services when they came on leave. I had an interview with Sir Gilbert Laithwaite, the Permanent Under-Secretary, who gave me a cordial invitation to visit the office whenever I felt so inclined during my leave to find out the latest developments in Burma. I told him that many of us felt that there would be no stability until a date for Burma's independence was fixed. His reply was that Britain was bound to consider world opinion and her obligations to the United Nations; if Burma was given her independence before she was ready for it, a stick would be put into the hands of the Communist countries with which to beat the West. Since those days many countries far less prepared than Burma to govern themselves have been given their independence by the British Government.

In Burma the political deadlock continued; the Governor was summoned home for consultation, and he left Rangoon a few days after I reached England. About the end of July it was reported that he had resigned, and it became clear that his resignation was to herald a complete change in the British Government's policy towards Burma. It was a natural assumption that it was because Dorman-Smith felt himself out of sympathy with the new policy that he submitted his resignation. It later became known, however, that he had himself been urging a review of the policy stated in the White Paper of May 1945, and that he had suggested that it might smooth the way for the change if he resigned; he was in any case a sick man. Sir Hubert Rance (who, as Major-General Rance, had been head of the Military Administration in its latter days) was appointed to succeed Dorman-Smith. In the circumstances in which Burma now found herself this proved to be an excellent appointment. Rance had worked with Aung San during the Military Administration, and from all accounts they got on very well together. As Governor, it was said, Rance used to tell Aung San bluntly, as one soldier to another, just where he disagreed with him, and Aung San appreciated this.

In August and September there was a strike of government employees in Burma, which involved all the police in Rangoon, some of those in the districts and some of the clerical staff. Officers of the Civil Service and the Police who were on leave were warned that, in view of the very serious situation, they might be recalled to duty. I was in Stockholm with George Merrells when we received this news, but in the event our leave was not interrupted.

Rance's first task was to come to a settlement with Aung San. The Executive Council was dissolved and a new one appointed; Aung San was appointed Deputy President of the Council (the Governor being President) and Defence Member, while the Home portfolio went to Thakin Mya, one of the AFPFL leaders. Tin Tut, the most brilliant Burmese member of the Civil Service, who had accompanied U Saw to England before the Japanese entered the war, had recently retired from the Service, and he became Finance Member. U Saw himself had a seat, and most of the rest went to members of the League. Thus the demand made by Aung San after the re-establishment of the Civil Government in 1945 was conceded. And there was a significant change in the character of the Council: instead of being purely advisory to the Governor, it became in effect a Cabinet controlling policy. To all intents and purposes therefore Burma now had a Burmese Government with a British constitutional Governor, though legally the Governor could still in the last resort take over the government in order to maintain law and order.

A split now developed in the AFPFL between the left and the right wings, between, that is to say, those who were strictly Communists and those who were primarily nationalists. The extreme Communists, led by Thakin Soe, who formed the Communist Party (Burma) or CPB – and were more usually referred to as the Red Flag Communists – went into outright opposition to the AFPFL. Their activities became subversive and their organisation contained a considerable number of dacoits. The less extreme Communists belonged to the Burma Communist Party or BCP – known as the White Flag Communists – which, though parting company with the AFPFL, became a somewhat more conventional opposition. The Red Flag organisation was declared illegal in January 1947, while the White Flags remained within the pale of the law; the leaders of the latter were Thein Pe and Than Tun, who have already been mentioned in these pages. The major remaining constituents of the AFPFL were the Burma Socialist Party (BSP) and the People's Volunteer Organisation (PVO) which, as I have said before, had strong Communist leanings.

I had been granted eight months' leave from the date of my departure from Rangoon in May 1946, but leave in England immediately after the war, when rationing of food, clothing and petrol was in full force, with new cars virtually impossible to buy, and with the barely civil 'take it or leave it' attitude of some shopkeepers, soon outwore its novelty, and I often regretted that I had not had just one leave in those spacious pre-war days. In November therefore I began to plan my return to Burma. I was unable to obtain a sea passage, but the government agreed to my returning by air, and I left towards the middle of December, after just six months in England. Sir Gilbert Laithwaite travelled in the same aircraft on a mission to assure the Burmese leaders of the sincerity of British intentions towards Burma.

I had reason to believe that I might be posted to Moulmein as Deputy Commissioner, and was pleased at the prospect. But on reporting at the Secretariat I was told that there was bad news for me. I at once asked whether I was to go to Pyapon, and the answer was 'Yes'. Ever since the reoccupation Pyapon had had a bad name, both for its record of crime and for its constant threats of political trouble. My friends in the Secretariat commiserated with me on my appointment. I went to see the Chief Secretary, who was now U Ka Si, my late Commissioner, the first Burman ever to hold the post. Now that there was virtually a Burmese Government ruling the country, it was clearly wise to have an experienced Burmese officer in the chief executive post. I do not imagine that U Ka Si found the job an easy one, but he was of an equable temperament, which was what was needed at that time of one in his position.

I again stayed with Ohn Maung, and my servant Tun Che, who had remained in Bassein when I went on leave, rejoined me in Rangoon. I spent about a week there, during which I called on the Governor and discussed matters relating to my new district with various heads of departments. I was told that the government was about to declare an amnesty for members of the various armed gangs who were terrorising the country, and that they would be given a fixed period in which to surrender themselves and their arms at the office of the local Deputy Commissioner.

Pyapon was the most easterly district of the Irrawaddy Delta and the nearest to Rangoon. Its population was recorded in the 1941 census as 385,000, and it was therefore considerably smaller than Bassein. The vast majority of the people were Burmese, though there were about 21,000 Karens. The district was as flat as a pancake and consisted of acres and acres of paddy fields. Its only product of importance other than rice was fish, which was caught both on the sea coast and in the Delta creeks.

Before the war it was a peaceful little backwater, causing no trouble to the administration, but it was very different now. It consisted of two Subdivisions with headquarters at Pyapon and at Kyaiklat further north. There were township officers at each of these places and also at Bogale in the western part of the district and at Dedaye in the eastern part, nearest to Rangoon. During the Japanese occupation one Mya Hlaing, who was half Burmese and half Chinese, had wielded considerable power in the district; in the interregnum between the retreat of the Japanese and the establishment of the British Military Administration he had ruled Bogale, and acquired control of a large number of arms. He set himself up as the local leader of the Socialist Party, and made himself pleasant to the first post-occupation British authorities. They on their part, anxious to enlist the co-operation of political leaders with the government, naturally welcomed his advances and hoped that they were sincere. Meanwhile, believing that he had lulled the suspicions of the authorities, he was privately hiring out his firearms to criminals who wanted them for the commission of robberies and dacoities. The crime figures for Pyapon District in 1946 must have been the highest in Burma. Dacoities alone, mostly committed with firearms, averaged seventy to eighty a month; in Bassein, a much larger district, the figure had been thirty to forty, and I had considered that high.

Very little progress had been made in the collection of government revenue. The first Deputy Commissioner after the return of the Civil Government had recommended that no land revenue should be collected for the year 1945–46, since he thought that payment would cause hardship to the people. He was told, however, that, while the government could not agree to any wholesale abandonment of revenue, remission might be granted in accordance with the normal procedure where crops had been damaged either by weather or by pests or as a result of military operations. Under this authority half the revenue was written off, and no undue pressure was used for payment of the balance.

Early in August 1946, a new Deputy Commissioner arrived, a senior Arakanese member of the Class II Civil Service. He found that only about 2½ per cent of the reduced land revenue demand had been collected, and he was taking steps to speed up collection when the strike of government servants took place. In Pyapon District this affected the police, the whole of the land records staff and, I believe, some of the clerks also. These events completely demoralised the Deputy Commissioner. He left his headquarters only twice during the four and a half months that he was in the district, and his subdivisional and township officers followed his example. For a month before my arrival he was expecting at any moment to be relieved, and the administration seems simply to have marked time, though the police, under an energetic European superintendent, were as active as was possible, having regard to the fact that the trustworthiness of many of their members was open to question.

I arrived in Pyapon by steamer after dark on the 23rd December 1946. I had arranged for a telegram to be sent announcing my arrival, but I preceded it and found no one to meet me at the jetty. A message was sent to my predecessor, who was entertaining some brother officers, and it was reported to me later that he danced round the room with joy on hearing that his successor had arrived. I was well able to appreciate his feelings when I learned six months later that my relief had been named and was actually coming to Pyapon.

My senior administrative officers were an Additional Deputy Commissioner, young, enthusiastic and inexperienced, and an experienced Headquarters Assistant, who was of great help to me in dealing with politicians; but within some ten weeks of my arrival both had been transferred and neither was replaced. The Akunwun (Chief Revenue Officer) was one of the very few Burmese officers whom I felt that I could entirely trust in that very political district, where so many administrative officials, seeing which way the wind was blowing, were taking good care not to fall foul of the local politicians. My old friend U Aung Pe had been transferred from Bassein and was now Subdivisional Officer at Kyaiklat, where he was a tower of strength.

The old Deputy Commissioner's residence was now occupied by the troops, and I shared a house with two police officers. Bestall, the Superintendent, was an Irishman, with a very considerable understanding of the Burmese – sometimes called the Irish of the East – and an intelligent appreciation of the change in their outlook since the Japanese invasion. Despite a certain quickness of temper, he was undoubtedly popular with his force as a whole, in so far as this could be said of any European official at a time when independence from British rule was the slogan, and he was making determined efforts to reduce the volume of crime. The other policeman was a young man called Ward who had recently come from India and was in charge, under Bestall, of what was known as the armed police.

The only non-official European in Pyapon was Lawrence Dawson, a Scot who had come to Rangoon originally as a lawyer. About 1910 he gave up his law practice and founded Dawson's Bank, which was to apply modern banking principles to Burmese agricultural finance. Its head office was in Pyapon, and there were branches in Rangoon and in some of the Delta towns. The Bank suffered from the agricultural depression which had followed the worldwide fall in cereal prices, and went into voluntary liquidation. It was later permitted to issue over five million rupees worth of debenture stock, and by the time of the Japanese invasion it was within sight of liquidating half the outstanding debentures. Like the Chettyars, Dawson's Bank had to take over large areas of paddy land, but it was an excellent landlord and managed its estates very well. Lawrence Dawson had left Burma when the Japanese came in, but had returned as soon as he could to save as much as possible from the wreck and, as he was constantly telling me, to protect the interests of his debenture-holders. He must have been at least seventy at this time, a grand old man. At first it was difficult to make him understand that we officials of the administration no longer had the power to do what we had done before the war; we were now serving what was in effect a Burmese Government and were unable to rely on the police to enforce the law against wrongdoers connected with the parties in power. Dawson came, however, in time to accept the position, and certainly there was no question of a breakdown in the administration. I met him for the last time in Rangoon, just before I left Burma for good; he gave me lunch and still seemed fairly cheerful.

The district clerical staff was the worst that had ever served under me. The Chief Clerk was a Karen; he and another Karen were the best of a bad bunch, and they had to do much of the work which should have been done by the other clerks. The Burmese staff were, almost without exception, lazy, uninterested and very much involved in politics. There were rumours at one time that they were going on strike, as a result of a government decision to discontinue a temporary cost-of-living allowance which had been paid by the Military Administration. I told the Chief Clerk that, so long as my officers and one or two office boys remained, it would not make the least difference to me whether the clerks struck or not, as most of them were not worth their pay. I hope that he passed this on to the staff; anyhow, there was no strike.

The police force at this time consisted of three branches: there were the ordinary civil police of peacetime, who now carried arms; the armed police, who were used mainly for patrol work and for operations against criminal gangs; and the special police reserve, who went through a course of training and were then drafted into the civil or armed police as vacancies occurred. There was some quite good material among all these branches, but the police strike of September had done irreparable damage to the morale and discipline of the forces throughout Burma, and the Pyapon District police force must have been one of the worst in the country. The section guarding the Treasury vault would often be found in the evenings squatting on their haunches and chatting to women, with their rifles propped against the wall of the vault. From time to time members of the force deserted with their arms or used them to commit crimes and later, when Bestall had been transferred and for a couple of months the district was left without a Superintendent, discipline deteriorated still further, and in outstations little work was done. In addition to this, the local force was strongly imbued with politics. The Pyapon police station was next to the house which I occupied and every day at sunset the police on duty were paraded outside it to sing the nationalist song 'Doh Bama' ('We Burmese'); there was always a horrible discord when the high notes were reached, which I suspected to be the contribution of the Karen policemen, who, though Karens generally had good voices, cannot have been greatly interested in 'We Burmese'.

When I first went to Pyapon, there were also two police flying squads based on Rangoon, whose main task was to track down the really big gangs operating in the district. They were not local men and, to that extent, they were more reliable. One squad did its work so well that it was hurriedly recalled to Rangoon, as I shall relate in due course.

The military garrison was a company of Chin Rifles under a young British officer. They were not interested in Burmese politics, many of them spoke no Burmese, and I think that they could have been relied on to carry out any orders given to them. But in February they were replaced by two companies of Burma Rifles; a platoon was posted to each of the three outstations and the rest were stationed in Pyapon. They belonged to a comparatively new battalion, composed largely of former members of the Burma National Army. They had had little training as we understand it, their discipline left much to be desired, and their sympathies were strongly AFPFL and Socialist. Their commanding officer Major Downs, who was an Anglo-Burman – and a cousin of Ohn Maung – was a pleasant enough fellow. He was not interested in politics, but he found it difficult to control his junior officers, who, like the men, were mostly staunch Socialists. Towards the end of his time in Pyapon, he found things so difficult in his mess that he arranged to have his meals with me.

A few days before I arrived in Pyapon the British Prime Minister

Attlee announced in the House of Commons that His Majesty's Government would receive a delegation from the Executive Council to discuss the steps necessary to give Burma self-government, either within or outside the Commonwealth. The delegation left for London early in January, among its members being Aung San, Tin Tut, Thakin Mya and U Saw. The month was an anxious one in Burma, and especially in the Delta districts and other parts of Lower Burma, where there was far more political activity than in the less sophisticated northern areas. The intention at this time was that elections to the Legislative Council should be held in April 1947; thereafter the country would have the same form of government as before the war with a Council of Ministers, and in due course a Constituent Assembly would be appointed to draw up a new constitution for a self-governing Burma. But this was not good enough for Aung San and his colleagues. Their aim was independence by the end of the year. There was a considerable undercurrent of unrest during the London discussions, and it was common talk that, if Aung San did not get what he wanted, he would give the signal for a rebellion. There is no doubt that arrangements had been made to this end, and in the neighbouring Myaungmya District the rebellion started off at half-cock before the result of the London conference was known. Bestall and I went on tour as much as we could, in the hope that the constant presence of government officials and police might deter potential trouble-makers, and we congratulated ourselves that our district remained quiet.

On the 27th January the Attlee-Aung San agreement was signed, whereby it was agreed that the April elections should be for the purpose of electing a Constituent Assembly, which should at once embark on the task of framing a constitution. Meanwhile the Executive Council was to be regarded as a Provisional Government. Aung San had therefore obtained recognition of the position which he had claimed when he first established contact with the returning British. On the completion of their negotiations in London, he and his colleagues returned to Burma, and we were free to apply ourselves to the more routine tasks of administering our districts, in so far as they could be called routine, when crime was rampant, and in many areas the people would not pay their taxes or repay their agricultural loans.

I have said that in my predecessor's time very little touring had been done by administrative officers. To my mind constant travelling was the only way of showing the people that there was still an effective administration and of finding out what was happening. This was particularly necessary in areas where some political gangster had established himself as the local gauleiter. The appearance of a strong patrol in his area would send him into hiding, and to some extent he would lose face with the people whom he tyrannised. I therefore arranged with Bestall for each of my subdivisional and township officers to be given an armed special police guard to accompany them on their tours. I also allotted our launches for fixed periods in each month, so that my officers could plan their tours in advance. By these means I hoped to get them out of their headquarters, and to a great extent I was successful, though some needed constant badgering.

This reluctance to leave headquarters extended also to the lower grades of government official. My field inspections showed cases in which the revenue surveyor had marked crops and areas under cultivation in his maps, but had quite obviously never been near the fields to check the correctness of his entries. The vaccinators, who were supposed to visit all villages, kept away from those which were not on the main waterways. It was the fear of armed gangs that deterred them from venturing out, and it was difficult to blame them when senior officers were not leaving their headquarters. Even headmen, if their tracts were bad ones and liable to attack, would live outside. We issued guns for village defence, and I increased their number and instructed my officers to organise 'defence guards' in each village tract, consisting preferably of young men, who would take it in turns to patrol the villages and the fields. We gradually

Village defence party

got most of the headmen back into their own areas, but the majority of them were unreliable: they were either themselves politically inclined or afraid of the political parties in their villages. I remember only two stout-hearted headmen, who refused to become embroiled in politics, assisted the police to round up criminals, and even at times brought in criminals themselves without police aid.

Local politics were dismal and sordid. There was not one political leader who combined intelligence with respectability. The AFPFL leader was, I think, sincere enough, but he was slow-witted and had no ideas which went much beyond his own district. My predecessor had discontinued meetings of the advisory committee which had been established after the British reoccupation. I was very much in favour of reviving it, and within a fortnight of my arrival I called a meeting. The AFPFL leader complained that in the past, when decisions had been taken at committee meetings, they were never put into effect by the authorities; if, he said, the same thing was going to happen again, it was a waste of time for members to attend. I explained that if members made suggestions which I could not accept, they would be told why I could not adopt them; but that where they could be put into effect and action was agreed upon by the committee, they would certainly be implemented. A date was fixed for the next meeting, but only one member appeared; thereafter, disheartened and somewhat irritated by the patent lack of any co-operation from the political organisations, I made no further attempt to revive the committee.

Shortly before my arrival in Pyapon an arrested dacoit had made a confession in which he stated that Mya Hlaing, the local Socialist Party leader, had hired out arms for the commission of crimes. This was the first clear evidence of these activities, and Bestall arrested him. He was released on bail for medical reasons and went to Rangoon to undergo an operation for appendicitis. Meanwhile evidence began to accumulate that he was preparing for a rebellion. After his operation he was sent to Pyapon hospital till he had completely recovered. While he was there, a police sub-inspector who was investigating the rebellion case visited him and placed him under arrest. According to the sub-inspector's story, he told a police guard which was posted on the lower floor of the hospital to keep an eye on Mya Hlaing – who was on the upper floor – while he went to arrange for another guard. In the interval Mya Hlaing escaped. It was fairly obvious that either the sub-inspector or the guard on the lower floor, or both, had connived in his escape. He joined a politico-criminal gang operating on the sea-coast, and ultimately made his way to Rangoon, where he surrendered under the terms of a 'political' amnesty extended to persons who had been engaged in rebellious activities against the government. He turned up again in Pyapon at the time of the April elections, and was reported to be holding his court in the town, arranging for the murder of those who crossed his path, issuing leases of land which did not belong to him in the name of the Socialist Party, ordering tenant farmers to leave their land, and so forth. I even learned that, while I was on tour, he was making use of my official jeep, for which I straight away dismissed my driver. It was difficult to collect direct evidence against him, and the police would do nothing unless they were continually prodded. When he surrendered under the political amnesty, I found that they were proposing to withdraw the cases against him of abetting dacoity and escaping from lawful custody; I told them that these were not covered by the amnesty and directed them to proceed with them. The first case was still being heard when I left the district. I do not know what happened ultimately to Mya Hlaing. He was a thoroughly disreputable character, and his following was gradually falling off: the man who was officially President of the local Socialist Party and who had been little more than a figurehead went off to Rangoon in disgust; the PVO fell out with him; and his own brother, one of Aung San's henchmen in Rangoon, was said to have disowned him.

The PVO, the semi-military component of the AFPFL, were mainly interested in trying to get hold of guns, ostensibly to enable them to help the police in combating dacoity. Early in January 1947, all Deputy Commissioners were instructed by the government to consider enlisting the aid of the PVO and other organisations for this purpose. Bestall and I thought this over, and decided to issue two Sten guns and a dozen rifles to the PVO in Pyapon town as an experiment. The understanding was that they would act either in conjunction with the police or on their own, but that in the latter event they would keep the police informed of their activities and of the areas in which they were patrolling. If we found that they were really proving useful, we would consider giving them more arms. Later, when the troops were withdrawn from Bogale, we gave a number of rifles to the PVO there, in order that they might help to protect the town. But in neither case was the experiment a success. The Pyapon PVO never told the police what they were doing, and appeared to use their arms solely for the protection of their own headquarters in the town; whenever a dacoity took place in Pyapon, they would fire off their rifles at random, frightening the townsfolk more than the dacoits. In Bogale one of the PVO used his rifle to commit a robbery; and when there was an outbreak from the police station lock-up by prisoners awaiting trial, among whom were four PVO men, the members of the organisation fired their rifles in the middle of the town, causing the police to think that there was a dacoity there and so distracting their attention from the lock-up. I withdrew their arms at Bogale and though at the request of the police the Pyapon PVO were allowed to retain theirs, they received no more ammunition.

Shortly before the elections in April a consignment of three hundred British service rifles was sent to us from Rangoon. The local PVO at once came and said that they understood that the arms were intended for issue to them. I had no intention of giving them any more arms if I could help it, and very fortunately the government omitted to inform me for whom the rifles had been sent, though I learned unofficially that they were indeed meant for the PVO. Every few days they would come and ask for them, but none had been issued by the time that I left. I had no objection in principle to arming the PVO, but I considered that the local members of the organisation were men of little character or reputation. They might have given some assistance to the police against criminals belonging to another political party, but that, I thought, was as far as any help could be expected. In all their interviews with me their eagerness to get their hands on firearms was apparent; they rarely mentioned any desire to combat crime. And experience in other districts suggested that they would not have proved amenable to discipline if we had tried to form them into an auxiliary branch of the police.

The Burma Communist Party (or White Flag Communists) had their main strength around Pyapon town, and they were not strongly represented in other parts of the district. They seemed to concentrate their activities on fomenting agrarian discontent, and organising mass meetings of cultivators with the object of causing embarrassment to the government. They would tell the people not to pay any land revenue nor to repay the agricultural loans issued to them by the government. Forcible ploughing was another of their favourite pastimes: if they disapproved of the lease of a piece of land by the owner to a particular tenant, they would arrange for a party of men to enter on the land, plough a portion of it and plant it with paddy on behalf of the man who in their opinion should have been given the tenancy. Like the AFPFL, the Burma Communist Party had a semi-military wing known as the Red Guard, consisting of young men wearing a uniform of sorts.

It was the White Flag Communists who organised a mass demonstration at my office within a few weeks of my arrival. The Commissioner, who was now an Arakanese member of the Indian

Civil Service, had come from Bassein on a routine visit, and I had taken him out in my jeep before breakfast. In the course of our drive I had observed large numbers of people walking towards Pyapon, some carrying banners, and had assumed that they were going to some political rally. After breakfast, when I was in the office discussing business with the Commissioner and Bestall, we heard the sound of many voices approaching. It soon became clear that the objective of the crowd, which numbered several hundreds, was the office. The police were already standing by, and I sent word to the officer in charge of the Chin Rifles.

In due course a paper was sent in which contained a number of resolutions. It appeared that a case of forcible ploughing by the Burma Communist Party had occurred in my predecessor's time and the police were prosecuting the culprits for trespass. The resolutions demanded the withdrawal of the cases and asked that I should receive a deputation. The crowd had now completely surrounded the office, standing several ranks deep, clearly with the intention of preventing anyone from leaving; but, as they were perfectly orderly, I was prepared to receive the deputation. The Commissioner, however, without reference to me, instructed my clerk to tell the crowd to go away and send a small deputation the next day. I enquired what he proposed to do if they refused to disperse. 'In that case,' he said, 'we shall have to think again.' I assumed that he probably knew his people better than I did and said no more, but back came the answer that the people would be busy the next day and insisted on my seeing the deputation now.

As the Commissioner had said that no interview would be given that day, Bestall and I decided that the next step must be to clear the exit from the office by a police charge. But, when a police squad had been organised with Bestall at their head, they refused to charge, saying that the crowd were not criminals and had done nothing wrong. My choice lay between ordering the troops, now drawn up outside the office, to disperse the crowd by force, and climbing down and receiving the deputation. At this stage I had no justification for the former course, and decided therefore to listen to the deputation. The Commissioner had by this time disappeared into an inner room, leaving Bestall and me to deal with the matter, and he did not emerge till it had been settled. The word soon went round the crowd that he had gone into hiding!

The deputation consisted of three or four youngsters, some quite polite, others patently rude. At intervals they would go out to consult the crowd, and then return to say that my proposals were unacceptable. It was now drawing near to sunset, and we suspected that the crowd intended to keep us in the office till after dark, when it would be very difficult to break them up. I therefore made a final offer to withdraw the pending cases and look into them myself, and said that, if the crowd had not gone within fifteen minutes, I would call on the troops to disperse them by force. I warned the officer in charge; thereupon some of the leaders of the crowd tried to address the Chin soldiers in English and ask them to take no action, but the Chins took not the slightest notice. At last, a few minutes before 'zero hour', the people began to move off with shouts of 'Victory', the demonstration was over and we could go home.

One amusing incident arising out of this affair was later recounted to me. At intervals the crowd were shouting slogans, the principal of which was 'Lutlatye' meaning 'freedom' or 'independence'. A certain Burman, who was not himself taking part in the demonstration, found himself standing on the outskirts of the crowd next to an old woman who was squatting on her haunches and shouting 'Lutlatye' as lustily as the rest. 'Old aunt,' he asked her, 'what is this "Lutlatye" that you are shouting for?' 'I don't know, sir,' she replied, 'but everyone else is shouting for it, so I am doing so too.'

The only other political party which I have not yet mentioned was the extreme left-wing organisation known as the Communist Party (Burma) or Red Flag Communists. Their stronghold was in Dedaye Township, but they went underground when they were declared by the government to be an illegal organisation in January. Apart from a case of rice-looting in Dedaye, when police and troops looked on and did nothing, they caused us comparatively little trouble. It was, however, the practice of the Rangoon politicians to ascribe the unsettled state of affairs in Pyapon District to the Red Flag Communists.

Crime and politics were inextricably mixed, and this applied to many parts of Burma after the war. In a remote area down on the sea-coast was a gang led by one Thein Pe, which had a close connection with the Socialist Party – one of the main components, as I have said, of the AFPFL, which was now the effective Government of Burma. Thein Pe was running a parallel administration, imposing his will on the people and assuming powers of life and death. Not long after my arrival I went down to the coast with Bestall and a police party, and we addressed the villagers. They listened to us, but clearly we did not make much impression on them; they knew of course that we should go back to our headquarters and that Thein Pe and his gang would continue as before.

One of the police flying squads in the district was sent down to corner Thein Pe, and the result was a spate of complaints from the local Socialists of the excesses committed by the squad, most of which, I was certain, were entirely false. The picture painted by these interested parties was one of a peaceful coastal region living under the benevolent protection of Thein Pe, the peace of which had been rudely shattered by the atrocities of the barbarous police. In the middle of January the flying squad was temporarily withdrawn in order to give Thein Pe the opportunity of surrendering under the terms of the amnesty extended to criminal gangs, but he is alleged to have told agents sent to him that the amnesty did not apply to him, as he was not a criminal but a nationalist. He took the opportunity of his temporary respite from the flying squad to pay off some old scores by murdering a headman and a headman's assistant, both of whom had helped the police; and he again set himself up as the virtual ruler of the area.

So the flying squad was again sent after him, and the troops assisted. As a result, about seventy unimportant members of the gang surrendered. The political sympathies of the troops – who by this time were Burmese and infected with politics – were too closely allied with those of the leaders of the gang for them to give very serious help in rounding them up, and their Burmese officers were reported to be spending much of their time asking villagers what they thought of government officials and of the police.

At the beginning of March it looked as though the flying squad had really cornered the gang; they had been beaten to a standstill and lack of food and water must have ended their resistance within a few more days. At this crucial moment Bestall was suddenly transferred and the flying squad was pulled out of the district, without the knowledge of the senior police command in Rangoon – save presumably the Inspector-General, who was at this time my old friend U Ba Maung of Tharrawaddy days, and who no doubt did what he was told. The whole thing was obviously a political move, engineered by the AFPFL Government to save Thein Pe from an ignominious defeat.

Negotiations were then opened for the remaining members of the gang to surrender under the 'political' amnesty. They were apparently determined not to surrender to a European officer; they waited therefore till they heard that I had gone on tour for a few days, and then came into Pyapon and surrendered to the subdivisional or township officer, bringing such few arms as they chose to hand over, and obtained the benefit of the amnesty. Thein Pe himself came in on the very last day of the amnesty, the 31st March, when I was again on tour; we had no direct evidence against Thein Pe of complicity in the murders and other crimes for which his gang had been responsible, and could not therefore arrest him. About one-third of the arms reported to be in the gang's possession were surrendered, and soon reports were arriving of their committing further crimes in the same area.

Bestall's transfer from the district at the beginning of March was a serious setback to the task of restoring law and order. His successor, a little Burman called U Hla Taw, had been given an assurance before he left Rangoon that he would not have to stay for more than three weeks in Pyapon, which was not a popular district with Burmese officials! It was no doubt intended during the three weeks to post another Superintendent permanently to the district. When this period expired, the government honoured its promise to U Hla Taw, but sent no one in his place. Control of the district police force passed temporarily – for Ward was a youngster with little experience of Burma – to the police Headquarters Assistant, whose duties were of a sedentary nature and who was not normally expected to tour; indeed it was virtually impossible for him to do his office work efficiently if he did not spend all his time in headquarters.

From about this time – or even earlier – the local political leaders had been making strenuous efforts to have me transferred and replaced by a Burman who would, they hoped, be more amenable to their demands. They would go to Rangoon to interview their leaders in the government, and return with the information that so-and-so was being sent to relieve me. I have no doubt that their information was entirely correct, and sometimes things reached the point at which a Burmese officer was officially posted. But in every case the posting failed to mature: one officer would suddenly fall ill; another would ask for leave when he heard that he was to go to Pyapon; another would 'work the oracle' and get his posting cancelled. I used to tell the local politicians that I was well aware that they wanted me to go, and that in this matter at any rate our views were identical. The position at the end of March, then, with the elections due to take place in a few weeks, was that I had no additional Deputy Commissioner, no Headquarters Assistant and no Superintendent of Police, and the length of my own stay in the district was problematical.

Another semi-political gang was now giving trouble. Its leader was Than Maung, and it centred round Wegyi, a village somewhat to the west of Pyapon town. Than Maung is said to have obtained his firearms originally from Mya Hlaing, but he later asserted his independence and refused to take orders from Mya Hlaing. Towards the end of 1946 Ward, the Assistant Superintendent, and his armed police conducted successful operations against the gang, and there was talk of their surrendering. Then came the amnesty offer and, in the usual way, the police were withdrawn in order to allow the gang to surrender. Negotiations for Than Maung's surrender were carried on through monks belonging to the Anti-Crime Association.

The chief character in the Pyapon branch of the Association was the monk U Thon, a sturdy Friar Tuck of a man, whose principal lieutenant was a skinny little monk. During the period of the amnesty they represented to us that they wished to co-operate and to persuade the gangs to surrender. We had considerable misgiving – Bestall and I – as to the extent to which we could trust them, but were willing to give them a chance to show that they really wanted to help. They wasted a great deal of our time. As evidence, presumably, of their bona fides, they brought us one Sten gun from the Than Maung gang – which the gang could well afford to hand over – and a promise from Than Maung himself that he would shortly come and surrender. Then one monk started working against another, each eager to obtain the kudos of having brought in this important dacoit leader. U Thon abandoned the field and decided to concentrate on Thein Pe, the leader of the other big gang. But he soon came to us with the story which I have already quoted that Thein Pe was not a criminal at all, but a nationalist who was helping the government by 'protecting' the area in which he was operating. We then abandoned all hope of receiving any help from these monks. It was obvious that they liked to be seen riding about in government transport, which we provided for them from time to time, and that they were very closely connected with the local Socialist Party.

Meanwhile Than Maung, if indeed he had ever intended to surrender, changed his mind. It was also said that the AFPFL high command instructed him not to surrender, in case he should be required to take part in a rebellion at the end of January, in the event of the Attlee-Aung San discussions in London breaking down. In February therefore the armed police were again sent against him, and at one time it was said that he was reduced to four rifles. But early in April, when the district had no Superintendent of Police, occurred the outbreak of under-trial prisoners from the Bogale police station – to which I have already referred – in which twenty-one firearms, including a Bren gun, were lost by the police. A number of those who escaped joined Than Maung, and this sudden access of strength enabled the gang to resume its activities.

During all this time arrangements for the elections were proceeding. Their organisation involved a good deal of detailed administrative work in addition to the compilation of the electoral rolls. Polling stations had to be sited at convenient centres and in some cases special buildings erected; launch schedules had to be carefully worked out so that the supervising officers would be delivered at the right place and the right time with the ballot boxes and the voting discs, and collected as soon as polling was over. There were three constituencies in the district, which returned two Burmese members and one Karen. I was able, through the good offices of my Karen chief clerk, to persuade a Karen candidate to withdraw, leaving the Karen seat uncontested. The Burmese seats were contested by the AFPFL and by some of their opponents who might, I suppose, have been called independents. There was no opposition party as such. The White Flag Communists boycotted the elections, and the Red Flags were now an illegal organisation. There were rumours that the Communists were planning to wreck the elections by burning down polling booths, by preventing voters from reaching them, and by other methods. I asked one of the AFPFL candidates U Win (who later became a Minister) what action he would advise in the event of the Communists adopting the favourite Burmese tactics of lying on the ground around the booths so that no one could record his vote. He replied with some amusement that, though in the past he had himself organised demonstrations of this sort, he was unable to make any suggestion as to how they should be dealt with!

In view of the possibility of disturbances in the forthcoming elections, I regarded it as essential that I should have a Superintendent of Police in the district. I had eventually to telephone the Chief Secretary before I could get any response to my requests, and U Hla Taw was sent back for about a week to cover the period of the elections. The only untoward incident was the burning of one polling booth on the eve of the elections, but there was sufficient time to erect another. Apart from this everything proceeded smoothly, and both the AFPFL candidates were returned with overwhelming majorities. Throughout the country the AFPFL met virtually no opposition, and the elections proved beyond a doubt that it did in fact represent the Burmese people.

The government had been so scared lest there should be any trouble during the elections that instructions were issued from Rangoon that fifty persons selected by the local Socialist Party should be enrolled in the district armed police. Half of them were at once sent to Dedaye to deal with any potential Red Flag menace. The remainder were supposed to receive training in Pyapon. Later, when I had time to examine the lists of those who had been appointed, I found that ten were former members of Thein Pe's gang, of whom four had never surrendered under the amnesty! This was duly reported to Rangoon, but nothing more was heard before I left

Pyapon. The original intention was that these 'political police' should be appointed only for the short period of the elections and their aftermath. They took orders from the Socialist leaders rather than from the police officers, and it was not long before they were suspected of being accessory to 'political' crimes.

Meanwhile the collection of revenue and the recovery of loans made to cultivators was giving a great deal of trouble. When I took charge of the district about one lakh of rupees – a lakh is 100,000 rupees or £7,500 – in land revenue out of a total of eight lakhs had been collected. My own opinion, after I had travelled about the district, was that the people were no less able to pay than those in Bassein, where there had been no difficulty in collecting the revenue; indeed U Aung Pe, who had been my Subdivisional Officer in both districts, thought that, if anything, Pyapon was the more prosperous. There was no doubt at all that it was political agitation which prevented the people from paying. I did what I could to press for payment and, when I left, collections had been trebled. Many of the defaulters were large landowners, some of whom argued not unreasonably that their principal source of income was rents from their land, which their tenants were not paying, and that they were therefore in no position to pay the land revenue to the government.

More than twenty lakhs of rupees had been issued to the farmers of the district in the form of agricultural loans. In due course the first instalment of repayment was demanded, but here again the local politicians interfered. They went round telling the farmers that there was no need for them to repay their loans; whether they paid or not, they would get further loans in the coming year. Both Socialists and Communists were responsible for this, but the latter were perhaps the more active. By the time that the elections were over, less than 1 per cent of the loans had been recovered. Despite this, the government allotted the district ten lakhs of rupees to be expended on loans in the year 1947. It seemed to me that this was simply pouring money down the drain – money too that was provided by the British taxpayer – and I told the government so. My allocation was thereupon reduced to one lakh, though I was given the option of applying for more if I thought fit. I was meanwhile doing constant propaganda during the course of my tours, assuring farmers that, if they did not repay their old loans, they would get no more. When eventually they realised that this was the truth, and that they had been misled by the political parties, there was a sudden move to pay up and, when I left, about 5 per cent of the loans had been recovered. It was doubtful whether much more would be forthcoming, for it seemed to be generally agreed that, though most borrowers could have repaid after selling their crop earlier in the year, they had listened to the politicians and spent their money on clothes and gambling, and were probably genuinely unable to find any more till after the next harvest. Having therefore extracted as much in repayment as I thought was likely to be available, I gave instructions to my officers to tell the people concerned that they could apply for postponement of payment of the balance, and to demand repayment immediately after the next harvest. Meanwhile they could accept applications for new loans.

About this time Thakin Nu passed through the district and sent word that he would like to meet me at Kyaiklat. He had been a Minister in the puppet Ba Maw administration, was now one of Aung San's right-hand men, and was later to become the first Prime Minister of independent Burma. I happened to be at Kyaiklat when I received his message. I had an interesting conversation with him, and took the opportunity to explain exactly how I felt about the collection of revenue and agricultural loans. I said that the government – that is to say, the AFPFL – was issuing instructions to Deputy Commissioners to collect the revenue while at the same time it appeared that the AFPFL was telling its political representatives in the districts to urge the people not to pay, or was at any rate conniving at their doing so. I told Thakin Nu that it was a matter of indifference to me personally whether government told me to collect revenue or not to collect it; I had, however, to obey my instructions and all I asked was that the instructions issued by the League through official and political channels should be the same. He said that he and his colleagues realised that the government must insist on the people paying their dues and that a statement was shortly to be issued. And in fact it was only a few weeks later that a statement in Burmese appeared over Aung San's signature, explaining to the people that the government could not function if the taxes were not paid, and exhorting them to pay.

I told Thakin Nu also how little co-operation government officials in Pyapon District were getting from the local politicians. I said that I was not myself unduly concerned if I was at loggerheads with them, for I should not be much longer in Burma. But I asked him to consider the position of my Burmese officers, who wanted to do what was right and yet could not afford to fall foul of the politicians, whose power would presumably increase so greatly once Burma achieved independence. I do not remember that he gave any direct answer to this, but I have no doubt that he took it in, for Thakin Nu was no fool.

Government's willingness to make further large sums available for loans to farmers, even though little attempt was being made to repay the previous year's loans, was undoubtedly due to the serious rice shortage in South-East Asia which confronted the re-established administrations after the defeat of the Japanese. Before the reoccupation of Burma it had been decided that the British mercantile firms should not return in their former completely independent capacity, but that some form of government direction should be enforced. The purchase of rice was now the overall responsibility of an Agricultural Products Board established by the government. This Board appointed agents in all the rice-growing districts to buy rice, mainly for export. Most of the agents were firms which had before the war been engaged in rice purchase, but for political reasons a few new Burmese firms were appointed. Pyapon was allotted to one of these Burmese agents, and soon the local politicians were complaining about it. It had only a small amount of capital, and relied on selling its first purchases before it was able to buy any more. I tried to persuade the firm to buy paddy rather than rice, so that the money would go to the growers rather than the millers, but this was not such an attractive proposition from its point of view. I pointed out to the complainants that they had asked for Burmese firms to be given some of the agencies; they admitted that they had, but said that they did not want 'this sort of firm'. The truth of course was that any Burmese firm at that time was bound to be very much less efficient than a European or an Indian one, for it had neither the experience nor the capital.

The government continued the subsidy scheme, whereby rewards in cash were given for increased cultivation of rice. Unfortunately, the Burmese name given to the subsidy – which meant roughly 'the reward for bringing uncultivated land under rice' – gave some farmers the impression that all that they had to do to qualify was to cultivate some land that was uncultivated in the previous year, regardless of whether the total acreage planted was greater than before.

In April, besides the elections I had the annual job of auctioning the fisheries in the district. I had already notified the date for the Pyapon auctions when some members of the Socialist Party approached me with the request that they be postponed. It transpired that they were trying to organise a syndicate with sufficient funds to bid for, and probably buy, most of the fisheries. I naturally refused to put off the auctions simply to suit their convenience. On the appointed day I duly took my seat on the bench in the court room, where the auctions were usually held. For the first two or three fisheries bidders appeared, but they were quickly approached by

members of the Party and persuaded not to bid. Lounging round
the court room doors were uniformed members of the PVO, clearly
there to see that in fact no bidding took place. It was impossible for
me to do anything about this, for I could expect no assistance from
the police if I called for it. I therefore went through the form of
calling out the name of each fishery, and at the end announced that,
as no bidders had appeared, I should now postpone the auctions
till a later date. This pleased the Socialists and to some extent saved
my face. It was, however, with some satisfaction that I learned later
that the negotiations for the formation of a syndicate had broken
down; and the postponed auctions took place without incident. But
when I was going to hold fishery auctions at Kyaiklat, I was again
asked by the Socialist Party to postpone them for the same reason,
and I again refused. 'But,' they protested, 'you put off the Pyapon
auctions.' 'Yes,' I replied, 'because you dissuaded people from bidding. If you want the same thing to happen in Kyaiklat, you will
have to come there.' Even they saw some humour in the situation,
for they laughed and said that they could not go all that distance
with their supporters. The Kyaiklat auctions and those in the township headquarters passed off without interference. The incident at
Pyapon goes to show, however, what things were like at that time
in some districts, when the local politicians could interfere with the
ordinary course of administration and the Deputy Commissioner
could do nothing about it.

From the point of view of law and order too the situation was
deteriorating. The number of dacoities and robberies, which had
begun to drop before Bestall's departure, was again on the increase,
with over one hundred cases reported every month, most of them
committed with the aid of modern weapons. Towards the end of
April the Than Maung gang, now reinforced as the result of the
outbreak from the Bogale police station, launched an attack on a
place called Setsan where there was a small police station. They
failed to surprise the station, but they looted the village at will and
the police did practically nothing. It will be recalled that, except for
a few days during the election, the district had been without a
Superintendent of Police since the latter half of March. And at this
juncture I was informed that it was proposed to withdraw the troops
from the district early in May and to leave simply one platoon of
Chin Rifles at Dedaye. Dedaye was now giving very little trouble,
but it was the area in which the Red Flag leader Thakin Soe was
hiding, and the AFPFL Government persisted in maintaining the
fiction that the trouble-makers in the district were the Communists,
when in reality they were their own Socialist Party supporters. At

the beginning of May all military detachments were withdrawn from the outstations in preparation for the Burma Rifles to leave the district. I decided that I must go to Rangoon to urge personally that the troops be kept till the situation was more under control and to ask once more for a Superintendent of Police to be posted permanently to the district. On the night before I was due to leave there was an attack on Pyapon town itself.

On that day (4th May 1947) arrangements had been made for some kind of show to be held on a piece of land between the government office and my house. Like most Burmese entertainments it was not due to start till the evening. That night I had had my dinner and was just settling down to listen to the 9 o'clock news from Rangoon when I heard a number of bangs. I at first took no notice, thinking that Chinese crackers were being let off as part of the show. The showground was about three hundred yards to the south of my house; Pyapon town was rather over a quarter of a mile to the north. Then, as the explosions continued, my suspicions were aroused. I went downstairs and found my servants all huddled together; they assured me that the noise was gunfire. I was certain that some at least of the shooting had come from the south and, knowing that there were some police on duty at the show, I went there first. I found the police and asked if they had been firing. They replied that they had; they had heard firing from the town, so had pointed their rifles into the air and done a little firing on their own account.

I then went to the police station next to my house, where there was little sign of activity. The police Headquarters Assistant was in bed with malaria, but he at once arose when he heard what was happening. We collected a number of police with rifles and proceeded cautiously into the town. As we advanced up the main street, we were met by machine gun fire from the centre of the town. There were supposed to be police in that area, and at first I thought that they were firing at us, under the impression that we were dacoits. A policeman standing next to me received a superficial wound, and it seemed that there was little more that a police party could do. I was about to call on the troops when Major Downs, who had heard the firing, appeared with his men and proceeded ahead of us into the town. We left the matter in his hands and returned whence we had come.

Later Downs came and reported to me. His men had exchanged shots with the dacoits, as they proved to be, and had driven them out. In the course of the engagement one policeman had been badly wounded and it was thought that two of the dacoits had also been hit. The policeman was taken to the hospital and later I went to see him. He was in a very bad way, and that same night he died.

Touring by boat

The night's incident made it yet more imperative that I should go to Rangoon the next day as I had planned. Soon after dawn an American Army officer presented himself in my house to ask if I could send him to Rangoon. It appeared that he had arrived in Pyapon the previous day, accompanied by an Anglo-Burmese girl whom he introduced as his wife, to collect the remains of certain Americans who had been buried in the district. He had not informed me of his arrival, but had gone straight to the Government Rest House, which was in the town. I do not remember that it was ever used by anyone else during my time in Pyapon, for visitors generally came to stay with me. He and his girl had of course been very nearly in the thick of the battle, and he told me that he did not think that Pyapon was a healthy place to remain in any longer! I told him that I was myself leaving shortly for Rangoon in my launch and that they could come with me. He had a number of sacks, labelled 'Harry', 'Tom' and so forth, containing remains which he had collected before he reached Pyapon; I asked him not to let my launch crew know what was in them, or they might refuse to have them on the launch. (My crew were entirely Burmese, which was unusual, for government launches were generally manned by Indians. They were a cheerful bunch, and one of my few pleasant memories of Pyapon is my launch tours.)

We stopped for the night at Twante, where there was a Rest House,

Touring by boat

and the American and his companion slept there, while I remained on the launch; there was not room for us all to sleep on board. Early the next morning we tied up in the Rangoon River. I reported at the Chief Secretary's office, and also went to see U Ba Maung, the Inspector-General of Police. A garbled version of the Pyapon dacoity had already reached Rangoon, and I was able to give the facts. U Ba Maung told me that a young police officer called U Khin Maung Maung was being sent to Pyapon as Superintendent, and would be leaving in a few days. I met him, and found that he was the son of a Burmese Government officer whom I had known when I was under training in Sagaing, and who had now retired.

I went to Army headquarters to discuss military dispositions in my district. The recent dacoity had strengthened my hand, and it was agreed that the troops should remain to operate against the dacoits until the end of May. I was told that Major Kyaw Zaw, formerly of the Burma National Army, would be sent to Pyapon to take command of them in place of Downs.

My last two months in Pyapon saw a considerable improvement in the situation. We learned that it was the Than Maung gang which had attacked Pyapon town, and that they had been using the Bren gun which had been looted from the Bogale police station; one of their number had died as a result of their engagement with the troops. During the second half of May military operations on a large scale were conducted against the gang. Before they began Major Kyaw Zaw asked me what promises could be made to those who wished to surrender. I told him that the amnesty had expired and that I had no power to extend it; anyone who surrendered would therefore have to stand his trial in the usual way, but in the event of a conviction I would report the cases to the government for a decision whether a sentence of death should be commuted or one of imprisonment reduced. The operations were most successful. In the next few weeks twenty-seven members of the gang (which appears to have numbered thirty-nine) were captured or surrendered, and the Bren gun and some twenty rifles were recovered. Than Maung himself escaped and made his way to Upper Burma, but his right-hand man was arrested in Rangoon. Kyaw Zaw, a ruthless looking man who rarely smiled, co-operated loyally with me, though his political background must have made it distasteful to him to have to deal with a European official; but he said that he had been told to trust no one but the Deputy Commissioner!

Khin Maung Maung shared my house, and settled down to the task before him with determination. He had to go slowly at first, as his police force was so demoralised. But he made good use of the troops and, whenever an operation had to be carried out in which military participation seemed desirable, he would not hesitate to call on them for assistance. At the end of May we were asked if the troops could be withdrawn, and I requested that they should stay for another month. In the end the Army accepted the fact that we should need them at all events till the end of the rains.

Towards the end of June a Headquarters Assistant for my office was at last posted; I had been without one since January. On the same day that he arrived came orders that I was to be transferred to Sagaing and that my successor was to be a Karen officer. It was with profound relief that I received this news.

My successor was not expected for a week or two, but I had applied for possible employment with the British Council in Burma after I left the government service, and had been asked to go to Rangoon for interview early in July. There seemed little point in my returning to Pyapon after this, and I obtained permission to hand over the district temporarily to the Headquarters Assistant and to leave it for good. I had at least the satisfaction of knowing that there had been a very considerable decrease in crime during my last month, owing to the operations conducted by Khin Maung Maung and Kyaw Zaw.

The government staff gave me a tea party in the municipal office on my last day, and on the 6th July I left by government launch for

Rangoon. All the senior officials were lined up at the wharf, and I delivered a little homily on the undesirability of a government servant having any close connection with a political party. I said that I fully appreciated the difference in outlook between a Burmese official who had to live in the country after it attained self-government and myself who was soon leaving it for good; but no political party remained in power for ever, and a government official who dealt impartially with all parties was much more likely to command respect and to retain his position than one who was known to have marked sympathies with one particular party. They all listened politely, and I left.

I had been in Pyapon for six and a half months, and it was the only district in Burma which I disliked. At times I had felt that I was little more than an 'Aunt Sally', condemned to suffer innumerable pinpricks from the local politicians, and unable to look for support to the police or even to the central government. Though I was in charge of what was recognised to be one of the most troublesome districts in Burma, for most of my time I was expected to do the work of about three senior officers, and for two months to manage without a Superintendent of Police. Once or twice I considered going to Rangoon to ask for an interview with the Governor, but I reflected that there was probably little that he could do, since the control of the country had been virtually handed over to his Council. All that we British officials could do was to soldier on till the day of independence arrived, and meanwhile there was some satisfaction to be gained from pitting one's wits against those of the local politicians.

CHAPTER FOURTEEN

On the Eve 1947-48

*A*s A RESULT of the overwhelming victory of the AFPFL in the elections of April 1947, Aung San was now the virtual ruler of Burma. Early in June the Constituent Assembly met, elected Thakin Nu as its President, and resolved that Burma should become an independent sovereign republic outside the Commonwealth. From the first the AFPFL had proclaimed its aim to be a republic. Some of its leaders saw advantages in retaining the Commonwealth connection, but it was generally supposed that India, which was to become independent in August, would leave the Commonwealth, and this doubtless had its effect in swaying the balance in favour of secession. On the 23rd June Thakin Nu left for London at the head of a mission to report the Assembly's decision and to discuss detailed arrangements for the transfer of power, and Tin Tut was appointed Burmese High Commissioner in London. An outline of the new constitution had already been presented to the Assembly and various sub-committees were appointed to draft it in its final form.

I spent nearly a week in Rangoon and for the last time stayed with Ohn Maung. My interview with the British Council representative seemed satisfactory, but it was later decided that no-one who had exercised administrative authority in Burma should work there with the British Council. In the long view this was no doubt wise, but the decision certainly deprived the British Council of the potential services of persons who knew and liked the Burmese. My interest in joining the organisation arose solely from my desire to remain in Burma after independence, and I thereupon abandoned all further thought of it as a possible career. It had already been made clear by the Burmese that they did not intend to retain the services of European government officials after independence except for certain persons with technical qualifications to whom they would offer contracts.

On the 12th July I left Rangoon by train for Mandalay, where I was met by transport sent from Sagaing. I had been pleased by my posting. It was clear that this was to be my last district, and there seemed to be something peculiarly appropriate in my returning at the end of my service to be Deputy Commissioner of the district in which I had been trained. Moreover, I was going back to Upper Burma – the real Burma – and I expected to have a much less difficult time than I had had in Pyapon. U Aung Pe, who had been my Subdivisional Officer in both Bassein and Pyapon Districts, had been transferred to Mandalay District about a month previously, and had written me a glowing account of conditions there: 90 per cent of the revenue collected and comparatively little crime.

I spent a night in Mandalay and left the next morning for Sagaing. One span of the Ava Bridge had been demolished by the British troops during their retreat in 1942, and traffic crossed the Irrawaddy in landing-craft. Sagaing looked very much the same, with the Civil Station strung along the bank of the great river. Most of the hospital had been destroyed during the war, and the American Baptist Mission house, which I had once shared with George Merrells, was now used as a hospital. The Club had disappeared and the Commissioner's house, not far from it, had been damaged. It was a pleasant change after the unending flat paddy fields of the Delta to see hills, roads, red soil and a variety of crops.

The Commissioner had arranged for me to live with him until the Deputy Commissioner's quarters had been vacated by my predecessor, U Ba Htay, who handed over to me within a few days of my arrival.

One of my first jobs was to check the arrangements for a forthcoming visit of the Governor. He was to come up from Rangoon to Mandalay, and then drive through Sagaing town and see the Kaunghmudaw Pagoda before proceeding on his way. I had been timing the drive from one point to another on his route when his tour was abruptly cancelled.

Just a week after I had bade farewell to Ohn Maung the Mandalay telephone exchange rang me in my office to say that Mrs Ohn Maung wanted to speak to me from Rangoon. The reception proved too bad for the call to be put through, but the operator told me that she sounded very distressed.

Later in the day rumours spread through Sagaing that Aung San and other leading Burmese politicians had been killed in Rangoon. Another report reached me that Ohn Maung was also dead, though it was not clear how, if at all, his death was connected with the others. That evening the Governor broadcast to the country. It appeared that Aung San and certain other members of the government were in conference in the Council Chamber in the Secretariat building when a number of Burmans dressed in uniforms entered and turned machine guns on them. Aung San, the Home Minister Thakin Mya and others had been killed outright. Ohn Maung's connection with the incident was still not apparent, but it later transpired that he had been called into the Council Chamber with some papers and had unfortunately been there when the assassins entered. I later received an invitation to his funeral, but was of course unable to go.

Ohn Maung had been a close friend of mine since Oxford days ten years before. Though we had met only infrequently in Burma, we had kept in touch by correspondence, and I knew and liked his wife and had watched his children growing up. He was an intelligent, hardworking and straightforward man. He had his country's interests very much at heart and, had he not been a civil servant, he might perhaps have become a nationalist politician. But he would never have been an extremist, and he had a number of European friends. In his likes and dislikes he drew no distinction of race. His death at this time was a great loss to Burma.

U Saw, who had held no position in the government since the April elections, was arrested in connection with this crime. It was proved beyond the shadow of a doubt that the assassins were his men. He was brought to trial and, shortly after Burma became independent, this colourful but thoroughly unscrupulous character met his death on the gallows.

Aung San was thirty-two years old when he died. He was an uncompromising nationalist, ruthless and unyielding in the pursuit of his aims. But no one could doubt his sincerity of purpose, and his honesty was never impugned. He was not anti-British, but he fought for the ending of British rule in Burma. He helped the Japanese against the British, because he thought that they would give Burma independence. When he found that all they gave was a mere shadow of independence, he turned against them too. He had the courage to criticise the Japanese in public, and secretly prepared his troops for the day when they would rise against them. He welcomed the returning British as allies, not as rulers. He commanded a following like that of no Burmese leader since Alaungpaya. He demanded Burma's independence from the British Government and obtained it. For the last ten months of his life he was virtually Premier. He had no illusions as to the weight of responsibility which rested on his shoulders, and fully realised his own youthfulness and inexperience. But he was prepared to learn. His forthrightness and sincerity impressed men like General Slim and the Governors with whom he came in contact, and he won the respect of the British civil servants with whom he worked. He represented a new spirit in Burmese politics, a spirit of service and honesty. Dare one say that this spirit was a legacy of British rule in Burma?

The sudden disappearance of so many leading members of the AFPFL did not have so calamitous an effect upon the League and the government as might have been expected. The Governor sent for Thakin Nu who, though he had held no post in the government, was commonly regarded as the brains behind the League, and offered him the leadership of the government, which he accepted. Thakin Nu was much less of a fanatic than Aung San. By temperament a scholar and a recluse, he would far rather have devoted himself to the translation of great works of Western literature into Burmese or to meditation in a monastery than to leading a government. But he did what he conceived to be his duty, and it was he who carried through the final negotiations with the British Government for his country's independence and became the first Prime Minister of the Union of Burma.

Once the excitement engendered by U Saw's great crime had died down, I was able to turn to the administration of my new district. Few of my Burmese officers had I previously known, but the District Office still had many of the clerical staff who had been there when I was under training. Compared with the staff in Pyapon, they were of high quality. I was amused when my Chief Clerk enquired on my first day in the office whether I would like to have petitions submitted to me with an English translation. I said that I thought my Burmese was sufficiently good for me to understand them.

Politics gave far less trouble than in Pyapon. The AFPFL had the strongest following, and its two principal representatives were both lawyers, who were level-headed men and willing to co-operate with me. There was admittedly a fairly active White Flag Communist organisation in the western part of the district, whose leader was a young graduate of Rangoon University, and whose aim seemed to be merely to make a nuisance of itself. My predecessor had told me that he had to spend so much time in his office listening to petty complaints by members of the various parties that he had to do his office work at home. He said that it was quite impossible to avoid seeing them, but I made it a rule that they were to go first to the Subdivisional or Township Officer concerned, and to come to me only if they failed to obtain satisfaction from him. The result was that comparatively little of my time was wasted by unprofitable discussions. It was of course easier for me to refuse to see party members than it was for a Burmese officer.

The PVO here, as in Pyapon, were a thorn in the flesh of the administration. U Ba Htay had, in compliance with the suggestion made by the government at the beginning of the year, enrolled one hundred members of the PVO as special police reservists and issued arms to them. (In Pyapon, it will be recalled, we had issued only a very few arms as an experimental measure.) One of their own men was placed in charge of them with the honorary rank of 'Special Police Officer'. U Ba Htay apparently enrolled them by direct arrangement with the local PVO command and without consulting the Superintendent of Police, and he continued to deal with them direct. When one of them died or resigned, the PVO nominated his successor, who was duly enrolled. They may perhaps have done some good work at first, but by the time that I arrived in Sagaing they were working against the police and sheltering wanted men. Some of them committed a robbery in Sagaing town; they later confessed to this, and said that the PVO leaders had shared in the loot. Indeed it was common knowledge that the PVO were responsible for much of the crime in the district. I drew the attention of the government to the fact that about seventeen thousand rupees a month were being spent on these PVO special police reservists and suggested that they should be disbanded, but I received no reply. It was very difficult at this time for district officers to know what was the government's policy: whether it was content to acquiesce in the PVO acting as they did, or whether it was afraid of them. I have no reason to suppose that the AFPFL leaders approved of these unlawful activities of the PVO, but the government had its difficulties: if the PVO were disbanded, it had to ensure that they did not go underground or into opposition, and that some alternative and useful employment was found for them.

Apart, however, from the considerable political activity and the marked increase in crime – though in Sagaing District dacoities and robberies numbered only twenty to thirty a month as compared with about a hundred in Pyapon – I found the district very much as it had been before the war. The collection of revenue gave very little trouble and I travelled about doing the same sort of work, and in much the same atmosphere, as before the Japanese invasion. It was pleasant to visit the villages which I had known eight years before. In the course of one of my tours to an area some miles down the Irrawaddy which could be reached by road, I was marooned by the river suddenly rising and flooding the surrounding country. I asked for a launch to be sent from Mandalay – for we had none in Sagaing – and then visited many of the places affected by the floods, to see what damage had been done. Fortunately for the paddy crop, the floods had come sufficiently early for most of the nurseries which had been destroyed to be replanted, and we assisted people in these areas with agricultural loans. On another of my tours I reached Monywa, another of my pre-war stations, and found my old Deputy Commissioner back again.

Village in flood

I once took a few days' holiday at the invitation of my friend U
Aung Pe – who, as I have said, was now in Mandalay District – to
go to the Taungbyon festival, which took place yearly in his area.
The story goes that the great King Anawrahta (1044–77), while
returning from an expedition to Yunnan, halted at Taungbyon to
build a pagoda. He gave instructions that everyone in his entourage
was to contribute to its building by bringing one brick. Two of his
most famous warriors, Shwepyingyi and Shwepyinnge – the sons
of a Mohammedan who had been shipwrecked in Lower Burma –
failed to bring their bricks and were put to death by the King. They
have now become *nats* (spirits) and are worshipped at the
Taungbyon festival. No one connected with the shrine will touch
pork, presumably out of regard for the religion of the father of the
two *nats*. This festival is one of the many examples of the overlaying
of Buddhism with a thick veneer of spirit-worship. It rained during
most of the festival and, as all the huts and stalls were temporary
buildings erected every year and there were no roads, it became
very muddy underfoot. Crowds of people came from all parts,
impelled by the twin urges of worship and trade. Much
good-humoured banter went on, for it was traditional at this festival
that men and women might address ribald remarks to each other

with impunity. There were the usual entertainments: *pwès*, spirit dances and sideshows; there was a fortune-teller who told me that, after returning to England, I should go overseas again, and was quite right; and, despite the rain and the mud, it was evident that all were enjoying themselves. It was indeed difficult to damp the ardour of a Burman who was determined to have a good time.

The Deputy Commissioner's house, in which I lived, was a large two-storeyed building and, as I occupied only two rooms and a verandah, I let my staff use some of the other rooms. I still had Tun Che; my cook was an old man, officially employed as an office peon, who had cooked for my predecessor. And I had two policemen attached to the house; one was a local Catholic who evidently had some knowledge of Western songs, and I often breakfasted to the sound from outside of Handel's 'Harmonious Blacksmith'.

I was soon busy with headmen's elections. I have explained earlier that, once a headman had been elected by his villagers and confirmed in his appointment by the government, he remained headman until he died, resigned or was dismissed. He was therefore virtually a permanency during his life-time. This practice attracted much criticism from political leaders of the younger generation, many of whom felt that the headman was the tool of the administration rather than the representative of the people. Orders were therefore issued by the government towards the middle of 1947 that three months' notice was to be given to all headmen and that, when the notice had expired, elections were to be held throughout Burma for new headmen. Headmen's elections were normally conducted by the subdivisional officer, but these mass elections meant that all administrative officers, from the Deputy Commissioner downwards, had to lend a hand. Needless to say, politics now entered into the elections, and in most areas one of the candidates was a party member. Half the Sagaing elections had been completed before I left, and it was interesting to see that the party candidates had by no means had things all their own way; indeed the indications were that, in this district at all events, the people preferred their old headman or his son or someone who was not connected with politics. One election which I supervised, in quite an important area, resulted in the defeat of the party candidate by one vote. Of course we had a recount, but the result was the same, and the defeated took it very much amiss when I said that I did not propose to hold a second election on the ground that the votes had been so close! No doubt he later appealed against the conduct of the election!

Since early in the year the Home Department of the government had been circulating to European members of the Government

Services information about other forms of employment which might become available to them when they left Burma. The India and Burma Offices in London had established a Services Re-employment Bureau. Many of the appointments notified were on contract terms. Only three interested me: the Foreign Service, the Colonial Service and the Home Civil Service. I was still young enough to be admitted to them, if I were successful, on permanent and pensionable terms, and I applied for appointment to them in the order which I have shown. By this time the terms governing the termination of our employment in Burma had been settled. Provided that we stayed until such time as it was considered to be in the public interest that we should go, we were to receive pensions proportionate to the length of our service, and in addition compensation for loss of career. The compensation depended on the length of service and was calculated on a sliding scale rising (for the Burma Civil Service) to £8,000 after sixteen years' service and then gradually falling. I, after nine years' service, should have qualified for a lump sum of £4,500. There was, however, a proviso that an officer who accepted appointment to another Civil Service under His Majesty's Government on a permanent and pensionable basis would receive no compensation, but would instead be eligible for a resettlement grant of £500. The equity of the proviso appeared later to be open to considerable doubt. Not only did those who obtained employment with non-government organisations retain their compensation in full; but those who were appointed to contract posts in a Civil Service did likewise, and some of these latter were admitted to the permanent establishment after three or four years, when it was too late to ask them to repay their compensation.

In due course I was notified that I was required in London in the latter half of October for interview in connection with my applications for entry to the Foreign, Colonial and Home Civil Services, and that an air passage was being booked for me in the middle of the month. I should have liked to remain in Burma until the handover of power to the independent Burmese Government, and I asked for permission to return after my interviews; but this was refused.

On the 10th October 1947, I relinquished charge of my last district after spending barely three months in it. That night I slept in the Circuit House in Mandalay, where I joined John McTurk, who had been in charge of Shwebo District, directly to the north of Sagaing, and was being transferred to Rangoon. Independence was now round the corner, and European Deputy Commissioners were being replaced by Burmans, and either being sent home for interviews or being posted to duty in the Secretariat. Mandalay was much changed since the war; I had passed through it on several occasions during the last three months. The old palace of the Burmese kings within the walls of the palace-city had been completely destroyed during the fighting of 1945. Parts of the town had been damaged by air raids and the bazaar, though still in existence, was but a shadow of its former self.

The next morning I was awake early and strolled out into the street, where I fell into conversation with some Burmese municipal employees who were assembling for their day's work. I told them that I was on my way to Rangoon to leave Burma for good, and that by the end of the year most of the European government officials would have gone. They were frankly incredulous: they did not really expect us to go and indicated that, if we left, they could not conceive how the administration would be carried on. This attitude of mind was, I think, prevalent among many of the less sophisticated Burmans in the villages, but it was interesting to find it even in the second city in the country. As in so many emergent colonies, the cry for independence came principally from the political-conscious minority.

The schedule of the train running between Rangoon and Mandalay had been so timed that it passed during the daytime through that part of Central Burma which was now largely under Communist control, and where vehicles travelling at night were liable to attack. I spent only four days in Rangoon. The city was full of young Burmans wearing uniforms and carrying arms. These were members of the PVO, who had become much more prominent since the murder of Aung San. I think that most of the Ministers now had their own bodyguard, and I saw Thakin Nu driving into town with a truck-load of armed men behind him. A government officer could no longer enter the Secretariat without passing through a wired passage and allowing the PVO guard to examine everything that he was carrying. I obligingly opened my bag and told the guard that I had no grenades in it, but he was neither grateful nor amused.

I called on Ohn Maung's widow, and went with her to the Jubilee Hall, where the embalmed and coffined bodies of the victims of the 19th July had been laid to be venerated by the people; on the front of Ohn Maung's coffin was a photograph of him, an enlargement of one which I had once taken at Oxford. We and other visitors lined up in front of the coffins. Then a young PVO man appeared before us and barked out a word of command, whereupon the whole assembly bowed; another bark and we raised our heads again. It was all carried out in the best Japanese military tradition. The bodies have since been placed in a specially built shrine on the slopes of the Shwe Dagon Pagoda.

There was a distinct air of hooliganism in Rangoon. The PVO would hold up buses at any place at which they wished to board them, and crowd into them regardless of whether they were already full. They would hold up traffic at crossings to allow their own vehicles to pass and, as they were invariably in uniform, the ordinary motorist could not tell from a distance whether they were police or not. On one of my last mornings, while I was having breakfast with a friend, a young PVO man came in to collect subscriptions for his organisation. The PVO had been a source of constant trouble to me for nearly a year, and there was something ironic in my being asked to contribute to their funds just as I was leaving Burma. But he was outwardly a polite young man and I am glad to say that we were still able to appreciate the humour of the situation and delve into our pockets for some small change.

The agreement reached in January between the British Government and the Burmese delegation had been subject to the proviso that the hill peoples should be permitted to choose for themselves whether they wished to join the new independent Burma or to continue to be administered by Britain. These peoples – the Shans, Kachins, Chins and the Karens of Karenni – had never in the past been subject to Burmese ministers; the Governor had held a special responsibility for them. In the succeeding months Aung San negotiated with the leaders of these races and was able to allay any fears which they might have had by virtually allowing them to write their own terms into the constitution. The new state was to be the Union of Burma, a union of the various races living in Burma. Only the Karens proved difficult, for they had suffered at the hands of the Burmese more than the other peoples, especially during the Japanese occupation. They demanded a state of their own, a demand which would have been impracticable of fulfilment for, save in the hill area of Karenni, Karens and Burmese were inextricably mixed and everywhere the Karens were a minority. Eventually their more reasonable claims were met, and it is generally agreed that in his negotiations with the other races Aung San displayed considerable qualities of statesmanship.

The constitution which was ultimately evolved is said to have borrowed features from a number of other constitutions, but to have been modelled mainly on that of Yugoslavia. The Constituent Assembly did not finish its work until after Aung San's death, but on the 24th September 1947, the draft of the new constitution was approved unanimously. Towards the middle of October Thakin Nu went to London for the final negotiations with the British Government for the transfer of power to an independent Burmese Government and for the secession of Burma from the British Commonwealth. On the 17th October a treaty was signed, in which His Majesty's Government recognised the Republic of the Union of Burma as a fully independent state from a date to be fixed by Parliament, and undertook to carry through Parliament without delay a Burma Independence Bill.

By this time I was on my way to England, having duly obtained a certificate signed by the Governor to the effect that it was in the public interest that I should proceed on leave prior to retirement. On the 16th October I said goodbye to my servant Tun Che, who had come with me to Rangoon, and boarded a BOAC flying boat with two of my colleagues who were also going to London for interview.

The Burmese astrologers were called upon to determine a propitious date and hour for the transfer of power, and at 4.20 a.m. on the 4th January 1948, the last British Governor of Burma, Sir Hubert Rance, handed over the administration to the first President of the Republic and left Rangoon. It was indicative of the desire of the Burmese that the other indigenous races should be fully associated with them that the first President was a Shan, Sao Shwe Thaik, the Sawbwa of Yawnghwe.

Chapter Fifteen

The Reckoning

ANYONE WHO HAS SERVED as an administrator in a dependent territory must ask himself certain fundamental questions. Was the colonial power justified in annexing the dependency in the first place? Did its administration prove in the long view to be a blessing to the people, or did it do more harm than good? There is no simple answer to these questions. It is easy to be wise after the event, and to point to some of the more obvious mistakes which were made, the effects of some of which could not possibly have been foreseen at the time. And we must beware of looking at the colonial activities of the nineteenth century, when imperialism and colonialism were considered not only respectable, but the only hope of salvation for the backward peoples of the world, through mid-twentieth century spectacles.

The first Anglo-Burmese War of 1824–26 was caused by Burmese aggression in Arakan, followed by incidents on the frontiers of British India, and finally by an advance of the Burmese troops into Bengal. For some years the Governor-General of India had tried to arrange a *modus vivendi* with the Burmese. He had sent no fewer than six envoys over a period of years, but the Burmese king had declined even to grant them an audience, on the ground that he could not receive ambassadors from a mere Governor-General, but only from his equal, the King of England. The coastal areas of Arakan and Tenasserim, which were annexed by the East India Company at the end of the war, were not parts of Burma proper. They were outlying provinces of comparatively recent acquisition, peopled by races who were akin to the Burmese but were not Burmese. In Arakan at all events the cruelty of the Burmese had been such that the inhabitants welcomed our deliverance from them, and our removal of the prohibition on export of rice which had been imposed by the Burmese soon brought a degree of prosperity to the province. But, apart from the fact that Arakan and Tenasserim formed a link between British India and the new British base of Singapore, their acquisition was of little immediate advantage either to Britain or to the East India Company, and the cost of administering Tenasserim was so uneconomic that in 1831 the Company actually considered handing it back to the Burmese.

281

It was only the fear that the inhabitants would suffer from Burmese vengeance which prevented them from doing so.

The Second Anglo-Burmese War of 1852 was the result of incidents affecting British sailors and merchants in Rangoon. These were hardly sufficient to justify the annexation of Rangoon and the Lower Burma hinterland (the Province of Pegu), and there was some criticism of this action by liberals in England at the time. But here again the East India Company annexed only a province of the Burmese Empire, which was peopled largely by Mons, the hereditary enemies of the Burmese, and which had been conquered by them less than a hundred years earlier. No attempt was yet made to occupy the Burmese homeland, but the effect of our now occupying the entire coastline was inevitably to leave the Burmese yet more insulated from happenings to the world outside.

The ostensible cause of the Third Anglo-Burmese War of 1885 was the victimisation of British business interests in Upper Burma; the real cause was Britain's fear that the French might forestall her, a fear which now seems to have had little foundation in fact. In terms of mid-twentieth century thought there was no justification whatever for Britain to invade Upper Burma, far less to annex it. But nowadays all states of the world have had experience of relations with other states, and it is hard to visualise the existence of a country, such as Upper Burma was at the time of the annexation, which had had virtually no contact for years with the outside world, and was totally ignorant of the normal forms of diplomatic intercourse. Her government treated the nationals of other states in a high-handed manner, recognised the existence of foreign representatives only when this suited her purpose, and ignored all representations made by other countries. Moreover, there was strong pressure in England for annexation on humanitarian grounds, for the cruelties practised by King Thibaw's regime, including the murder of most of the members of the royal family, had revolted civilised opinion. In retrospect, one cannot help feeling that, if Britain had to interfere in the affairs of Upper Burma, it was unfortunate that she could not establish a sounder and more progressive government and then withdraw her troops, leaving the country under British protection with British advisers. But there was no suitable member of the royal family left who might have been placed on Thibaw's throne.

The effect of the impact of a highly-developed industrial civilisation on a traditional society is now generally appreciated. It was not, however, and could not have been, foreseen in the heyday of colonial expansion, in the latter half of the nineteenth century. As I have explained, the first parts of Burma to be annexed were the outlying dependencies of the Burmese Empire. As a result of the general devastation which had accompanied their conquest by the Burmese, organised society had largely broken down, and considerable areas of Lower Burma were depopulated. There was therefore no existing social structure, with all its concomitant class distinctions, on which the British might have learnt to build. Consequently, when Upper Burma was annexed in 1886, they assumed that the same state of affairs existed there. The result was that they undermined the highly complex social organisation of the Burmese, which they did not understand, and attempted to replace it by the British system based on the secular state, the rule of law and the liberty and equality of the individual.

A Buddhist monarch, such as the King of Burma, though he might not himself be an ecclesiastic, had certain of the attributes of a divinity, and was head of the Church. In Burma he governed the Church through an ecclesiastic called the *thathanabaing* and a commission composed of both monks and laymen. The *thathanabaing* was something between a primate and a king's chaplain. Both he and the members of the ecclesiastical commission were appointed by the King, and between them they administered religious endowments, conducted clerical examinations and exercised disciplinary control over the priesthood. Shortly after the annexation of Upper Burma the primate and a number of his colleagues offered to preach submission to British rule throughout the land, provided that their jurisdiction over the priesthood was confirmed. This the Government of India refused. The refusal was due partly to misunderstanding of the established order of things in Burma, partly to reluctance to grant such wide powers, partly to the traditional British principle of not interfering in matters of religion. As a result, though the British continued to appoint a primate, his actual powers were negligible; the priesthood, freed from all restraining influences, deteriorated, and before very long monks began to meddle in politics, and monasteries to harbour criminals and fugitives from justice dressed in the yellow robe. It was indeed mainly in the monasteries of the large towns that this collapse in religious discipline and morals occurred. In most of the villages the monks were simple – often saintly – men, devoting themselves to meditation and the education of the young, and justly revered by the people. But it was the large towns which were the potential centres of trouble, and many of the subversive movements against the British were led by monks.

On the secular side too the breakdown of the traditional social restraints had disastrous consequences. Under Burmese rule the administration of the countryside was in the hands of a hereditary squirearchy of headmen and superior headmen (*myothugyis*). Land belonged to the family and could not be sold to an outsider. Here again the British failed to understand the social structure of the country which they had conquered. They came with preconceived ideas acquired in India. They allowed the *myothugyis*, who were the natural leaders, to die out; they introduced the Indian system of village administration, with an elected headman appointed by the government for each village unit, who was in effect a subordinate government functionary collecting taxes and exercising certain police powers, instead of the hereditary leader of the community. And, by insisting on freedom of contract, they encouraged the Burmese to buy and sell land.

Under Burmese rule the individual occupied his appointed place in a tightly-knit social system. The common people were kept in their place; they had to work hard, were paid no wages, could not wear fine clothes, and constantly suffered from the exactions of the local officials. Violent crime seems to have been comparatively rare. The British annexation introduced liberal ideas such as that of the freedom of the individual, and led to a staggering growth in economic development. The Burmese peasant could now earn as much money as he wished if he chose to work for it and, freed from customary prohibitions, could spend it on dress or on liquor as he pleased. There was a rapid rise in the standard of living, but it was achieved at the expense of the traditional social restraints.

The result of the breakdown of the old Burmese social system on both the religious and the secular side was most clearly seen in the phenomenal increase in crimes of violence: murders, robberies and dacoities. In the years before the Second World War there was an average of 900 murders a year; England and Wales, with nearly three times the population of Burma, had 140. Dacoities (gang robberies) averaged nearly 500 a year. The major upheaval caused by the Japanese invasion and subsequent expulsion, and the existence of large numbers of modern weapons which had been abandoned by two retreating armies, led to a yet further increase in violent crime after the war.

The Government of India imported the British-Indian criminal law into Burma. It was a much more humane law than the old Burmese law, which had used torture, ordeal and savage punishments. But it was alien to the people of Burma, and so a lawyer class grew up to represent them before the courts. In the early days the lawyers were mainly Indians, but it was not long before Burmans took to the law. The profession was grossly overcrowded, and it was to the financial advantage of the less able and less scrupulous lawyers to encourage litigation and to prolong it as much as possible. Pleaders could be seen outside the courts touting for work, and a great many of the cases which occupied the time of the magistrates need never have come to court at all. As I have said earlier, the vagaries of British justice were incomprehensible to the average Burman. Some British judges gave the impression of leaning over backwards to find grounds for acquitting an accused person, in their anxiety to ensure that he received a fair trial, and cases were frequently thrown out on some legal technicality. The people could explain an apparently perverse decision only on the assumption that it had been bought. It is acknowledged that very many of the subordinate judges were corrupt, but the Judges of the High Court and the District Judges who were members of the Class I Service were, irrespective of race, honest and honourable men. But this did not alter the fact that the processes of justice were slow and the results frequently not understood by the people.

From the economic point of view, the worst legacy of British rule was the problem of agricultural debt and land alienation. This was a problem which was virtually confined to Lower Burma. The Upper Burman peasant produced a wide variety of crops: rice, wheat, cotton, sugar cane, sessamum and groundnuts (for their oils), tobacco and pulses. This diversity of crops provided some insurance against disaster, since it was unlikely that a bad season would affect them all equally. The Upper Burman was generally a smallholder. He too required money for his agricultural operations, and he borrowed it on the security of his land, and sometimes the moneylender was forced to foreclose and take possession of the land; but, since the land laws of Upper Burma prohibited the alienation of agricultural land to a non-agriculturist, the moneylender who was permitted to acquire land would be himself an agriculturist, and consequently he was generally a Burman.

In Lower Burma the cultivation of rice – the only crop of any importance – was practised on a commercial scale. The expansion of rice production in the delta areas was one of the most remarkable economic achievements of British rule. Much of Lower Burma was, as I have said, depopulated when it was annexed in 1852. In 1855 the total acreage under paddy in British Burma – and this of course included the Arakan and Tenasserim strips annexed thirty years earlier – was under one million. Twenty-five years later it had reached ten millions out of a total for the whole of Burma of some twelve and a half millions. But this great expansion had been achieved only at the expense of Burmese peasant ownership of land. The demand for field labour in the early days was such that great numbers of Indian immigrants arrived. Their much lower standard of living enabled them to compete on favourable terms with the Burmese for land tenancies. Moreover, the Burmese cultivator's need for capital soon drove him and his land into the hands of the Indian moneylenders. The government's attempts to help him by providing loans at low rates of interest were ineffective. Co-operative societies were encouraged, but most of them failed during the economic depression of 1929 onwards, though a determined attempt at reconstruction on a sounder basis was beginning to bear fruit.

It was indeed not until Burma had achieved responsible government after her separation from India in 1937 that any real effort was made to tackle the problems of land alienation and agricultural indebtedness. A Land and Agriculture Committee was appointed in 1938, and one result of its work was the passing of the Tenancy Act in the following year. More far-reaching, however, was the aim behind the Land Alienation Act, which extended to Lower Burma the prohibition on the transfer of agricultural land to non-agriculturists. Its main defect was that it came some fifty years too late, for it was not to apply to existing land mortgages, and by this time probably not more than fifteen per cent of the agricultural land of Lower Burma was owned by genuine agriculturists and unmortgaged. The Land Alienation Act was not enacted until 1941 on the eve of the Japanese invasion, and there was therefore little opportunity to enforce it and to study its effects before the British relinquished their responsibility for Burma.

It was from many points of view a tragedy that Burma was ever administered as a province of British India and so for many years lost her identity. This was no doubt inevitable in view of the fact that the annexation was carried out by the Government of India with British Indian troops. The early administrators of Tenasserim did indeed come from Penang, which was closer than Calcutta, but it was natural that Arakan which adjoined Bengal should be regarded simply as another territory added to the East India Company's vast Indian possessions; in the early days of British rule – incredible as it may seem – the language of its court was Persian, because this was the language in which the judicial records of India were at that time kept!

Lower Burma was rapidly overrun by Indian immigrants, who came to work in the delta rice fields and in the ports. Had it not been for them, the economic development of Burma could not have proceeded at such an astonishing pace, but the social problems raised by the presence of ultimately over a million immigrants of alien race and religion and a lower standard of living were considerable. Not only were Indians employed as labourers; many were brought over by the British to staff the lower ranks of the new administration, and even in the last days of British rule the majority of the subordinate officials in such departments as the posts and telegraphs, the railways and public works were Indians. There was no love lost between the Burmese and the Indians.

Until 1937 Burma remained a province of the Indian Empire, and she had little control over her own finances. The Government of India retained much of the surplus revenues of the provinces to meet emergencies, which were of frequent occurrence, such as famine, frontier warfare or internal disorder. After her separation from India in 1937 Burma kept her own revenues and had complete control over their expenditure. Far too much, however, seemed to be spent on administration, and the new Burmese government had little time to consider a more balanced distribution of its expenditure before the Second World War and the Japanese invasion were upon it. In 1939/40, out of a total expenditure of 15.6 crores of rupees (1 crore = 10 millions), 2.7 crores went on general administration and police. By comparison, less than one crore was spent on education, half a crore on health, one-fifth of a crore on agricultural and veterinary services.

Big business was largely in British hands. The biggest forest leases were held by British firms; the oilfields in central Burma, the largest tin mines of Tenasserim and the Namtu silver mines were all worked by British companies; and the best rubber estates were British. The big importing and exporting firms were British, Indian and, to a lesser degree, Chinese. The activities of all these foreign businesses developed the country's resources and put money into the pockets of the Burmese; for, though a proportion of their profits was naturally absorbed in the payment of dividends to overseas shareholders and overseas taxation, the amount spent in Burma in taxes, wages and production costs was far higher. The nationalist politicians claimed (as do nationalists in all dependent territories) that Britain exploited the natural resources of Burma for her own benefit. But Burmese firms had not the capital required to finance big business, and it is instructive to note that in the neighbouring independent state of Siam industry was also in the hands of foreigners using foreign capital and remitting profits to foreign countries.

It may not be realised what a very considerable degree of control the Burmese had over the government of their country in the later days of British administration. Under the system of dyarchy introduced in 1923, the 'transferred' subjects (local government, education, public health, agriculture, excise, public works and forests) became the responsibility of two ministers who were answer-able to the legislature. The 'reserved' subjects (law and order, irrigation, revenue and finance, and general administration) were administered by two members of the Governor's Council, one of whom was always a Burman; they sat in the Legislative Council, but they were not elected like the two ministers and they could not therefore be dismissed by the Council. The main defect of the system was that the control of finance lay with the non-elected members.

But the next constitutional advance of 1937, which accompanied Burma's separation from India, gave the country a cabinet of min-isters which was responsible for everything except foreign affairs, defence, currency and the administration of the non-Burmese hill areas, for which the Governor retained personal responsibility. The Burmese cabinet now had far greater powers than the cabinet of any Indian province, for the latter had to relinquish certain powers to the central Government of India. It is true that the Governor still had ultimate responsibility for the internal security and financial stability of Burma and could in the last resort suspend the constitu-tion and assume the government himself. But he would have been most reluctant to intervene in the actions of his ministers, for his instructions were that he was to 'be studious so to exercise his powers as not to enable his ministers to rely upon his special responsibilities in order to relieve themselves of responsibilities which are properly their own'. From 1937 onwards therefore Burma had virtually internal self-government. It was not until the break-down of the administration in the face of the Japanese invasion in 1942 that the Governor exercised his special responsibilities and took over the government.

The civil services had for years been predominantly non-European. At the outbreak of the war in 1939 there were 403 European officials, all in the Class I services; non-Europeans numbered 200 in the Class I services and 827 (Burmans, Anglo-Burmans and Indians) in the Class II services. The premier service, the Burma Civil Service (Class I), which received its first Burmese member in 1921, had 90 European officers out of a total of 169; the Burma Police (Class I) had 56 Europeans out of 82. The other Class I services, though still contain-ing a majority of Europeans, were recruiting very few more, and one or two had Burmans at their head, with Europeans serving under them.

In the other professions Burmans were gradually making their way, but it was unfortunate that those who could not aspire to enter the government services almost invariably drifted into the law, politics or journalism. Here standards were lamentably low, self-advancement regardless of others or of the good of the country being the general rule. A Committee on Bribery and Corruption was appointed soon after I went to Burma, consisting of four Burmese members of the House of Representatives and two European officials. After long delay its report was published in 1941, but certain sections which implicated ministers had to be excised on the ground that the Committee was concerned only with the conduct of officials!

The British came to Burma, as to their other dependencies, with the profound conviction that parliamentary democracy on the Westminster pattern, which had proved satisfactory in Great Britain, was the ideal form of government for all peoples. Burma had for centuries been accustomed to a despotic type of administration, but the British tried to establish a modern liberal state, and the result was frequently not liberty but licence. Many British officials considered that the type of government which would best suit Burma would be a benevolent dictatorship. The Japanese introduced the Burmese to a new conception of government, based on the support of armed force, and the young post-war leaders of Burma surrounded themselves with private armies, which soon got out of hand. This too was not the answer.

Though the British undoubtedly made mistakes in Burma, some of which are easier to perceive now than when they were made, though many of the effects of their administration were unhappy, yet, when all is said and done, the old Burmese type of society could not have continued to exist in the modern world. It would have had to be radically altered and adapted to modern conditions, and only a Western power had at that time either the knowledge or the resources to undertake the transformation, either by taking over the administration or by supplying its nationals to act as advisers and agents to a nominally independent and sovereign state. That Burma fell under the direct rule of a Western power, unlike Siam, was of course a natural source of grievance to the nationalists who, like their fellows elsewhere, took the view that self-government was preferable to good government. And the Burmese had been a proud people, unused to living in subjection to an alien race, and throughout their history had generally been the conquerors rather than the conquered.

The more obvious benefits of British rule would no doubt have come in time to Burma, but if the British had not brought them, some other nation would have done so. (The example of Japan cannot be regarded as typical. After emerging from her oriental seclusion in the middle of the nineteenth century she deliberately set herself to build a modern industrial state on the Western pattern, and within fifty years had won recognition as a great power. Her task was made very much easier by the existence of coal, copper and iron ore deposits.)

Apart from the so-called Burma Rebellion of 1930 and occasional communal disturbances such as the Burmese-Muslim riots of 1938, Burma enjoyed internal peace during the period of British rule until she was invaded by the Japanese. Roads and railways were built and excellent water transport services were provided, and internal as well as external trade was developed.

Public health services were poor by Western standards, since hospitals and public health staff (other than vaccinators) were seldom to be found in rural areas outside township headquarters. But nonetheless the benefits of Western medicine were brought to vast numbers of the people of Burma, and their expectation of life was greatly increased.

In the sphere of education the British found that the monastic schools had made Burma one of the most literate countries in Asia; but literacy had not led to much beyond the mere ability to read, write and do arithmetic, and much was still to be done. Considerable strides were made, but they were far from adequate. About 500,000 children, less than a third of the total population between the ages of six and eleven, were taught in the 6,800 primary schools; these schools taught in the vernacular and were controlled by the District Councils, many being privately-owned. About eighty per cent of the pupils were withdrawn after a year or two by their parents, who needed their services in the fields. Above the primary schools came the Anglo-Vernacular middle and high schools, where English was the medium of instruction in the higher classes, and a few English high schools, where English was used throughout. These were all in the towns, either maintained or aided by the government, but there were only 270 of them, and the proportion of children who ever attained this level of education was abysmally low; they had about 55,000 pupils in all. In 1920 Rangoon University was founded on a fine site and provided with buildings of which Burma was justly proud, where students could study arts, science, medicine, education, agriculture, engineering and law. It had about 2,700 students, but standards were kept high, and only about 400 graduates were produced each year. About sixty per cent of the undergraduates failed to stay the course and should never have been admitted; many of them went to swell the ranks of the politicians and journalists.

The long-term effects of British rule in Burma have been made more difficult to assess by the breakdown of the British civil administration during the years 1942 to 1945, a heart-breaking experience for those officers of all races who had spent their lives in the service of the country. It was re-established only a little more than two years before sovereignty was transferred to a fully independent Burmese state. This was not long enough for the damage done by the Japanese occupation to be repaired and the pre-war machinery to be put again into full working order. A large quantity of modern firearms had fallen into the hands of criminal gangs, who kept the attention of the administration distracted from some of the more urgent tasks of reconstruction in the short time that was left.

Another factor which augured badly for the future was the rift between the old and the young Burmese leaders. Aung San told a European colleague of mine that he was acutely conscious of the burden of responsibility which rested upon him and the other leaders of his generation, and of their lack of experience. But, as he said, few of the older politicians had any real wish to work in the best interests of the country; under the Japanese occupation it was the young ones who had taken all the risks and the hard knocks. The truth was of course that the young men wanted change, while the old ones did not, unless its pace could be properly controlled by them. The prestige of the older generation of politicians had suffered a serious setback during the Japanese occupation, and our unsuc-cessful attempt to restore it after our return only aroused the suspicions of the younger set.

If we had had about six years to clear up the débris and the political antagonisms left by the war, with military assistance on the security side, we might have succeeded in welding together the old and the young and handing over Burma in good working order to a sound and broad-based Burmese Government. We should, how-ever, had had to get rid of the European die-hards, most of whom disliked the militarised young men with whom they now had to deal, and who were equally disliked by them. But the time was not given to us. The nationalists wanted independence as soon as possible and at any price, and they got it.

It used to be said that, when British rule in Burma had passed away, the only thing which would preserve its memory would be the football. But other characteristics of our administration have been retained by the independent state. The independence of the judiciary from interference by the executive, the general shape of the district administration, the social services whose foundations we laid, and the high standard of public service in the superior branches of the civil service, all these remain.

Relations between Burmese and British were good. The common people generally preferred a European district officer to a Burman, and I remember a senior Burmese officer remarking on this and wondering why it was so. One reason may have been that the European was at all events impartial, whether he was dealing with parties of more than one race or with Burmans only. It was not necessary to bribe him, though the path to him was frequently smoothed, without his knowledge, by douceurs to his subordinates. Unfortunately, however, he was never kept long enough in any one district to know and be known by the people. This was partly due to his periodical departures to Europe on leave, partly to deliberate policy on the part of those responsible for postings not to leave an officer too long in any one district, lest he should begin to identify himself with it and lose the faculty of dispassionate appraisal of circumstances. The administration tended therefore to be impersonal, and not many of the people of the district ever learnt the names of their European officials. My experience was that British and Burmese officials in the districts got on well together though, as I have said earlier, close social intercourse was frustrated by the inability of the womenfolk to speak a common tongue. The politicians and other non-official members of the intelligentsia regarded the British as haughty and stand-offish. Ohn Maung, when I first met him in Oxford, used to assure me that I was quite unlike the general run of Europeans in Burma; but that was simply because he knew me better. In Rangoon, admittedly, things were different. There was a large European community of unofficials there, many of whom never went outside Rangoon or were brought into contact with the Burmese in the course of their work. Rangoon itself was a cosmopolitan city with the Burmese in a minority, and each community tended to keep to itself. An educated Burman wrote some years after the end of British rule: 'The relation of the ruler and the ruled is hardly one to conduce to a proper understanding or knowledge of each other.' There is some truth in this, but it is noteworthy that the British did not leave behind among the Burmese such sentiments towards them as the Dutch unfortunately left in the Netherlands East Indies or the French in Indo-China.

Whatever the Burmese may have thought of the British, I think it is true to say that most British officials (and non-officials too), who had regular dealings with the Burmese, had a very real affection for them. Though capable on occasion of acts of atrocious cruelty, they were an intelligent, cheerful and hospitable people with many loveable characteristics. A British official who later served in another Colonial territory realised only too soon what he had lost by leaving Burma.